IN SEAI
TI
PARANORMAL

25 YEARS HUNTING GHOSTS ACROSS GREAT BRITAIN AND THE UNITED STATES

RICHARD ESTEP

For Laura, with deepest love

and,
in loving memory of

My mum, Lynda
My father, Rick
My grandparents:
Gordon and Lucy White,
Irene and Fred Perkins,
Christopher and Doreen Shakesby

...and the big-hearted Steven Arden

Clear skies.

CONTENTS

INTRODUCTION TO THE SECOND EDITION

Life doesn't always give you second chances.

In 2014, I had been investigating claims of the paranormal for close to twenty years. I began toying with the idea of writing a how-to book, describing methods, techniques, and theory, in the hopes of assisting those who were new to the field.

The publisher I submitted my book proposal to, sent me a very nicely worded rejection letter (most authors do not receive this courtesy) stating that unfortunately, they didn't think there was a market for that sort of book at the time, because "most people learn ghost hunting from TV."

It is an unwritten rule of book proposals that you should never respond to a rejection letter. Fortunately, I was ignorant of the fact when I emailed the acquisitions editor back and, after thanking them for their kind reply, asked earnestly what type of book there *was* a market for.

"True ghost stories and paranormal encounters," came the reply. "Do you have any of those?"

Did I *ever*.

"Then send us three sample chapters and an outline," the editor said, "and we'll see."

Drawing on some of my more interesting cases on both sides of the Atlantic, I spent the next three months writing on my lunch hour. I worked night shifts for an I.T. company, and this was my psychological hack to avoid rejection. No matter what they might say outwardly, deep down, pretty much all writers are terrified of rejection — understandably so. Nobody likes rejection, but it cuts very deeply when you put your heart and soul into a creative project, only to have it turned down after investing months of hard work.

As I wrote my way through the last few decades of my life, essentially putting together a paranormally-themed memoir, I found the project to be extremely enjoyable, but I was never quite able to shake impostor syndrome — the sense that, no matter how hard I tried, my words were never going to be quite good enough. As a species, writers tend to have fertile imaginations. Mine kept conjuring up mental images of another rejection email coming back after I finished the manuscript, destroying my dreams of ever being a published author.

Writing on my work lunch time was a psychological hack to offset this fear. I was getting paid by my employer to write for an hour a night, I told myself, so at the end of the day, if the book was rejected and I could not interest another publisher, then I was still a *paid* author. My time would not have been wasted.

I wrote the first three chapters and a structural outline, receiving a provisional thumbs up from the publisher.

So far, so good. Now it was starting to get real.

Taking a deep breath, I opened my email, attached the document, and hit send...and so I plodded on, line after line, paragraph following paragraph, until finally, I reached the end.

The wait was interminable. And excruciating.

Finally, after an eon or two had passed, I received a response. My manuscript was accepted...but there was a caveat.

The publisher requested changes. Which was a nice way of saying that there were going to be changes, period. This is a standard and entirely acceptable way of doing things in the publishing world. On the one hand, you had me, the first-time author who had precisely zero experience of marketing and selling books. On the other, a publisher with a massive distribution network and hundreds, if not thousands of books under their belt. It would have been arrogance on my part not to agree with them and make the changes they were asking for.

With the benefit of seven years' worth of hindsight, I can see that they were right on many of those things. I was overly critical regarding some aspects of the paranormal field, and ran the risk of alienating the book's core audience. A vein of healthy skepticism ran through the manuscript, but at the same time, readers are not (for the most part) interested in an author's work if it seems too judgmental or preachy.

Other things came out simply because they didn't quite fit with the overall theme, or were simply too outlandish, such as the lady who emailed me after one of the cases detailed in the book, to complain that, by investigating a haunted location in the vicinity of her home, I had somehow opened a portal to the underworld. This allowed the ghosts of dead miners to come through and sexually harass her while she was taking a shower. At this, I could only scratch my head. I continued to receive harassing emails from this individual until finally, there was talk of involving my lawyer.

I must confess, part of me would have loved to have seen my attorney's face when it came time to construct a case.

(For the record, I do not find claims of sexual harassment or assault to be remotely funny. Regarding the case in question, I genuinely believe that the unfortunate lady should have started by evaluating non-paranormal concerns first, including an evaluation by a qualified physician).

Much that was cut out of the first edition of In Search of the Paranormal was, I suspect, best left that way. One of my biggest regrets, however, involved the book's length. The book was restricted to somewhere between 60,000 and 65,000 words — no fault on the part of the publisher, this was simply the standard length for a book of its type, and also a function of the paperback format. There was so much more that I wanted to tell, however, and while many of those cases ultimately made it into the next book in the series (Trail of Terror, which is due to receive its own second edition in the not-so-distant future) I had wanted to give the reader a little more bang for their buck.

Fortunately, I was able to redress this in the version you are now reading. In 2021, the publisher wrote to inform me that In Search of the Paranormal had completely sold out. The entire print run was gone. Surprisingly (to me, at least) they were not going to produce any more copies, meaning that the book would now be out of print.

They were nice enough to return all rights to the book to me, something they were by no means obligated to do, and an act of kindness for which I will always be grateful. The only thing I did not get to retain was the cover, which I rather liked: a black background, with an old house and a chair sitting in front of it. However, I have a kick ass cover designer on retainer, and he produced a cover for this second edition which I absolutely love.

This new, updated version of In Search of the Paranormal has been expanded by about 25%, some 16,000 words of new text. The lion's share of this covers a pair of iconic North American locations: the Waverly Hills Sanatorium, in Louisville, Kentucky, and Bobby Mackey's Music World in Wilder, also Kentucky. My intent was to take readers behind the scenes of both the history and haunting of each place, and give my personal take on what it was like to walk those haunted hallways in person.

The observant reader will notice that my writing style has changed somewhat in the almost eight years between editions of this book. I hope that this does not prove to be too jarring for the reader. Having written some 28 more books in that timeframe, it was inevitable that my "signature" would look a little different this much further down the line. I have not altered anything in the original manuscript, so the only changes made in the second edition are additions, not subtractions.

You never forget your first love, as the old saying goes. This is as true in publishing as it is in romance. In Search of the Paranormal was my first published book. A lot of water has gone under the bridge since it was released.

I like to think that I could do it better now, given the chance to write the book again, but I resisted the urge to tinker. The book has a lot of heart, and I'm both proud and fond of it in equal measure.

Now, put your feet up, enjoy a glass or cup of your favorite beverage, and let's set out on a dark and haunted road together.

Richard Estep
Longmont, Colorado
24 January, 2022

INTRODUCTION

Locked inside London's oldest prison, where the apparition of a masked plague doctor is said to walk. Staking out an abandoned graveyard, and its desecrated historic church – from which other ghost hunting teams have
fled, a mysterious cloud pursuing them to their car. Spending the night in a lonely mountain inn, on the trail of a long-dead former occupant. These are just three of the nights I have spent in search of the paranormal.

For as long as I can remember, ghosts and hauntings have fascinated me.

My name is Richard Estep, and I am a dedicated ghost hunter and paranormal investigator. I am also the co-founder and current director of the Boulder County Paranormal Research Society (BCPRS) operating out of Boulder, Colorado.

The Boulder County Paranormal Research Society

Along with my wife Laura, I founded the Boulder County Paranormal Research Society in 2006. BCPRS is a volunteer organization, staffed by some

very talented and dedicated individuals who are all professionals in
various other fields. I earn my living as a paramedic and as an educator, who also happens to be a firefighter in my spare time, and occasionally deploying on national emergencies with a Federal Disaster Medical Assistance Team.

Our ghost hunting team is made up of an eclectic mix of individuals, with a diverse set of skills and life experiences. All of this contributes to the melting pot that is BCPRS, and every member brings something unique to the table which can assist with investigating claims of the paranormal.

Please allow me to introduce you to Kate (retired telecommunications engineer), Charlie (emergency medical technician), Joey (I.T. engineer), Jenna (Counselor and Therapist), Catlyn (Professor of Philosophy, Religion, and Women's Studies), Lucilla (Healthcare office manager), and Sean (mechanic).

The group has also attracted its fair share of married couples, for whom the term "date night" has taken on an entirely spookier new connotation than those of most husbands and wives. Apart from myself and my wife Laura (medical insurance professional), we also have Kira and Seth (web comic designer and massage therapist), Jason and Linda (both healthcare professionals), and finally, Jeff and Miranda (a computer networking engineer and an electrical engineer).

As you can see, we're quite the motley bunch. But we all share a common goal: to investigate claims of paranormal phenomena, assess their validity, and above all else: *to help people*. We're passionate about helping the living and hunting the dead...and, let's face it - there are worse ways to spend your free time...

I began to seriously investigate claims of the paranormal back in the mid-nineties, when I was living in my native England. The next four years were spent learning the paranormal investigator's craft, and stand out in my memory as being truly fulfilling ones.

It is important to remember that the paranormal research scene looked very different in the late nineties than it does today. In Britain, the night vision-shot, profanity-laced adventures of *Most Haunted* had yet to grace television screens. Two plumbers from Roto-Rooter had yet to get an American TV deal and launch the smash hit show *Ghost Hunters.*

Paranormal investigation was still the exclusive domain of a relative few. We were often perceived as being rather odd by Joe Public, willing to give up a Friday or Saturday night to spend crawling around darkened buildings rather than hitting the pubs, clubs, and restaurants. It was truly a fringe scene, and walking into a bookstore would present you with no more than two or three shelves of paranormal reading choices, as opposed to the explosion of material that is out there today.

None of us knew about K-2 meters, Mel meters, or infra-red thermometers. We weren't aware of a possible link between paranormal activity and EMF levels. EVP research was in full swing, but had been for decades, and was conducted with factory-fresh audio tapes rather than digital voice recorders. Our cameras had to be loaded with film, because they didn't contain a hard drive. Most teams used equipment that was affordable and sometimes held together with duct tape and bailing wire.

On the flip side, the absence of a bewildering array of gadgets meant that investigators were forced to rely on old-fashioned critical thinking and basic techniques. Fewer flashing lights and blinking gizmos made for more work, and that forced you to do your background reading. Hours and hours prior to and after an investigation would be spent in the public library.

Caveat emptor – *let the buyer beware* – has never been truer than when applied to the field of paranormal investigation.

The miracle of modern technology today lets anybody punch such terms as "ghost hunter" or "paranormal investigator" into a search engine, and in the blink of an eye, they will receive hits from numerous individuals and teams within driving range of their home or place of work. If you're looking for help with a paranormal problem, you might think that more choice is a good thing. But you would be wrong.

On moving to the United States in 1999, I brought my passion for ghost hunting along with me. I continued to investigate cases of haunted places, objects, and people, eventually founding my own paranormal research team here in Colorado's beautiful Front Range.

The book you are now reading documents my journey from enthusiastic but unskilled rookie to seasoned professional paranormal investigator. It collects some of my favorite cases from the past two decades. I'll take you from historic stone buildings that are hundreds of years old, into living rooms of modern-day houses in sleepy residential neighborhoods. From London to Denver, you'll sit beside me in darkened corridors and travel haunted highways, as my team and I seek to uncover the truth about all things ghostly.

So, pull up a chair, get comfortable, and settle down for a trans-Atlantic tour of the paranormal.

Whatever you do, though...don't look behind you.

CHAPTER ONE

SIDEWAYS STEP

I was not quite sixteen years old when I saw my first dead body.

The insistent ringing of a telephone woke me from a deep sleep, brought on by a long night at work. It was just past noon on a weekday. I was still half asleep when I answered. The voice on the other end was immediately recognizable as my grandfather's neighbor, a kindly old lady who made it a point to keep an eye on him since he had become widowed. She sounded very upset.

In broken English, she hesitantly told me that my grandfather was "not good" and that she had called for the police. I felt like I had been punched in the gut. My mother had only spoken to him the evening before and everything had sounded fine. He had complained of no more than the usual aches and pains that were commonplace in a man of his age.

My grandfather had lived alone since my grandma died, in a small single-story home with a beautifully blossoming garden that was his pride and joy. He redirected all of his energies into tending that garden and making it flourish. To this day, I've never seen such a spectacular array of plants and flowers that were the sole work of just one person.

Rain or shine, he would drive over to my parents' house each morning and work hard at tending *their* garden, before heading back home to care for his own yard. We'd make each other mugs of steaming hot tea, and when he thought I wasn't looking my grandfather would add a splash of whiskey to his – strictly for "medicinal purposes". I loved him as much as a self-centered teenage boy could ever love his grandfather, but it remains one of the greatest regrets of my life that I took him far too much for granted.

My parents both worked during the day, so I made hurried phone calls to my mother and stepfather at their respective workplaces and then called for a taxi to take me over there.

There can be fewer things more stomach churning in life than arriving at the house of somebody you care about and seeing a police car parked outside. Paying off the taxi driver, I hurried down the driveway to be met by a burly police sergeant who looked exactly like the actor Dennis Quaid. It's strange that, even to this day, the fact that he looked like the star of *Tombstone* stands out in the forefront of my mind. Under situations of great stress, the mind often tends to fixate on that which is familiar.

"Your grandad's dead, son." The sergeant placed a fatherly arm around shoulder and steered me towards the open kitchen doorway.

As quickly and as simply as that, my entire world changed for the worse. I felt completely numb, too stunned to even begin crying. Following the time-honored tradition of the local British copper during times of emotional distress, he filled the kettle with water and made me a cup of tea.

My grandfather, Gordon – known to his friends by his middle name of "Nev" – had lived alone in the house since the passing of my grandmother a few years earlier. He was a strong and proud man, who made it his life's work to spoil me rotten.

Sitting in my grandfather's kitchen, shell-shocked and suddenly flooded with tears, the world started to close in. This familiar environment had been a safe place for me through my entire childhood. I can remember playing with *Star Wars* action figures in that kitchen, and snagging the sticky mixture from my grandmother's cake tin when I was barely old enough to run.

But now, he was cold and dead on the floor in the next room.

Fortunately for me, I was being looked after by a copper from the old school, who had done this often enough that he knew just how to treat me. The hot sugary tea was a start. That's often the standard English response to any emotional crisis...put the kettle on, make a cup of tea. It's how I handle any major personal crisis to this day.

Then the sergeant started to talk. He was comforting without being condescending or patronizing. *You're a big lad,* the conversation went. *You should look at joining the police, it might suit you.*

He was not only distracting me. He was building me up a little emotionally, not something I would have expected from a police sergeant who was built like a tank. But it was working. I quickly began to calm down and straighten my posture. My breathing slowed and the tears stopped. I wondered if my grandfather was standing in the room right now, unseen. The books I had read about ghosts suggested that it might be possible. I didn't want him to be disappointed in me, crying my eyes out in front of the police!

My stepfather arrived shortly after that, and he fell into conversation with the sergeant. Taking a deep breath, I stepped outside and moved around the house to the large glass patio door that looked into the living room.

I could see a slipper, upside down on the carpet beside the couch. In the slipper was a foot, dressed in a beige sock.

My eyes continued upwards, drawn unconsciously along the length of my grandfather's body. I couldn't have looked away if I had wanted to. His pant leg was crumpled upwards towards the knee, presumably where he had fallen to the ground. The skin was white on top, but was mottled a deep bruised purple at floor level where gravity had drawn all the blood after his heart had stopped beating. It would be another ten years before I learned the name of this condition: *dependent lividity.*

It was striking to me then – and I haven't shaken the feeling even today – just how unnaturally *still* a body looks when the life has left it. Something looks plain *wrong* about it to the eye. Your subconscious mind is very aware that the body isn't just sleeping, because there is literally *no* movement at all.

The couch arm blocked my view of grandfather from the shoulders up. If I had taken just one sideways step to the left, I would have seen his face. But I didn't want to, and don't think I could have moved if I *had* wanted to.

My feet were rooted to the spot. I wanted to remember my grandfather as he was, not as a lifeless body face-down on the living room carpet.

I never took that sideways step.

I'm still glad that I didn't.

Twenty-five years have passed since then. Sometimes I wonder where the time has flown to. During the course of my duties as a paramedic and volunteer firefighter, I have attended more than my fair share of deaths. Some have taken place peacefully, whereas others have been marred by violence. I can remember certain ones with crystal clarity of thought, and others have faded into the background haze of my long-term memory.

None of them are burned into my mind's eye like that first time, when I was a teenager.

CHAPTER TWO

A GHOSTLY ROAD

I was raised in the beautiful English town of Syston, nestled in the heart of the county of Leicestershire. When other kids my age were running around kicking a soccer ball, I was far more likely to be found curled up with a spine-tingling book about ghosts and haunted houses, or creepy works of fiction in which the spirits of the dead returned from the world beyond to terrify the living and exact revenge.

Leicester has seen a great deal of worldwide media attention lately, due to the body of King Richard III being unearthed in a car park in the city center. The area has no shortage of ghosts and legends, and I was fascinated to learn about them all.

For example, the city's Guild Hall is renowned for multiple ghosts. A spectral police officer has been reported there, as have a grey monk, a ghostly cat and dog, and a pair of disembodied legs! A huge black hell hound with blazing red eyes reputedly haunted Black Lane. The central railway station is home to the ghost of a mailman. Leicester's old Haymarket Theater was supposedly haunted by the apparition of a child wearing a sailor outfit. And the brick alleyway running alongside the old ABC movie theater, where my friends and I spent many happy hours immersed in the movies, was said to be haunted by the spirits of two children dating back to the Victorian era.

My mother and stepfather were both working parents, so I saw a lot less of them than most kids see of their parents. But they and my grandparents all recognized my bookish streak at a very early age and kept me well-supplied with stacks of age-appropriate books. Children's books about ghosts always went to the very top of the pile. I loved the chill that crept down my spine when reading them with a flashlight under the covers late at night, long after the lights were supposed to be out.

It wasn't long before I discovered the magic of the public library, and got myself a junior reader's card. I was soon checking out books on all aspects of the paranormal – UFOlogy, ESP, lake monsters, cryptozoology, spontaneous human combustion, and alien abduction were just some of the subjects that I devoured thanks to the "supernatural" section of the Syston library. By the age of ten, I had read many of the acknowledged classics in the field, such as the works of ghost hunters Harry Price and Andrew Green. My favorite author by far was Peter Underwood, president of the Ghost Club and author of *The Ghost Hunter's Guide*, a copy of which sits on my bookshelf at home today.

I would dream of following in the footsteps of these pioneers, creeping through haunted houses in the dark and tracking down the spirits of the unquiet dead. Everybody knows that life can take strange and bizarre turns sometimes, but I had absolutely no idea that I would spend the better part of two decades investigating haunted houses on two continents. My boyhood self would have been equally shocked and ecstatic to hear it!

One of the benefits of being a stepchild is that you get three sets of grandparents. I had really lucked out, because all of mine were wonderful. My stepfather's parents lived in the city of Hull. Grandfather Chris was a lovable, larger-than-life bear of a man, who had fought the Japanese in Burma during World War II. He encouraged me in my love of all things military and kept me well-supplied with comic books that had

exciting names such as *Commando! Battle!* and *Warlord!* In fact, lots of other comic books whose titles ended with an exclamation mark came my way thanks to Chris. He and my grandmother Doreen were part of that greatest generation that had
seen off the Nazis and given Hirohito a bloody nose. Doreen had raised a brood of children and held down the fort at home while her husband was dodging bullets overseas.

We stayed with Chris and Doreen very rarely, because they lived several hours' drive away from Leicester. It was always a big adventure to visit them, and became an even bigger one when I found out that they lived in a very haunted house. This was the first haunted house that I ever visited, to the very best of my knowledge.

Their home on 8th Avenue in Hull was your average everyday single-family residence, lovingly maintained but certainly nothing unusual...until you dug a little deeper. For some reason, it seemed to be inundated with apparitions, poltergeist activity, and enough other ghostly activity to terrify an impressionable and imaginative young lad of my age.

Sadly, my grandfather Chris died several years ago, and I miss him still. But Doreen still lives in the house in which they spent the majority of their adult lives, keeping it spotlessly clean and tidy. More than thirty years ago, when my nose was buried in a junior book about haunted houses and ghosts, they made note of my interest and sat me down to tell me about the events which had taken place in that very same house. When my stepfather and his siblings were young children, they were regularly tucked into bed at night by a kindly old lady who would float through the room and make sure that they were all safe. They felt no sense of fear or menace from this apparition, who behaved in a very maternal way, treating the children as a grandmother or nanny would treat her charges. Once the children were all tucked up safely under the sheets, she would simply disappear, either into thin air, or gliding through the brick bedroom wall into the corridor outside.

Chris and Doreen took this in their stride, and did not seem at all alarmed about the fact that the ghostly old lady was caring for their children at night. As the children grew up, the visitations became less and less frequent, until they finally stopped altogether when the children matured and moved out of the house to follow their own paths in life. An interesting coda to this story is that, when my stepfather moved away from home and traveled the country as a drilling worker, he maintains that the ghost actually followed him, turning up in his rented accommodation at night and scaring him half to death as he lay in bed. My stepfather used to talk about the ghostly old lady quite freely, with neither embarrassment nor embellishment, in that plain-spoken and factual manner in which many people from the North of England speak.

Their account of the ghostly old lady closely fit the textbook behavior of an apparition that is attached to a person or persons, rather than to a specific place. Generally, experts in the paranormal field agree that there are three broad categories of haunting: haunted *places,* haunted *objects,* and haunted *people.* It might explain why, over the entirety of my childhood visits to the house on 8th Avenue, I never encountered this ghost even once.

Oh, I used to lie awake at night *looking* for her! In a way, it is probably a good thing that she failed to materialize and tuck me in, because I would most likely have been terrified of her. Despite having an interest in the paranormal that bordered on the obsessive, I was paradoxically terrified of actually running into a ghost some dark and stormy night. I would probably have wet my pants!

I would lay there, bedclothes pulled up to the bridge of my nose, pretending to be asleep but cracking one eye halfway open. Kids of my parents' generation were obviously made of sterner stuff, because my stepfather's siblings all sounded completely unfazed when discussing these supernatural nocturnal visits.

Looking back with the benefits of hindsight, it might be tempting to conclude that my leg was being pulled. Perhaps the adults were concocting a scary story to frighten a young boy? But it is important to understand that my family's story has remained absolutely consistent for the past thirty plus years. This tale has not grown in the telling, as such stories are often prone to do. All of the witnesses involved have described the lady in exactly the same way, and they describe her regular appearances in the same way: with greatly affectionate nostalgia, and a slight air of bemusement. There is not so much as a whiff of falseness to their story, and I still believe it unreservedly.

This friendly and maternal old lady has turned out to be the first ghost that I was unable to catch. She would not be the last.

My stepfather's brother once encountered the apparition of a man in the hallway of an upstairs bedroom. The man, dressed in a suit and raincoat, looked stern and forbade him to enter the room. Upon fetching his mother, they discovered that after heavy rains, water had seeped into the walls and had rendered an exposed electrical wire potentially lethal. Once the wiring was repaired, this apparition was never seen again. My uncle insists that the ghostly man saved his life that day by denying him access to the bedroom.

As if this wasn't enough, a third apparition was seen by my grandmother one day when she was hanging wet laundry on the clothesline in the back yard. On looking back at the house, she saw the figure of an old lady standing in the open back doorway. The figure had folded arms and appeared to be watching her sullenly. Doreen wasn't sure if this apparition was the same as that which visited her children in the night, or perhaps a different entity. There had been talk of a previous owner of the house having hanged herself on the property, and Doreen wondered if this might be the apparition seen in the kitchen doorway. My grandmother described the ghost as exuding an air of profound sadness, matched by a downcast facial expression and slumped body posture. Like the stern but protective ghost seen upstairs by the children, this upset specter simply disappeared before her eyes.

When victory over Japan was declared, my grandfather returned from overseas combat and went back to civilian life. Both he and my grandmother told me of a spontaneous outbreak of poltergeist activity which took place in the house at that time, along with several other weird occurrences.

As they lay in bed together at night, it was not at all uncommon for my grandparents to hear the sounds of what seemed to be a party or some sort of social gathering, going on downstairs in the living room. The first night that this happened, shortly before midnight, Chris raced downstairs under the impression that there was a break-in in progress. Charging into the living room, he found everything to be dark and quiet, exactly as they had left it.

Chris went back to bed and turned out the light. Almost immediately, the sound of voices and laughter could be heard coming from downstairs again. The next morning, my grandparents dressed and went downstairs to make breakfast. They discovered picture frames turned at crazy angles on the walls, with some pictures taken down completely and left lying in the middle of the floor. Articles of furniture such as cushions or ornaments were moved around the room, scattered haphazardly as if by the hand of a playful but mischievous child.

This happened so frequently that my grandparents stopped remarking on it. Eventually, almost as if a battery were winding down its charge, the activity first tailed off and then stopped completely. After that, the house seemed to be absolutely normal, and remains that way to this day as far as I know. During my time spent there, I never experienced anything out of the ordinary. But that didn't stop me from playing the junior ghost hunter, begging my stepfather to repeat the tales over and over again, hitting him with questions from different angles and pestering him for more and more detail.

I didn't realize it at the time, but I was unconsciously aping the interviewing techniques of the ghost hunters I had been reading about, like the great Peter Underwood and Harry Price. The twin forces of skepticism and a burning desire to believe were pulling me in two opposite directions at the same time.

It's good to know that some things never change.

It was around the age of eleven that I went to a secondary school called Roundhill, since renamed "Roundhill Academy". American readers would recognize aspects of the secondary school system from the *Harry Potter* books and films. On the first day of school, we new students were all sorted into our houses, each named for a famous historical figure in Leicestershire history. We wore uniforms – shirt, blazer, tie, slacks – and were awarded or docked "house points" and "merit points" for academic achievement. Think of it as Hogwarts, but without the magic.

Roundhill unsurprisingly sits atop a fairly large round hill. The school itself is situated about halfway from the summit. At the very top of the hill is an old house that bears a creepy resemblance to the Bates Motel. Every school in Britain (and probably in the world) has an urban legend of some sort attached to it, and Roundhill was no exception. The house was supposedly haunted by a former student named Amy, who had died under mysterious but tragic circumstances that varied drastically depending on which student was telling you the tale.

Some said that she had been kicked to death by a horse in the adjoining stables. Others, that Amy was murdered by a teacher or janitor many years ago, when she spurned his advances. The story was passed by word of mouth to each successive generation of first year students in an attempt to scare the crap out of them on the long, lonely trek up the hill.

I first heard the tale of Amy back in 1983, and used to look for her in the tall glass windows on the upper floor when I approached the house for my lessons. A couple of older children were gleefully spreading the story of Amy's demise (in my version, she fell from an upstairs window and broke her neck on the driveway below). It was absolutely true, they insisted confidently, because *they* knew a guy who knew a girl who knew a third-year girl who had seen the ghost, waving to her from a window with her head cocked at a creepily unnatural angle. Of course, when pressed for details, the boys became increasingly circumspect, finally running away and laughing.

I returned to Roundhill in 1997 for some adult community college classes in economics, and made a point of looking up some of my old teachers. Sitting down with a former English teacher, who looked a lot less intimidating now that a couple of decades had nearly passed, I asked him about the story of Amy, and whether there was a germ of truth at the heart of it all.

"As far as I can remember, the story has been going around this campus when the new first year hordes come screaming on board. I've never heard of there being a genuine death happening up at the house.

"Then again," he contemplated, "they *were* telling that story when *I* was a first year here."

And they're still telling it now.

Thanks to the Internet, keeping in touch with friends and classmates of yesteryear is now easier than ever. First years are *still* being told the same story, or variations of it. And yet, everybody seems to know somebody *who knows somebody* who has seen the ghost of tragic Amy. I have yet to hear of an actual witness to the apparition coming forward. But I like to think that the legend of Amy, whether fact or fiction, will continue to have first years quaking in their shoes long after I am six feet under!

I have spent many years investigating reports such as this one. Sometimes there is a grain of truth to the story, a small kernel of fact that takes on a life of its own and explodes dramatically into urban legend and drama. The savage murder at Macky auditorium is one example of just such a case, where a genuine tragedy has been spun into a ghostly tale worthy of a Hollywood movie. Even the wildest, craziest ghost story is worth looking into – just in case there is a nugget of credibility hidden at its core.

Graduating from Roundhill and moving up to a school called Wreake Valley at the age of fourteen, it didn't take long for the seniors to spread a new urban legend about that school. Wreake Valley had a theater complete with a stage and auditorium seating. Legend had it that, if you were to sit in a specific seat in a specific row, the ghost of a big black dog would materialize on stage and run out through the back wall of the theater.

It's a fun story, but one for which I can find no witnesses to corroborate it. However, during the course of researching this book, I spoke with an old friend who used to work at the school until not too long ago. She hadn't heard the tale of the ghostly dog, but related to me a conversation she had with a member of the maintenance department. The closed-circuit television cameras are said to have recorded a shadowy black form, which seems to be drifting along the exterior walls at the back of the school. I would dearly love to get my hands on a copy of this footage. Is it imaging artifact, a trick of the light, natural shadow...or could it be something otherworldly?

• • • ● ● • ● ● ● • •

I am, and always have been, a massive geek at heart. Science fiction and fantasy conventions are my idea of a blissful weekend vacation, and my bookshelves groan under the weight of genre authors such as Heinlein, Asimov, and Tolkien.

As a survival mechanism, teenage geeks and nerds tend to band together during high school. I spent a lot of time hanging out with a great buddy named Travis Adams. We went on to become great friends – and remain so to this day, despite living on different continents. Apart from a mutual fanaticism for all things futuristic and fantastic, we shared a passion for the paranormal and formed a well-intentioned but ultimately short-lived ghost club. I'd read about the actual Ghost Club, the oldest and arguably most prestigious paranormal research organization, in the books of Peter Underwood. I didn't think that they accepted members as young as fourteen, so decided to go one better and start my own with Travis.

We spent a lot of time talking, watching bad horror movies, and reading about the paranormal. Sadly, precious little time was spent actually *doing*. We spent one less than stellar evening randomly knocking on people's doors and asking if their home was haunted, and tried to drum up the courage to do the same at a local church, but nothing ever really came of it.

Travis's neighbors had a ghost story that intrigued the hell out of us. They were a nice middle-aged couple whose name escapes me. The former tenant of their house was an old man named Arthur, who had died suddenly and unexpectedly in the home itself. Arthur had left a walking stick behind that stayed with the house after its sale. The neighbors told us that Arthur was now haunting their house. They heard footsteps crossing the kitchen floor when they were in bed at night. Most disconcerting of all, the walking stick would often levitate in the air, floating as if guided by an unseen hand, and performing sweeping movements in front of the incredulous couple.

We got to examine the stick, which seemed perfectly normal as far as we could tell. With hindsight, I've always wanted to ask that couple why they didn't keep a camera close to hand (or better yet, borrow a video camera) to capture some solid evidence of the floating, dancing walking stick.

By the time I turned twenty, life was going pretty well. I was renting a single room in a shared house with a couple of other single professionals, and working as a welder in a factory. I hated the job – it was mindless, and I was bored by nine a.m. But, the money was good and the overtime was plentiful.

Books continued to stack up by my bedside, many of them having a paranormal theme. On TV, *The X-Files* was taking both Britain and America by storm, encouraging me and a new generation of paranormal enthusiasts to grab a huge flashlight and find out whether the truth was actually out there.

Unbeknownst to me at the time, I was actually about to take a step closer towards finding out.

CHAPTER THREE

THE WRIGHT STUFF

One night during the mid-Nineties, I happened to pick up a copy of a local newspaper, the *Leicester Mercury*. Flipping idly past the TV listings, my eye was drawn to a headline that was guaranteed to provoke my interest:

RETURN TO THE DEMON CHURCH

Instantly engrossed, I devoured the entire article. The gist of it was that a team of ghost hunters led by a man called Andrew James Wright had recently spent the night at a haunted church in Lincolnshire. If the article was to be believed, they had witnessed paranormal activity on an unprecedented scale, which some eyewitnesses described as being demonic in nature. Andrew and his team were plotting a return visit. The remainder of the article was taken up with comments from a local priest, warning the investigators of the danger to their immortal soul if they attempted to tangle with the forces of darkness without being protected by the holy armor of God.

Wow!

This was the sound of opportunity knocking, loud and clear. Here was a chance to get involved, to actually get some experience if I played my cards right. I wasted no time in contacting Andrew Wright to ask permission to join his team as some kind of apprentice or probationary investigator.

A gruff voice at the other end of the phone line asked me if I had any experience with night vision equipment or other technical abilities. Thinking desperately, I came up with the fact that I had used some night vision equipment in the Territorial Army. Once.

There was a thoughtful pause. "Alright, you're in."

YES!

Andrew had founded an organization called SPECTA (short for "Search for Physical Evidence and Compilation of Theory into Apparitions") which was the first ghost hunting team that I ever joined. Although it sounds like the sort of underground international spy network that James Bond would have encountered during the Seventies, it was actually one of the very few reliable and trustworthy resources that people call could on for help during the Nineties if they were having paranormal problems.

I was walking on air when I put the phone down. I was finally about to get my wish and do more than simply read about ghosts in the pages of a book. There was a possibility that I would actually get to meet one.

Try to imagine Keith Richards of *Rolling Stones* fame, crossed with the singer Rod Stewart. Sprinkle in a dash of Eric Dylan, and you're imagining somebody that would look a lot like Andrew Wright. I sincerely believe that he missed his calling in life and should have been a rock star or at the very least, a roadie for one.

Andrew dresses flamboyantly, and during the nineties he could have stepped directly from the set of an MTV production. His standard uniform is a mullet, skinny jeans, a brightly colored shirt, and sneakers. Agent Mulder this was not. But underneath the surface lies one of the most experienced ghost hunters to haunt the British scene at the close of the Twentieth Century (Andrew has since retired, surfacing occasionally to do charity overnight events). Andrew worked with some of the greats in his time, such as Maurice Grosse of Enfield Poltergeist fame, and has an almost encyclopedic knowledge of British ghost lore. He is also an accomplished author, with several respected books on the subject of ghosts and haunting to his name.

Old school to the core, Andrew saw ghost hunting as every bit a social activity as it was a scientific research pastime. If there was an opportunity on any investigation to drop in at a nearby pub (or better yet, to investigate a haunted pub itself!) he would be in there like a shot. SPECTA met in the bar of a small, out-of-the-way hotel on the outskirts of Leicester city center. Andrew chaired the informal meeting, and introduced me and several other new members to the existing group. I hit it off with Eric and Tracey, two level-headed investigators who had worked with Andrew on investigations before. Amanda, a psychic, and her teenage daughter Tessa would also be accompanying us, along with some other first-timers who we would meet on the day.

There was an air of almost palpable excitement as Andrew briefed us on the details. St. Botolph's church is located in the county of Lincolnshire. The church was decommissioned in the 1970s and since then had fallen victim to desecration and vandalism by not only local teenagers, but also what is believed to be a Satanic coven.

St. Botolph's wasn't particularly well-known for its ghostly activity until the publication of a book entitled *Ghostbusters UK* by Robin Furman. I was familiar with this book, and had found the contents rather interesting to say the least. The section that centered round St. Botolph's church detailed the ghostbusting team encountering a wide range of disturbing paranormal phenomena both inside the church and out in the surrounding grounds, which were supposedly littered with the corpses of animal sacrifices. The the action climaxes with a ghostly mist emerging from a tomb and pursuing the paranormal investigators to their car, despite one of them firing a "tractron gun" (some kind of multi-colored light beam gun, designed to fight off ghosts!) into the mass before making good their escape.

An investigator called Colin Veacock had recently investigated the church after the "Grimsby Ghostbusters" had fled. To quote Colin directly on the matter, as described on his blog *ghost-quest.blogspot.com...*

"During our overnight stays we experiences footsteps crisscrossing the church, incredibly loud crashes, stone throwing, the grass and bushes in the graveyard moving in a weird way, a transparent figure stood in the altar, and on more than one occasion, doors slamming shut in front of our faces."

Andrew maintained that Colin was a trustworthy source and that his word was solid. It looked as if St.Botolph's church was a hotbed of paranormal activity, and I couldn't wait to experience it firsthand. An investigation was scheduled for a few Saturdays hence.

Although I wouldn't come face to face with a ghost, one would certainly crop up right behind my back...

We rolled up the long driveway to St. Botolph's church on a warm Saturday afternoon in the summer. The church was nestled amongst beautiful surroundings, rolling green flatlands reminiscent of a picturesque postcard.

Parking the cars next to a gatehouse covered in plants, our group entered the churchyard and began to unload boxes and bags of equipment.

Remember that this was the Nineties, long before the cheap EMF meter explosion rocked the world of paranormal investigation. Tape recorders, flashlights, and still cameras formed our basic kit. If you were really lucky – and we were – then you might be able to scrape up a VHS camcorder or two. Portable walkie-talkie radios were our communications link with one another.

Looking around at the quaint stone church and tower, I was struck by how peaceful everything seemed – not in the least bit creepy.

"This place changes after dark," Andrew remarked. "Just you wait, mate. You'll see."

At the time, we had no idea just how right he was.

Rumors abound to this day about the use of St Botolph's for rituals performed by those who are interested in the occult. While I can't say for sure whether this is true, our first sweep of the location did lend credence to rumors of ritualistic practice and animal abuse.

At the rear of the property stood six gravestones, dating back to the Second World War. There lie buried several unidentified sailors, crew of a steamship – the *S.S. Orsa* - that was bound for Bordeaux on Saturday, October 21st, 1939, with a cargo of coal. The *Orsa* was sunk by a German mine with the loss of sixteen crewmen. The bodies of some of those drowned crewmen washed ashore on a nearby beach at Saltfleet.

The area surrounding these war graves had a very peaceful atmosphere, but it didn't take long for one of the investigators to discover something out of place. Several decapitated chicken torsos were scattered in the long grass.

I thought that it might perhaps be a fox or some form of local wildlife. Taking a knee, Andrew shook his head. He pointed at the chicken necks for emphasis, indicating that they were artificial rather than natural. The wounds had most definitely been inflicted with some kind of sharp slicing implement, rather than torn by the teeth of some nocturnal predator. The chicken bodies were also intact, without evidence of other wounds or bites. And the heads were missing. A hungry animal would have eaten the bodies and left the heads.

We took pictures and left the scene undisturbed, then fanned out to search the churchyard.

Gravestones had been shattered, cracked, and desecrated. Human excrement was smeared across several of them. Flowers were uprooted and scattered around the cemetery. Obscene graffiti defaced the back of many grave markers. Was this vandalism the work of unruly local kids, or something more sinister?

I followed Tracey and Andrew inside the church. The sturdy wooden doors had been wrenched off and burned inside the church, according to the caretaker, a Mr. Beaufort. Stepping into the stone-clad shadowy interior, I suddenly felt cold – entirely understandable, given the change in environment. None of the windows contained glass, leaving the church entirely open to the elements. Given how cold it was now, I was glad I'd brought a sleeping bag and some warm clothing to see me through the night.

We split up and began to take photographs while the daylight remained strong.

Even today, I still insist that the human eye and an inquiring mind are the most indispensable tools of any paranormal investigator. A notebook and pen are not far behind. Everything else is negotiable. The true pioneers in this field relied on little else, and achieved some truly impressive results.

Tracey called us over to the nave. Several pentagrams were visible, staining the flagstones and the walls. Some were obviously orange spray paint, but others looked disconcertingly like blood. Burned-down candles congealed into piles of wax at the corners. More human waste was smeared across the walls and flagstones. It appeared relatively fresh, no more than a day or two old.

Somebody had obviously gone to great lengths to desecrate this truly beautiful old church. It made us all angry, but there was an underlying current of nervousness setting in as well. Would whoever it was return to find us here after dark?

At the far end of the building was the entrance to St Botolph's tall stone tower, a wooden trapdoor in the ceiling that would only be accessible with a large ladder. We hadn't brought one with us, so nobody was getting up there. The last group to investigate this place (which Andrew had been a part of) had claimed to see two red eyes in the outside windows to the tower, and hear an inhuman growling coming from up there. The group's sensitive, Amanda, insisted that a demonic entity was lurking in the tower. She referred to it repeatedly as "The Beast."

Twinkling ghostly lights had also been reported from the tower windows by local residents and former investigators. It seemed to be the focus of paranormal activity in the church. Amanda warned the team that we must not stand in contact with any of the walls, as she believed that "The Beast" might be capable of using this as a method of possessing an investigator.

It wasn't long before Amanda told us that she was beginning to experience a vision of some kind. She described seeing a tall, cowled figure, which seemed to be wearing a monk's robe. To my mind, her description conjured up an image of a monk or friar. Amanda went on to tell us that the figure pacing up and down the center of the church, jingling something at his waist which appeared to be a ring of keys. She believed this male entity to be a monk who had never left the church behind after his death, a lost soul. She was confident that the monk would leave us alone if we left him alone.

Evening was drawing in and we were starting to lose the daylight. Having investigated the church before, the plan of attack was mostly Andrew's baby. Teams of at least two people would be posted both inside and outside the building, some of them acting as static observers, and some of them roving about the grounds. The idea was that at regular intervals, everybody would hunker down and go quiet.

Being fairly new, I tried to keep my mouth shut and my ears open as much as possible. As plans went, it was a good one. But I was forgetting the time-honored military maxim that no battle plan ever survives first contact with the enemy. This would certainly prove to be the case at St. Botolph's.

Andrew wanted the tower to be under observation at all times. A team was stationed at the front gate, with a good view of the tower, the church front door, and a large part of the cemetery. Other teams were placed at corners of the building, the idea being that we would have almost 360-degree coverage of the place throughout the night. No team would be out of sight of at least one other team, for safety reasons.

Depending on your point of view, the interior teams either drew the short straw or really lucked out. One team would be positioned in the middle of the church itself. Most of the time they'd be alone, but if things really started hopping, then the idea was to send in a second team to back them up. This team would have to be pulled from the outside perimeter though, leaving a blind spot.

It might be a stereotype, but English paranormal overnights are fueled almost entirely by hot tea (with a side order of caffeinated soda). We'd all brought flasks of tea to see us through into the early hours and to help stave off the biting cold. The first steaming hot cups were broken out at dusk, as the whole team gathered at the gatehouse and began to compare notes.

Andrew was holding court, a sketch map of the location spread out on a horizontal tomb stone in front of him.

We all agreed that the plan made good use of the personnel and resources that we had available. Fresh batteries went into the flashlights and walkie-talkies, and radio frequency checks were carried out, making sure that we could all talk to one another.

Dusk turned into full dark with surprising speed. The stars came out, a beautiful English summer sky that was mostly cloudless. All was peaceful and calm, the natural sounds of early evening lulling everybody into an easygoing confidence. Uninvited, Andrew's comment popped into my mind.

This place changes after dark.

We began to gear up. I wanted something utilitarian and warm, settling for leather boots, jeans, and my military camo jacket. Ten pounds of equipment was scattered throughout the various pockets or dangling around my neck on a strap.

I must have looked like a total idiot.

However, at least my hands were free, and I wouldn't have to go back to my kit bag for spare equipment. So, it wasn't all bad.

It was full dark, and fog was starting to descend on us. As the temperature began to drop, the fog was rolling in off the sea. The churchyard looked for all the world like the set of a 1970s-era horror movie, discolored gravestones scattered crookedly like broken teeth in the mouth of a methamphetamine abuser. If you've seen the Tim Burton movie *Sleepy Hollow*, then you can picture the scene exactly.

Andrew had been right – the atmosphere *did* change at night. Traffic on the main road was minimal, despite it being a weekend. The hushed silence was genuinely eerie. Sounds traveled farther than they did during the daytime, and echoed in strange ways from gravestones and natural features. There were some weird acoustic effects going on.

Of course, a lot of this feeling was psychological. We all recognized that for what it was, and we had prepared for it mentally as best we could. But there's a big difference between having the intellectual knowledge that you're in a dark and supposedly haunted churchyard in the fog, and actually *being* there. It's difficult to switch off the nagging voice in your ear that constantly says, *Hey, you've seen so many horror movies that began like this!*

Tracey and I – recently dubbed *Team Three* - were posted in a quiet corner of the churchyard down by the war graves, getting our bearings in the darkness and settling in for an hour's watch. It wasn't long before Andrew's voice came over the airwaves and told us that there was an intense white beam of light cutting across the fields.

We set off for the gatehouse at a slow, deliberate pace, picking our way between gravestones and despoiled monuments. This was no time or place to stumble and twist an ankle in the dark. I also really didn't want to step in some of the nastiness we had seen earlier. The nearest medical attention was a good few miles away. Come to think of it – and this concerned me more – so was the nearest police presence. We really were isolated out here in the middle of nowhere. And this was years before everybody sported a cell phone.

Andrew's diminutive figure suddenly appeared out of the fog. He pointed in the direction of the main Louth road, whispering that some type of light beam had flashed up from there and hit the side of the church tower.

It was only a few seconds before a blinding white light sliced through the fog. The searchlight beam was tight, and moving quickly enough that it must have been mounted on some kind of vehicle or held out of a car window. We collectively held our breath, watching as the beam played across the side of the church tower and across the surrounding gravestones.

Everybody was thinking the same thing. I know this for a fact because we confirmed it afterwards, talking on the car journey home. But nobody wanted to give voice to it.

What if those Satanists were back?

It was a valid concern. The chicken corpses had been mutilated with a knife, or similar sharp implement...definitely a weapon of some kind. If the rumors proved to be true, and a Satanic group was practicing rituals at St. Botolph's church, just how territorial might they turn out to be if they found us on their turf?

The churchyard was suddenly a very lonely place to be.

I rummaged in the webbing pouch that usually housed my military gas mask, digging out the pair of cheap binoculars I'd brought with me. Bringing the source of the light beam into focus through gaps in the drifting fog, I could just make out a car braking to a halt at the end of the long church driveway. At least two figures could be seen milling about the boundary fence, which we'd padlocked under strict instructors from caretaker Beaufort.

I asked Andrew and Tracey if I could go and check it out a little more closely. They shrugged.

In a low crouch, I kept to the natural depressions in the ground and skirted the field's far left border. I don't think the camouflage jacket made much of a difference, but the fog shrouded me right up until I arrived at the main road fence.

I squatted, catching my breath, mouth open, and listened.

Laughter, was my first impression. And not the sinister cackling of the Hollywood horror villain, as played by Vincent Price or Boris Karloff. This laughter had more of the cheerfully inebriated than the Satanist about it, suggesting a few alcoholic beverages had been consumed this evening. My hackles were dropping by the second.

I crept up to a battered Ford Escort which had seen much better days. Its occupants turned out to be a man and a woman, both in their mid-twenties. They were giggling as each took a turn to shine a powerful portable searchlight across the churchyard. We were obviously providing them with some free entertainment on their way home from the pub. I was starting to get annoyed, not just with the pair of them, but with myself for getting afraid of nothing.

I was no longer feeling very charitable, and was just getting ready to step out of the fog in the most sinister way that I could muster, when my radio screeched into life.

Andrew wanted a status update.

Fantastic timing, Andy. Thanks.

As one, they both shrieked and leapt backwards. The air turned blue with swearing as they saw me, saw that I was alone, and wasn't intent on harming them. The man wanted to know why I was lurking in the fog late on a Saturday night. The woman – we learned later that she was his girlfriend – was visibly shaking, holding onto the Ford for support.

On occasion, I've been known to think on my feet. Although it was stupid to come down here on my own to confront what might have been a mob of knife-wielding strangers, I'd gotten lucky and been confronted with two slightly drunk locals instead. Let's call them Dave and Sharon. Dave told me that he and Sharon had enjoyed a couple of drinks at home and were on their way for a few more at the local pub with their friends, when they'd noticed lights and cars up at "the old haunted church." So, for a laugh, Dave had pulled over and tried to spook what he took to be a bunch of bored teenagers who he thought were damaging the church for kicks.

I was on the verge of telling him the truth about our purpose at the church, but some kind of hunch stopped me. Thinking it through, I realized that if my new "friends" became aware that a team of ghost hunters were staking out the churchyard, it would be the first thing they'd tell their drinking buddies when they got to the pub. And, with people being people, the gossip would spread among the locals like wildfire.

It was getting on for nine o'clock by now, which left a solid couple of hours drinking time at most pubs. By the time the pubs closed just before midnight, we would probably be inundated with a crowd of drunk and giggling thrill-seekers who wanted to mess with us. The whole investigation would be ruined before it ever really got off the ground.

Fortunately, my second brainwave of the evening was a real zinger. A plan started to form in my mind. It would rely upon three things to work. Firstly, my own natural ability to bullshit a couple of half-drunk people. Secondly, the willingness of my friends and colleagues to recognize what I was trying to do and to back me up on the fly. And lastly, a healthy dollop of good luck.

I decided to go for it.

Reaching for the walkie-talkie, I keyed the transmitter and let loose a sentence of absolutely meaningless rubbish.

"Copy your transmission, four-zero-X-ray-delta. Have made contact with two local citizens. Will advise shortly. X-ray niner, out." Reading all of those Tom Clancy novels hadn't been entirely useless after all.

Dave and Sharon gave me a curious stare. Plastering on my very best *"hey, you can trust me!"* grin, I launched into a tale that was both convoluted and completely made up as I went along.

The gist of my story was that I worked for a private security company, hired by the Redundant Churches Commission to stop vandalism and desecration at St. Botolph's church. And I wasn't alone, oh no sir and no, ma'am. I had a crew of security guards with me to help install a security surveillance system in the derelict building, in the hopes of catching the vandals red-handed and gathering evidence for the police to prosecute them. After all, why else would I be wearing a camouflage jacket and webbing on a Saturday night in the middle of nowhere?

No doubt the alcohol smoothed things along, but Dave and Sharon readily bought what I was selling. This was where things got tricky. If they left for the pub now, their story could be met with disbelief and a "let's see for ourselves!" reaction. Like any good lie, I needed to show them a nugget of truth in order to make it believable. I offered them a guided tour of our "security operation" to tell their friends about. But I was also using the carrot and stick approach, and made sure to tell them that any further intrusions over the next twenty-four hours would be treated as trespass and result in an arrest.

The faces of my teammates were an absolute picture when I escorted Dave and Sharon through the gateway into the churchyard. *My* face, on the other hand, seemed to have developed a muscular twitch. I was winking desperately at every one of them whenever we made eye contact.

Referring to Andrew as *boss*, I explained that Dave and Sharon were two civically minded locals who were concerned that we might be desecrating the church. The fake grin was still frozen on my face, but was beginning to feel increasingly desperate.

God bless Andrew and Tracey for playing along. I could see their mental wheels turning.

Dave and Sharon nodded and smiled a little bit nervously, but seemed to be convinced. The video camera propped against the gravestone at Andy's elbow wasn't hurting our credibility either.

I escorted them on a quick tour of the church interior, making a great show of expressing sorrow and disgust at the pentagrams desecrating this beautiful old building. Dave and Sharon were wide-eyed throughout, catching sight of the interior team just as they were placing tape recorders with external microphones underneath the tower trapdoor. We must have looked like the world's cheapest private security outfit.

The plan worked like a charm. I waved goodbye to Dave and Sharon at the locked gate fifteen minutes later, leaving them a fun story to tell their friends and eliciting a promise not to return tonight. We'd made a couple of new friends, and hoped it would make them think twice about coming back for more after the pub closed.

Things started happening just before midnight.

Lights in the tower were reported by two of the teams. Blue lights, which seemed to be twinkling. One minute they were there, and the next they were gone. Video cameras rolled, but subsequently none of the lights were recorded on tape. I didn't see them personally, but four witnesses in two separate locations reported seeing them from opposite corners of the graveyard.

In order to mix up the personnel dynamic a little bit, Andrew paired me up with Steven, another new guy, and told us to walk the perimeter of the church building and check for anomalies. Tracey switched over to work with Eric, who had been standing at the gate with Andrew until then. Changing teams around is a standard procedure in most paranormal research groups.

I was happy to stretch my legs, and told Andrew that I planned to take some photographs on each side of the building. He warned all teams over the radio that there would be some flash photography on all sides of the church over the next few minutes. This was good practice on his part. Flashes of light coming from an unknown source are often reported on paranormal investigations. The first and most obvious thing to rule out is flash photography by your fellow investigators. Putting the warning message out over the airwaves meant that nobody was going to mistake my camera flashes for anything of paranormal origin.

Steven and I were designated "Roving Team" for the duration of this assignment. For a young guy, he seemed to have a level head on his shoulders. Perhaps a little nervous, but that was understandable in these circumstances. Flashlights on, with red lens filters in place to help preserve night vision, we set off on a counterclockwise circuit of the building.

Systematically, we photographed the main doorway and worked our way towards the graves of the dead sailors. Then our roving team checked in with the static teams located on the building corners, making sure that everyone was OK and enquiring about unusual activity. Apart from the lights seen in the tower, nothing objective was reported. But half of the team members we spoke to, experienced a strange sensation of *heaviness,* as if an oppressive atmosphere was blanketing the location. At the time, I chalked it up to the psychological components of drifting fog and the creepy environment.

With the benefit of hindsight, I am not so sure.

Having carried out our instructions, it was time to head back. Steven and I rounded the final corner, passing a dark stand of trees on the way. I nearly jumped out of my skin as my walkie-talkie began to squawk again.

It was team one, two of the associated investigators that I didn't know very well. They wanted to know who the third member of our team was. Steven and I looked at one another in confusion. What third member of our team were they referring to?

The tall man, they told us, who had just followed the pair of us around the corner of the church.

Every literary cliché you've ever read descended on me at the same time.

My blood ran cold.

My mouth went dry.

My heart was pounding in my chest.

Steven and I turned round so fast, it's amazing that we didn't get whiplash. Nothing was there except a cluster of gravestones.

Team one proceeded to tell us that they had followed our progress around the church corner, watching as we appeared between the church wall and the stand of trees. My 6'2" frame and Steven's smaller, thinner one were easily recognizable. But a third figure had followed us, maybe three or four steps behind us.

Shaken, I asked them what the figure had looked like.

Taller than me, I was told. Robed and cowled. Very tall, and very thin. And the figure didn't so much walk as *glide*. It seemed to disappear into the fog, but did not run or bolt. My mind shot back to Amanda's story about the cowled monk pacing the church interior. Perhaps I owed her an apology for feeling slightly cynical about it earlier.

Tracey pressed a mug of steaming hot tea into my hands. The night was becoming colder, although we were lucky that there was little wind to speak of. Leaves rustled gently in the trees. There was no sign of the fog lifting.

Midnight passed by in relative peace. We began to settle down in our watch positions, with everybody keeping an eager eye out for tall, robed figures gliding through the churchyard.

A torrent of noise shattered the silence sometime after one o'clock. Our team of observers stationed by the merchant navy war graves started calling for help. Andy and Eric descended on their location, while the other teams stayed in place.

Silence settled in again. A quarter hour passed before Andy, Eric, and the two observers they had gone to assist joined us in the gatehouse. Andy called everybody in for a discussion. It didn't take him long to tell us what had happened.

Behind the war graves lay a small ditch, and beyond that was a field of long grass. The observers had noticed some odd sounds coming out of the field, as if something large and bulky were stomping through the grass and flattening a path as it went. At first, they had figured it for a fox, badger, or some other nocturnal animal. But as the noise grew steadily louder, it soon became apparent that the cause of all this noise had to be something bigger than even the largest English countryside animal.

The observers were both becoming more and more concerned for their safety as the crashing sounds reached a crescendo, racing towards them through the long grass. If not an animal, could this be a person (or persons) attempting to spook them or cause them physical harm?

Hearts in their mouths, both observers stood up, broke light discipline – with good reason, in my opinion – and lit up the field with their high-powered flashlights.

The long grass was undisturbed in all directions. Not a blade or stalk was out of place. No wind swayed the grass. The team was adamant that whatever had made such a considerable disturbance *must* have battered its way through the field, and should have left a trail of crushed grass in its wake.

But there was absolutely nothing.

By two o'clock, everybody was getting tired.

It had been a long day for each of us. The long drive from Leicester had meant a fairly early start. I hadn't managed to sleep in, mostly due to the excitement and anticipation of working on this case. Based on the conversations that I had shared with my fellow investigators, I wasn't the only one.

But now, it was starting to show. Even with hot, sweet tea and caffeinated soda in massive quantities, people were starting to flag. Attention spans were diminishing and minds starting to wander. It's a natural physiologic response to being awake when your body clock thinks you ought to be asleep. The nervous system gets cranky and likes to remind you of that at every opportunity.

I'd gone to gloves and beanie hat in order to stave off the cold. I was starting to really feel the chill now, and most of the hot tea was gone.

Tracey and I were standing outside the main entrance, quietly discussing the incident that occurred over by the war graves. Steven had drifted off to sleep, propped up against a gravestone five feet away from us. Although it seemed a little disrespectful, we didn't have the heart to wake him...and this was far from the worst form of disrespect that St. Botolph's had been subjected to recently.

Steven startled both of us by sitting bolt upright and crying out in alarm. He suddenly reached out and clung to Tracey like a scared child clinging to his mother. She did her best to soothe him and asked what was wrong.

Steven was working himself up into a minor panic. He'd felt sleepy and settled back against the gravestone, just for five minutes, to rest his eyes. I nodded sympathetically. It was getting harder and harder to stay awake, despite the now biting cold. He had been suffering what he could only describe as a horrible, nightmarish dream, and then woke up when he heard and felt somebody breathing heavily in his ear.

Steven was insistent that something physical – and more worryingly, something *malicious* – was messing around with him. He believed it meant him genuine harm, rather than simply being playful.

Tracey tried to allay his fears, telling him that it was probably just a nightmare brought on by their surroundings and by his state of physical exhaustion. But Steven was inconsolable and wasn't having any of it. This was his last investigation, he was done with all this, and that was final. *Fair enough,* I thought. You had to respect his wishes. Paranormal investigation isn't for everybody, and it's better to find that out sooner rather than later. We sent him off to the car to try and get some sleep in relative peace. He slept with the inside light on until sunrise.

With one man down and an uneven number of team members remaining, a cooperative decision was made to centralize everybody *inside* the church building. The interior team had been reporting odd shuffling sounds for the past few minutes, and what sounded to them a little like footsteps crisscrossing the stone floor.

Nobody needed any arm-twisting to talk them inside out of the cold fog. By now my teeth were beginning to chatter and I'd begun to shiver, so I snapped my sleeping bag out with a flourish and crawled inside, sitting with my back propped up against one of the interior church walls. As the early morning wore on and the temperature dropped further still, I ended up loaning out the sleeping bag to a few other people for short periods of warming up. The problem was that the flagstones would just leech the heat right out of you. It's only a slight exaggeration to say that our tape recordings ought to have recorded several sets of chattering teeth as background noise.

Sometime between three and four o'clock in the morning, I nodded off to sleep. Everything was quiet inside the church except for the cooing of pigeons nesting in the rafters. Heads were starting to nod and loll as exhaustion finally took its toll on most of us.

Tracey dug me in the ribs with her elbow. I'd been snoring.

SCREEEEEEEEEEEEEEEEAAAAAAAAAAAAAARRRR RRRCCCCCHHHHHHH!

I slammed bolt upright with a start. What can only be described as a high-pitched animalistic shriek was coming from the center of the church, right before our astonished eyes. Dawn was starting to brighten the sky outside the empty window frames, providing a reasonable backdrop of ambient light to see by. Several investigators had flashlights still shining. Despite the presence of a few small and shadowy nooks, there was no part of the church interior that we couldn't see into clearly.

The screeching was coming out of thin air.

Grabbing my flashlight, I swung it around to face the origin point. Nothing at all. Sleepy investigators had been jolted awake instantly and were likewise trying to pinpoint the source of the screech, which had now stopped. Puzzled (and more than a little unnerved), I unzipped the warm sleeping bag reluctantly and climbed out, walking out into the middle of the room. Breath misted the air in front of me. I looked up, flashlight beam sweeping along with my gaze. All that I could see was an empty ceiling.

Eric, Andy, Tracey, and I formed a huddle. Our tired brains struggled to conjure up a rational explanation.

A bird of prey? A previous investigator thought that he had seen a kestrel, lodging somewhere inside the church. We ruled this flying suspect out on the basis of our not having seen anything larger than a pigeon in the rafters when we searched the place, and hadn't heard a flapping of wings to accompany the screech. We were in agreement that the screech originated somewhere around eye level, not from up in the rafters. It really did seem to be coming out of thin air.

No other explanation appeared to fit the bill. To complicate matters even further, when we reviewed the audio tapes afterwards, nothing was picked up on them other than the commotion made by us in reaction to the screech. We had all heard it, but had recorded no objective evidence to back it up.

Dawn was just a few short hours away, and the decision was made to wrap things up. I was in favor of trying to bed down and get some kind of sleep before the long journey home at daybreak, and nobody wanted to argue. Tiredness was starting to affect everyone. It was written plainly on every face I looked at.

Soft snoring began to echo throughout the church. Another hour passed without incident. Amanda claimed to have been touched on the arm by something invisible, but went right back to sleep again. The next thing I remember was sunlight streaming through the tall skinny windows, burning off the night's fog. St. Botolph's looked a great deal less sinister when accompanied by sunlight and birdsong, but the memories of our eventful overnight there still lingered.

Yawning and stretching, the crew packed up all of our equipment and took some last-minute photos of the place before hitting the road. We had far more questions than answers.

It took a good stiff drink or two for me to properly relax after our experiences at St. Botolph's. I slept for what felt like a week, and found myself to be utterly exhausted for four or five days afterward. My body felt drained and didn't want to move more than five feet away from the couch for most of the week. The skeptical part of me thinks I was just feeling a little under the weather, but there's a nagging feeling that perhaps there was more to it.

Had we brought something more than a few drained batteries back from St. Botolph's church?

We never did explain the screeching, which was not picked up on audio tape. If it had been a bird nesting in the church, we would have seen it, and all eight sets of eyes failed to see anything that would account for the noise. The tall, thin figure that glided around the corner behind Steven and I, has also never been satisfactorily explained. Could it relate to the psychic vision that Amanda had reported? There is no way that somebody could have pranked us. All team members were accounted for. And what of the way in which it disappeared into the mist, leaving absolutely no trace behind?

If pushed, I will tell you that I believe we encountered a ghostly monk on that foggy night. The tone of voice and demeanor of the witnesses I spoke to was very real and entirely convincing to me. Both witnesses were adamant about what they saw, and I have no reason to disbelieve them. Their stories matched exactly. Talk about looking in the wrong place at the wrong time...

I made a second, almost entirely uneventful return visit to the church with SPECTA later that year. We encountered none of the inexplicable activity that characterized our first investigation, and I was tempted to think that the activity had simply died away like an old battery running down. But in the almost twenty years since we visited St Botolph's, the Internet has allowed me to keep an interested eye upon the place, and it is my avowed ambition to go back there again one day in an attempt to get to the bottom of the mysterious events that still plague the church to this day.

The church caretaker told the *Louth Leader* newspaper in 2004: "Satan worshipping has gone on. They come from Grimsby in the evenings, light fires and write symbols on the walls.

"I have gone to the church at three in the morning to try to move them on, but they swear at me so I don't like to go. I might get knifed."

According to the article, the altar has since been painted black, and daubed with the words "Carla and Amy sacrificed here." A local resident believes that a coven of witches has begun to practice in the derelict building, citing the existence of stone circles found inside and large numbers of cars parked outside the church at night. It is important to bear in mind when reading newspaper articles and listening to public opinion, that no distinction seems to be made between those who worship the light as opposed to those who worship the darker side of nature.

Another January 2004 article in the same local newspaper detailed an overnight investigation conducted by the Bassetlaw Ghost Research Group. Parapsychologist David Wharmby is quoted as saying, *"We heard many strange unaccountable noises, saw flashes in the sky when the weather was calm and experienced weird feelings. We saw small babies among the gravestones and grass.*

"We have had reports of people seeing apparitions of monks, and there is much folklore surrounding Skidbrooke Church, including spells, witchcraft, and about it being put under a curse."

The article goes on to quote a local village resident (who requested anonymity): "I felt such bad vibes. The whole place really freaked me out. People may think it's a load of nonsense, but there is such a thing as black magic and it's dangerous." The unnamed villager even went so far as to bring in a priest to conduct a blessing on her house.

Matters came to a head at Halloween of that same year. Wearing fluorescent high-visibility jackets and wielding flashlights, angry villagers blockaded the church entrance with their cars. The worm had finally turned. Locals were sick of the church being abused, and turned away over thirty people on Halloween night of 2004. But if they thought that the final page in the church's tale had been written, they would be forced to think again.

Daniel Codd's book *Mysterious Lincolnshire* mentions a 2006 visit in which several witnesses heard footsteps crunching on the stone floor, when the church was quite visibly empty. Fires and rituals continue to be reported even now, along with hooded monk-like figures floating through the ruins. I encourage you to run a web search on "St.Botolph's Skidbrooke" or to browse past articles on the *Louth Leader* website. There is no shortage of anecdotal accounts, some leading right up to the time of writing. It seems that St Botolph's church is still paranormally active.

Grace Dieu Priory

No matter how haunted a location is claimed to be, sometimes the ghosts simply won't come out to play. Such was the case with the ghostly white nun of Grace Dieu Priory, who provided my first real lesson in disappointment.

Located in a north-western wooded region of my native Leicestershire, near the small town of Thringstone, the crumbling ramshackle remains of this former priory have been the scene of many incredible ghost sightings and unexplained occurrences going back to the 1920s. The busy A512 highway runs directly adjacent to the ruins, which might explain why so many witnesses have experienced otherworldly events as they journey through this area.

The most common spectre to be seen here is the classic "lady in white," an archetypal ghost that is reported in many cultures from all around the world. Folklore speculates that in this case, this is the figure of the priory's founder, Roesia (sometimes written as *Rhosese*) de Verdon, whose order of nuns established Grace Dieu priory in the year 1239. As an Augustinian

Order, historians would normally expect the nuns of Grace Dieu to appear in black habits, as was their common custom. This would make the appearance of a lady in white seem a little unusual. But this particular order took the unusual step of wearing white robes, being known locally as "The White Nuns of St Augustine."

Grace Dieu ceased to operate as a priory in the year 1538, with the site being purchased by a wealthy family and a large manor house constructed a few hundred yards to the south. The priory buildings were partially demolished in the 1700s, left to rot. The manor house and the priory ruins are two separate buildings.

Conducting newspaper research into this location reveals an absolute treasure trove of ghost sightings over the past eighty years.

The first recorded sighting that I could track down took place during the 1920s, when a family traveling past the priory ruins in a horse and carriage were stopped dead in their tracks by some unidentified force. With their horse shaking in terror, the family were just as horrified to encounter six ghostly white robed figures emerging from the trees on the opposite side of the road, crossing it and heading up towards the priory. Perhaps the most frightening aspect of this sighting, which was documented in the *Coalville Mail* back in 1996, is that the nuns were all faceless...and had no feet.

Many stories revolve around the brick bus shelter which stands across the highway from the ruined priory. Witnesses tell of the day in 1954 when a bus driver stopped at the shelter because a lady dressed in white was standing there, seemingly waiting for a bus. In those days, bus drivers were accompanied by conductors, responsible for collecting fares and issuing tickets to passengers. As the bus braked to a stop, both the driver and the conductor were chilled to discover that the lady in white had mysteriously vanished without trace. At least one passenger on the bus has since corroborated the two men's story.

A grounds worker reported to the *Leicester Mercury* in 1964 that he had witnessed a white female apparition while going about the course of his duties. The figure disappeared before his eyes. A similar story comes to us from a council warden working at the site in 1997, but this is made somewhat more disturbing by the fact that the ghostly white nun was first seen staring fixedly at the warden, and then pushed him. Understandably, the warden dropped his gardening tool and fled.

Nor are the ghostly nun's wanderings restricted to the priory ruins. We do not lack for eyewitness sightings of her in the surrounding fields and woodlands. The village constable ran into her in 1961, when walking his dog. The police officer's dog reacted angrily, hackles rising with a warning growl, as the cloaked and hooded white figure passed into a thick hedge. He reported that a preternatural chill had fallen on them both during the experience, which immediately disappeared with the ghostly figure's passing.

By far the most frequent people to encounter the ghostly lady in white are drivers and motorcyclists traveling the A512, as this is one spirit who doesn't look both ways when crossing the road. An off-duty police offer biking back to Thringstone saw her in 1981, at half past midnight on a summer's morning. He described the feeling of intense cold during a 1997 interview with the *Coalville Echo*, and witnessed the phantom figure crossing the A512 at a glide. This police officer's trained eye also noted that the apparition was missing both feet (much as the family of eyewitnesses observed in the 1920s) and seemed to be wearing a hood or cowl. Showing considerable bravery, the officer stopped his motorcycle at the bus shelter to investigate further, but the white lady had already vanished.

One local historian actually reported running the ghostly white lady over, only realizing that he had encountered the ghost when he saw her in his rear view mirror, crossing the road behind him without a care in the world.

Other witnesses report encountering the ghosts of grey nuns in the priory ruins, but those of the white variety seem to be most popular. I now have a very thick file of eyewitness testimony pertaining to this case, going back over the past several decades. There is a remarkable consistency to the ghostly sightings.

It was a beautiful summer evening, seasonably warm and without too much of a breeze to disturb the countryside, when a crew from SPECTA carpooled out to the abandoned ruins of historic Grace Dieu priory.

Tracey and I were unpacking equipment from the trunk of the car. Andy emerged behind us toting a shoulder bag for a video camcorder. The idea was that we would try and capture footage of the mysterious "white lady of Grace Dieu." I heard the sound of a bag unzipping as I was setting up my own camcorder, popping in a fresh tape and battery, followed by the ker-chunk sound of a ring being pulled on a can of something liquid. Looking around, I was just in time to see Andrew cracking open a can of Stella Artois lager, one from a pack of four that were kept stored in the video camcorder/makeshift beer cooler bag. He nodded and toasted us with a dip of the can.

Shortly afterwards, we sat in the long grass opposite the priory and watched butterflies cavorting in the air on this lazy summer's eve. The sun dropped slowly below the horizon as night began to fall. Andrew suddenly leapt to his feet and stalked up the road in the direction of the village. He was off to "do some research" in the village pub, he said with a cheery over-the-shoulder wave. He reappeared several hours later, cheerfully relaxed but with no additional information. The locals were "very cagey", he reported as we settled down to continue our night watch, and really didn't want to discuss their local spook.

This was my first true taste of the disappointment that comes along with so many investigations. Despite having an outstanding paranormal pedigree stretching back for nearly one hundred years, it seemed that we had come to the right place at the wrong time. The ghostly lady in white wasn't going to show her face. I have been back to the ruins several times since, both with and without equipment, hoping for a glimpse of the elusive White Nuns of St Augustine, but to no avail.

Appearances of the ghostly white nun continue to reach my ears, flowing in a steady stream via the newspapers and Internet. A family of four experienced what can almost be called an ambush, just before midnight on a night in 2002, when their car was surrounded by a rapidly moving cloud of fog outside the priory. The father braked to a halt immediately, and narrowly avoided hitting a human-shaped figure that passed directly in front of them. The fog immediately lifted, and no figure could be seen anywhere around them.

The atmospheric ruins of Grace Dieu Priory are still a favorite haunt for ghost hunting groups today, and sightings of the lady in white are becoming supplemented by those of other ghosts. Some fascinating photographs have surfaced recently, including one taken in 2005 which seems to show a male figure standing in the ruined archway of the old priory ruin.

It is my intention to return to Grace Dieu one summer night in the not-too-distant future, in the hope that the
lady in white doesn't stand me up yet again!

Private Case: Conjuring Evil
It was only a matter of weeks before I heard from Andrew again. A help case had turned up on his desk that sounded intriguing.

Help cases are the bread and butter of most ghost hunting teams. They involve helping out families in their own homes, rather than investigating somewhere historic or commercial. People have a fundamental right to feel secure when they go to bed at night, not vulnerable and afraid of the unknown.

Charlotte was a single mother with two young children who lived in government-subsidized housing in the town of Loughborough. I knew Loughborough well because I was currently serving as a Territorial Army Reservist there. It turned out that Charlotte's house was right around the corner from my barracks.

Andrew, Tracey, and I arrived in Loughborough one Friday evening after work. We were met by Giles, a potential new recruit for the team. He was an interesting character, whose big passion was UFOlogy, anything and everything to do with flying saucers, alien abductions, men in black, and conspiracy theories. Ghosts and hauntings were further down on his interest list, but he was very well-read and could discourse intelligently on the subject.

Giles always dressed smartly for an investigation, and I admired his professionalism in that regard. Wearing a shirt, tie, and patent leather shoes, he seemed better suited to a day at the office than a ghost hunt.

In addition to herself and the children, Charlotte's brother also lived in the house. There was a somewhat tense domestic atmosphere, which is very common in cases of supposed hauntings. One theory is that single-parent families experience a greater level of emotional stress, creating potential energy that acts as a fuel source for paranormal activity – much like a charged battery.

A darker aspect soon reared its head. Charlotte wasted no time in telling us that her brother had developed an interest in black magic, reading lots of books on the subject. She suspected (but couldn't prove) that he had performed rituals in the house, and had perhaps summoned a sinister force of some kind.

We made ourselves comfortable and enjoyed some tea in the living room while Charlotte related the rest of her story. One incident that frightened her greatly occurred when she was taking a shower in the bathroom. On finishing up, she grasped the door handle and tried to open it – but the door wouldn't budge. Something heavy slammed into the door on the far side, making her jump backwards.

Charlotte tried turning the handle again, twisting with enough force to turn her hand white. The door wouldn't budge. She ultimately spent half an hour trapped in the bathroom, terrified and becoming claustrophobic. Then, without any warning or apparent cause, the door sprang open and released her into the upstairs hallway.

I didn't get the sense from Charlotte that she was a fantasist, or lying to us in order to gather attention. There was no motive for her to do so – Charlotte explicitly stated that she did not want any publicity surrounding our investigation. She just wanted answers to what had invaded her home, and why. That desire for privacy impressed me a great deal, and scored some major sincerity points as far as I was concerned.

We took a guided tour of the house, a modest but clean three-bedroom single family dwelling. Then Charlotte, her children, and her brother, left us the keys and went away for the night. This could turn out to be a double-edged sword. On one hand, having the family leave for the night left us with a controlled environment, free of potential trickery. But on the other hand, if family tension was a contributing factor to the paranormal activity, removing the source of that tension could make for a very quiet night. Only time would tell for sure.

Waving them good-bye, our team wasted no time in preparing the house. Sealing all external door and window frames with thick masking tape allowed us to exclude drafts from the building. We locked down all doors and windows, ensuring that nobody could gain access to the house from the outside. Even if they had a key, the frames were taped shut.

Poking around the brother's room, I uncovered a copy of the Satanic Bible and several other tattered paperback books covering the same subject area. The brother was also obviously a fan of horror fiction, and had a taste for dark movies, based upon the videotapes that we found in his room. If the brother was indeed practicing black magic rituals, it seemed entirely possible that some kind of dark force might have been summoned into an already stressed environment.

Cameras and tape recorders with external microphones were set up at key positions throughout the house. Our attentions were focused on the upstairs bathroom, the master bedroom, and the brother's bedroom, all of which were readily accessible from the upstairs landing. We soon had a pot of tea on the boil and set about devising our plan of action.

By general consensus, Charlotte didn't seem to be exaggerating or misleading us in any way. Everything about her rang true – her story, consistency of facts, apparent sincerity, and general demeanor. It also shows no small degree of trust to allow a bunch of strangers to have overnight access to your house while unsupervised. Our gut instinct, we all agreed, was that Charlotte was on the level.

We wanted to investigate the bathroom door situation in a little more depth. We looked carefully at the way in which the wooden door fit into its frame. There was no evidence of the wood having swollen or distorted over time, as it swung freely and easily open and closed with a light push from two fingertips. The locking mechanism worked smoothly, latching into place without much effort and releasing in the same way. We even ran the hot water through the shower stall, to see what effect the steam might have on it. Nothing, so far as we could determine. Somebody would have to hold the door shut tightly from the outside, applying physical force against the handle, in order to duplicate the trapping effect that Charlotte had described to us.

With just two teams of two, this was shaping up to be a small and intimate investigation. We settled into a steady routine of watching, listening, and monitoring as the hours ticked away until dawn. One group observed upstairs, paying particular attention to the bedrooms and bathroom. The other group remained downstairs, in slightly more comfort, and was in charge of that most critical of tasks: keeping a steady supply of tea and coffee on the go. Walkie-talkieradios kept both groups in contact, and we changed partners every hour.

Midnight came and went. I was downstairs with Andy, with me struggling to keep awake on a seductively comfortable couch, while Andy brewed tea for what felt like the tenth time so far. Everything was quiet throughout the house.

The radio crackled.

I cocked my head, expecting to hear Giles and Tracey speaking from upstairs. But it wasn't.

It was...breathing.

It was regular, slow and rhythmic. Each exhalation ended with a content, almost childlike sigh. This was certainly not adult breathing, it was much too high-pitched.

Excitedly, I beckoned Andy to come over and listen. We stared at one another in puzzlement. Who in their right mind would be broadcasting their own heavy breathing over a radio at one o'clock in the morning? It made no sense to us.

Andrew went to the bottom of the stairwell and hissed for Tracey and Giles to join us. They were equally perplexed. The breathing had become a low moan by then, drawn out but still child-like in nature. The moan returned to breathing after a few seconds. And then, a female adult voice was heard, speaking indistinctly but soothingly in the distance. Episodes of this same pattern went on for the next hour.

Tape recorders were brought out and the breathing was recorded for posterity. But it didn't take long for

Tracey to debunk this nocturnal breather. She was the first to realize that, every time the breathing became a moan and the adult voice was heard, a light went on in the upstairs window of a house visible through Charlotte's rear window.

"You know what that is!" Tracey said. "It's a bloody baby monitor!"

Light dawned on our tired brains. Of *course* it was. A baby monitor was broadcasting its microphone output to its base unit on what happened to be the same commercial frequency used by our walkie-talkies. The bedroom light that we could see going on whenever the baby moaned would be the child's mother going in to check on the kid, and that explained the soothing adult tones that ended each cycle.

Disappointing, but debunking something that at first seems to be paranormal in nature is the paranormal investigator's bread and butter. Full credit to Tracey for keeping an open mind and putting two and two together!

None of us can remember what the exact time was, but at some time between four and five we must have all drifted off to sleep.

In an ideal world, we would all be independently wealthy and able to sleep in on the day of an investigation. But in reality, every one of us had day jobs that we had been working at the day before. Charlotte's house must have been filled with gentle snoring from the four of us.

At a quarter past five, all hell broke loose.

The harsh slam of something hitting metal jolted us all awake. Groggily, I tried to figure out why the room was suddenly bathed in harsh white light.

Hands scrabbled for cameras and flashlights. I was out of my chair like a shot, fumbling for the button on my trusty Nikon.

A bright light was streaming in through the rear curtains. It was artificial, definitely not daylight yet. Andy yanked open the curtains and saw that a motion-activated security light was the source, mounted just above Charlotte's back door. Something had triggered the motion sensor...but what?

There was no sign of anything that might have caused the metallic-sounding crash we had all heard. I ducked into the kitchen and quickly verified that the seals on the back door and window frames were still intact. They were. Nothing had gotten into the house from the outside. But there were no metal items outside the house that could account for the noise.

We never did figure out what caused the crash. Our tape recorders did pick it up, and it sounds almost exactly as if the lid of a metal trash can were picked up and flung violently at the ground. The problem being, Charlotte's trash can was made of plastic, and made an entirely different sound when struck aggressively. I know this because I did it several times the next morning with my boot.

Level-headed clients like Charlotte are my favorite to work with. She took the news that we had found no paranormal phenomena in her stride.

"I know what happened to me," she said matter-of-factly. "I'm not crazy."

Investigators from SPECTA went back a few more times to Charlotte's house for further overnight investigations. She and her children remained at home, allowing the opportunity for an investigation to take place in the controlled environment of an empty house initially, and then in the normal household environment afterwards.

We couldn't help but notice that things seemed to calm down substantially when her brother eventually moved out and got a place of his own. I still wonder if this caused a release in the tension that had been slowly building up within the home and family, or whether the fact that he was no longer dabbling in occult practices inside the house could account for the newly found tranquility. I suspect a mixture of the two factors might be the answer here.

As so often happens in residential help cases, the paranormal activity eventually trailed off into nothingness, we parted our ways amicably, and Charlotte's family went on with the rest of their lives. When you think about it, it really is quite silly to expect a single overnight investigation (even two, or three) over the course of a year to yield conclusive evidence of a haunting. For starters, we still don't know for sure what the factors are that will cause paranormal activity to manifest. We do have a few reasonable suspicions. The time of day or night, phase of the moon, ambient temperature and weather conditions, may all play a role. The number of witnesses should be taken into consideration, and it is also important to determine whether there is anybody present who does *not* witness the supposedly paranormal phenomena. Do the witnesses believe or disbelieve in

the paranormal? After all, a predisposition towards belief might bias the evidence. And is the situation emotionally charged? Outbreaks of poltergeist activity are frequently associated with very strong emotion taking place, such as a marriage breaking up or the onset of puberty.

There are many, many other elements to be considered. All that we can say for sure is that a complex series of undetermined factors need to align in a very precise, specific way in order for paranormal activity to manifest.

Sometimes, as with the phantom figure in the graveyard at St. Botolph's, everything falls into place and something paranormal not only takes place, but also happens to be *experienced* by people at the scene. This is the ghost hunter's Holy Grail moment, the one thing for which we are all constantly searching, and trying to capture and substantiate as hard evidence.

One day, we are going to figure out precisely what those necessary factors are, and exactly how they must intersect and interact in order to produce a ghostly manifestation. Somewhere, hidden deep amongst all of the data and ghost stories that investigators have collected over the years, there is a pattern which we are not yet seeing.

But, we *are* still working on it...

CHAPTER FOUR

THEATRICAL SPIRITS

The more cases that I worked on, the greater my confidence became. I continued to read every ghost-hunting book that hit my local bookstore, and learned a great deal from talking to others working in the same field.

Before long, I was jointly running my own group in conjunction with Tracey. Calling it "Midlands Paranormal Investigations" (due to the fact that we'd mostly be operating the part of the country known as "the Midlands"), we enlisted a few enthusiastic volunteers, and substituted enthusiasm for depth of experience in our journey into the unknown.

We had both learned a lot from our time with Andrew and SPECTA, but felt the need to branch off and march to the beat of our own drum. We took on smaller cases that would require a minimal number of investigators, and looked for ways in which we could develop our craft.

There was the Northamptonshire pub, which was built upon an ancient stone foundation, whose owners couldn't get the resident German Shepherd dog to go down into the cellar under any circumstances. Liberating

some chopped up prime steak from the pub kitchen, I laid a trail by placing a chunk on each step leading downstairs. The dog chomped the first two from his position at the top of the cellar steps, but with

flattened ears and a
high-pitched whine, flatly refused to go down even
one single step.

Intrigued, I took a flashlight and poked around the
dank cellar myself, stepping gingerly between beer
barrels and boxes of snack food. Despite cellar space
being at a premium, I noticed several recessed ledges
carved into the stone wall that weren't crammed with
any items at all. Curious, I asked the landlord about
them. He told me in a completely matter-of-fact way
that hundreds of years ago, there was no mortician in
the village. They used to lay the bodies of the newly
dead out on those ledges until they were ready to be
buried, because it was very cold down there, and the
bodies would take longer to decompose and begin to
stink.

Chilled at the thought, I resolved to spend the night
sleeping on one of the ledges. Breaking one of the
main rules of ghost hunting, I was investigating the
pub on my own. I tried a little EVP experimentation,
and then listened as the building cooled down above
my head. I passed a peaceful night in the dark, curled
up in a sleeping bag on the cold stone ledge.

What a great shame that the only anomalies found
on my tape recorder that night were my own
exhausted snores! But the undisturbed night's sleep
did teach me a fundamental lesson of paranormal
research: just because a place seems as if it *ought* to be
haunted, doesn't necessarily mean that it *will be*. The
pub was an excellent case in point. If you have ever
seen the movie *An American Werewolf In London*, with
its stereotypical countryside pub (*The Slaughtered
Lamb*) then you can easily picture this pub in your
mind's eye. There was a definite vibe of "don't go
onto the moors at night!" about it, although it was
perfectly charming during the daytime. Considering
the fact that so many bodies had been stored on those
stone ledges down in the cellar, it would make
absolute sense for the pub to have a resident ghost or
ten.

But I have learned over the years that some of the most spectacular cases in paranormal lore occur not in the historic castles and ancient inns, but rather in modern day family houses and apartments. It really does not pay to judge a book by its cover.

• • • ● ●•●●●••

Harborough Theater

Ghosts and theaters seem to go hand in hand, on both sides of the Atlantic. Everybody loves a good ghost story, particular in the winter months of the year, when the dark nights draw in and the shadows grow long.

What is it about the acting profession itself that seems to attract ghosts? America, Britain, and the rest of Europe are positively inundated with haunted theaters! My own belief is that the strong emotion which theaters generate, among both the performers *and* the audiences, may act as an energy source of some kind which may help to imprint certain events on the atmosphere, and the play them back in some way under the right set of circumstances.

Theater stages see simulated situations of love, hate, murder, sex, incest, ghosts...and that's just counting Shakespeare! Abraham Lincoln met his untimely end in a theater, and he is far from the only victim to die in such a place. Backstage feuding and violence have been commonplace throughout the history of the acting profession, and many theaters boast a resident spook. One classic example in London is the Theater Royal in Drury Lane and its eponymous "Man in Grey", the apparition of an actor seen to be wearing period clothing who appears in an upper balcony. He is renowned for creeping up behind actors on the stage who may not be delivering their best performance, and delivering a swift sharp kick to their backside! One long held Theater Royal superstition insists that if the man in grey appears on the opening night of a new production, then that show will be blessed with a long and prosperous run. The belief persists to this day.

When Andrew Wright called me with the news that he was running an investigation at a haunted theater in the town of Market Harborough, we jumped at the chance to attend.

Staff at the Harborough Theater reported hearing disembodied footsteps when the building was empty. It was here that I first learned about the theatrical tradition of leaving a "ghost light" shining on the center of the stage when the theater is in darkness and closed up for the night. Although the practical reason to do this involves health and safety, the more colorful explanation involves ghosts. Many actors are superstitious by nature, and the role of the ghost light is to allow ghosts to perform their own plays on the stage when the theater is unoccupied overnight, thereby preventing them from growing bored and causing mischief to the living actors!

I fell in love with this fine old tradition as soon as I saw the ghost light and heard the tale behind it. Perhaps it is the spine-chilling image of walking past a theater after midnight, and being totally unaware of a stage show being performed by a cast of dead actors, watched and silently applauded from the stalls by an audience of ghostly patrons...

Because the ghostly footsteps at Market Harborough were reported to come from the stage, we set up our camcorders in the stalls facing the entire stage front. We wired the stage for sound with remote microphones, and had cameras set up on tripods ready to shoot at a moment's notice. If something paranormal happened up there, we were going to catch it!

We were spoilt for choice when it came to selecting comfortable seating. The stage manager kindly dimmed the auditorium lighting to a low ambient level, leaving the stage brightly illuminated. Settling in for the night, our small team of investigators took turns staking out both wings of the stage.

At this point, Tracey tapped me on the shoulder and wordlessly pointed behind us both. I turned around and mouthed something unprintable. I could not believe my eyes. The door to the theater lighting and music box was swinging wide open on its hinges. We had securely closed and locked that door after performing a cursory check of the box, which looked like a glass cage filled with electronic equipment. *Something* had unlocked that door, had turned the handle, and then opened the door outwards...all without our hearing a single noise.

And, in a spectacular stroke of bad luck that every ghost hunter experiences at least once in their career, every single piece of video recording equipment we had set up just happened to be pointing the wrong way.

I suddenly realized that my camera was dangling uselessly from its strap around my neck. With the sudden jolt of adrenaline, I had completely forgotten to take a photograph of the yawning open doorway. Somewhat embarrassed, I fired of a few flash photographs, just in case. They turned out to reveal nothing of a paranormal nature, but they still serve as a pointed reminder that a paranormal investigator must always be on their guard.

Treading The Boards at Vance Brand

It isn't just historic Great Britain that hosts haunted theaters. I was called upon to investigate the Vance Brand Civic Auditorium in Longmont, Colorado, back in 2008. Named after a Longmont-born astronaut, numerous
websites list the auditorium as being haunted, although the details tend to be very vague and generic (I was even able to locate a variant of the "sit in a

specific seat, and a ghostly black dog will appear"
urban legend – that's the Internet for you).

Talking to the auditorium manager however, added
an interesting twist to this particular tale. I was told
that during the construction of the auditorium, a
balcony collapsed. One of the construction workers
died as a result of this terrible accident, and it is his
ghost that is believed to haunt the auditorium today.

Staff members seem to agree. For example, the
technical supervisor told me that disembodied
footsteps can quite often be heard inside the
Auditorium when all is otherwise quiet at night.
Puzzled staff members have actually tried to chase
down the source of the footsteps, believing it to be a
trespasser, and yet nobody is ever found inside the
locked building. Bangs and crashes are also often
heard, seeming to originate from empty parts of the
structure. The staff members have simply gotten used
to this bizarre activity, writing it off with a shrug and a
wink as "the ghost playing his tricks again."

We were privileged to investigate the Auditorium
on a balmy night May evening. A couple of BCPRS
investigators accompanied me, along with one
employee of the auditorium, who locked us in and
helped secure all the entrances and exits. Baselines
were all as flat as a pancake, and it looked as though we
were in for a quiet and low-key evening. And so it
was, until just after a quarter past eleven, when a
colossal *crash* came from backstage. It sounded as if
something big and heavy, such as a bookcase, had
been flipped over and dropped violently to the
ground.

I'm proud to say that I must have learned
something since my investigative paralysis at the
Market Harborough Theater back in the nineties.
Upon hearing the slam, my crew and I reacted
immediately, pounding backstage to investigate.
Everything was completely in order back there.
Nothing had fallen, and nothing was stirring. The
Auditorium staff member poked his head out of the
office in which he had been watching television when

the crash was heard. This door had been in plain sight of those of us in the stall seats and on the stage, so there was no way that he could have been responsible for making the sound.

We were unable to figure out what had caused the crash, and when we reviewed them later, our locked-off cameras had detected no movement backstage. Squinting for mice, rats, squirrels, birds, and other critters turned out to be fruitless. To this day, we have no idea as to what caused the crash.

Almost half an hour passed quietly. Our small team of researchers were huddled in the cold stalls, watching the stage (and its ghost light) idly and allowing a digital voice recorder to run. Twenty minutes before midnight, everybody froze. There was a mass intake of breath, as five distinct, measured footsteps creaked across the main stage. The hackles rose on the back of my neck as I peered into the dimness, straining my eyes to try and make out the source.

I say "footsteps" with full awareness that there were no feet visible making the noise. It might be more accurate to say, "five *creaks*", but everybody knows what footsteps *sound like*. To my ear, and to those of the other investigators present at the time, the creaks were spaced perfectly regularly and moved across from the back of the stage to the front, in plain sight. Close your eyes and listen to five footsteps as somebody paces the room, and you are experiencing pretty much the same thing – except that nobody was there to make them.

Of course, creaky floorboards are nothing new and certainly nothing paranormal. But when have you ever heard five definite, regularly spaced creaks moving in sequence across a floor? What we were dealing with in this case was most assuredly *not* the ordinary settlings of a building during the cooler evening hours. Could these be the disembodied footsteps that Vance Brand Auditorium staff have reported hearing tread throughout the closed and locked building?

On reviewing the evidence, our digital voice recorders did indeed pick up the faint creaking sounds. The members of the investigative team were all agreed that we would be hard pressed to interpret them as anything other than the deliberate tread of an adult-sized human being.

• • • ● ● • ● ● • • •

Murder at Macky

A week later, BCPRS (along with our colleagues from another team, Brad and Nichole) found ourselves in yet another theatrical venue, albeit with a far more sinister history.

The Macky Auditorium, located on campus at the University of Colorado in Boulder, is an imposing masterpiece of Gothic-looking architecture, which looks like it ought to be the backdrop for a horror movie – and in fact, it actually has been! A low budget horror feature film was shot in the basement, sometime back in the nineties.

Completed in 1922, the cavernous auditorium has played host to college graduation ceremonies, lectures by a diverse range of speakers, and musical performances ranging from orchestras to rock bands. Indeed, the auditorium's official website lists performances by Harry Belafonte, Penn and Teller, REM, the Dalai Lama, and Archbishop Desmond Tutu – it doesn't get any more diverse than that! The site also mentions a riot that occurred in 1971, when a mob of students gatecrashed a Neil Young concert, clashing with police who ultimately turned fire hoses on the crowd.

But the most tragic event associated with the Macky auditorium involves the supposedly haunted room located in the western tower. The true story behind what has become an urban legend ghost story, took place in the summer of 1966, when a young zoology student was last seen eating lunch on the university campus grounds. A few hours later, her blood-soaked body was discovered in room 304 up in the western tower. A piece of wood, also covered in blood, was found abandoned at the crime scene. According to the coroner, this innocent young lady had been battered repeatedly about the face with the wooden board, inducing multiple fractures of her skull and facial bones and knocking out a number of teeth. The subsequent autopsy also revealed bruises and lacerations covering her neck, throat, and buttocks. Homicide detectives at the scene analyzed the blood trails and determined that the helpless victim must have attempted to drag herself out of the room, but her assailant grabbed her by the feet and swung her violently, battering her head against the wall.

A campus janitor was arrested for the brutal crime, turned in by his own children who noticed him carrying a bucket full of blood-soaked clothing on the day of the murder. Palm prints on the murder weapon matched with his, and the murdered was imprisoned for life, where he died in 2005.

The murder room is now used for junk storage. Touching inscriptions of remembrance have been carved into the walls and door over the years. It should come as no surprise to learn that class after class of students have passed on a story of the room being haunted by the ghost of this poor girl. The tale has now become a part of popular culture, referenced by the local tour guide as he makes his rounds past campus.

I spoke with the very level-headed technical manager at the auditorium, who made no bones about his feelings towards the haunting. He was less than thrilled to recount that around every Halloween, students try and break into 304 to give one another a good scare. An urban legend on campus leads them to believe that the dead girl's ghost will appear, despite the fact that there is no record of any such thing ever happening.

This was corroborated when the campus police dropped in to wish us luck. I spoke with a businesslike no-nonsense patrol officer, who told me that in the period around Halloween, police units do indeed respond often to calls of lights being turned on in the empty western tower, but the explanation is completely prosaic: students seeking thrills and chills.

Room 304 is essentially a big, dusty storage room. Despite its fearsome reputation, the atmosphere within is perfectly calm and tranquil. Exposed and unshielded wiring did generate some EMF spikes, but nothing that couldn't be explained quite simply. The room was a little on the warm side, and remained that way throughout our investigation. Particulate breathing masks would have been a good idea, because pretty soon we were all coughing and wafting away dust mites from in front of our faces. Fortunately, the air was still enough that the dust would soon settle once everybody stopped moving.

An atmosphere of absolute calmness and tranquility pervaded the room during the course of our stay. We all felt extremely peaceful, and our investigation proceeded in a professional but relaxed manner. Everybody was aware of the seriousness and brutality of the crime which had taken place in room 304, and took great pains to be respectful despite keeping our sense of humor as the night went on. But no impression of the terrible murder seemed to remain on the atmosphere. I could quite easily have closed my eyes and drifted off to sleep on the spot.

In the middle of an EVP session, my question was suddenly interrupted by a mournful whistled tune. We tracked it to the main entrance hall of the auditorium. The momentary excitement was punctured when this turned out to be the returning technical manager, who had seemingly forgotten our request for advance warning before coming back into the locked building.

It was a tired bunch of investigators that trooped back to our cars that night. Evidence review turned up no answers to our EVP questions, though we did record hundreds of "orbs" – easily explained in this case by the dustiness of the room itself.

In the end, only one frightening thing turned up during that night in room 304: a 1980 copy of "Prison Life" magazine. *Prison Life?* Who on Earth subscribes! But as for room 304 itself, not a trace of the western tower's horrific history lingered in the atmosphere on the night of our stay. This is one campus ghost story that should be left to rest in peace.

CHAPTER FIVE

A CLASH OF ARMIES AT EDGE HILL

The paranormal case lore is rife with instances of recording-type "anniversary" hauntings. Consider the Battle of Edge Hill, the first major clash of arms in the English Civil War. On October 23 in 1642, the army of loyalists that backed King Charles I engaged the army of Parliamentarians (the government forces) on the field of Edge Hill in Warwickshire. The combat was bloody, beginning with a barrage of cannon fire and massed volleys of musketry, before progressing to hand-to-hand fighting using pikes, swords, and axes. Soldiers on both sides were poorly trained and lacking in experience, so the casualty lists were understandably horrendous.

After three hours spent of carnage, Edge Hill ended in a stalemate, with neither side gaining a decisive advantage. That night was freezing cold, and as October 24th dawned, the dead and wounded of both sides were abandoned on the battlefield after being stripped of their clothing and looted of their valuables. Both armies returned to their respective camps to lick their wounds and count the human cost of battle. The Parliamentarians and Royalists disengaged the following day, neither having the stomach to prolong the slaughter. Royalist cavalrymen descended on the village of Kineton, which was sheltering many wounded Parliamentarian soldiers, and put them to death by the sword.

The story of Edge Hill should have ended there, a footnote or at most a chapter in the annals of the English Civil War. But things took a strange turn on Christmas Eve of that same year, when shepherds crossing the Edge Hill battlefield underwent a strange and terrifying experience. In the night sky above them, the Battle of Edge Hill was being played out once more by two armies of spectral soldiers. As the horrified men watched in fascination, phantom Parliamentarian and Royalist soldiers charged one another above their heads, to the accompanying roar of cannon and musket, the whinnying of frightened horses, and the agonized screams of the dead and dying.

The ghostly experience of these shepherds turned out to be only the tip of the iceberg. In the following days, many of the villagers from Kineton witnessed the ghostly spectacle in the skies above Edge Hill. So common was this event to become that a local printer, one Thomas Jackson, published a pamphlet on the subject in January of 1643 entitled *"A Great Wonder in Heaven, shewing the late Apparitions and Prodigious Noyses of War and Battels, seen on Edge-Hill, neere Keinton in Northamptonshire."*

Jackson's text makes for fascinating reading. The shepherds immediately proceeded to see the Justice of the Peace (William Wood) and also the local priest (Samuel Marshall), both of whom believed the shepherds to be drunk or delusional. These two pillars of the community nevertheless gamely accompanied the shepherds back to Edge Hill field the following evening, which was Christmas Night (on this same day in London, a child was born who would turn out to be arguably the greatest scientist ever produced by the human race – Sir Isaac Newton).

Fully expecting to be disappointed, the Justice and clergyman waited until the stroke of midnight, when they were stunned to hear the *rat-tat-tat-tat* of distant drums, slowly drawing nearer to their position. Nothing else disturbed the coldly clear night air on this field of battle, abandoned for the past two months. The drumbeats were soon accompanied by *"the noyse of soulders, as it were, giving out their last groanes."*

Wood, Marshall, and the shepherds suddenly discovered that the Battle of Edge hill was breaking out with full fire and fury in the skies above them. Armies charged and counter-charged to the accompaniment of full

surround sound; the witnesses described hearing drums beating, horses neighing, muskets and cannons firing. Cannonballs blasted entire files of pikemen into little more than bloody rags. Musket balls punched holes in the unarmored flesh of soldiers on both sides. Wickedly sharp pike heads thrust into enemy bodies, twisting and goring as they were pulled out. They watched the tragedy unfold over the next three hours, until finally the Royalist army withdrew from the field. Both armies faded away into the starry night sky, leaving behind nothing but the eerie melancholy of a deserted battlefield.

All remained silent and peaceful for the following week. Then, on Saturday and Sunday evening, the spectral combatants returned with a vengeance. Once more, the Battle of Edge Hill was re-fought to the same inevitable, bloody stalemate in the Warwickshire skies. As regular as clockwork, the ghostly battle was re-enacted on subsequent Saturday and Sunday nights throughout early 1643. Word finally reached King Charles, who gave the matter sufficient credence to dispatch a Royal Commission (a team of trusted observers) to Edge Hill, in order to show a royal interest in this fantastical occurrence.

Three military officers and three "gentlemen of credit" duly traveled to Edge Hill, and settled in as darkness fell on the following Saturday evening. Like clockwork, the drumming kicked off at around midnight, leading into another full-scale ghostly rendition of the battle. The observers of the Royal Commission were able to positively identify a number of the participants, including several that had been slain on the 23rd of October in the fighting.

It is an interesting quirk of fate that, due to the Royal Commission's sworn testimony in support of the ghostly re-enactment of the Battle of Edge Hill, this incident remains to this very day the only case of a ghost or ghosts being officially recognized by the Public Records Office in Britain.

As a typical anniversary recording haunting, the Battle of Edge Hill continued to be fought and re-fought in the night sky over the battlefield. Crowds would gather, traveling from miles away in order to witness what was basically the "Saturday night movie". But the incidences of this large-scale apparition began to slowly dwindle over time, appearing less and less frequently until they finally stopped happening at all.

Ghostly noises continued to haunt the vicinity, and indeed are still reported today. Modern residents tell of hearing musketry, screaming, the clash of sword on armor, and the general cacophony of battle throughout the area to this very day, growing more frequent and intense around the time of Halloween... this makes sense when we consider the fact that the battle occurred on October 23, and also that people tend to be more receptive to ghost stories and paranormal experience around this time of year. It is a hallmark sign of anniversary hauntings that activity seems to ramp up as the anniversary date rolls around, coming to a peak in the days immediately surround the anniversary, and then tapering off afterwards.

On a side note, the Edge Hill battlefield is also said to be haunted by a phantom white horse, which has seeped its way so deeply into local tradition and folklore that a nearby road was named after it.

I had first heard about the ghostly replay of the Edge Hill battle as a boy, avidly reading up on the case in several of my treasured ghost books. The mental images conjured up by the narratives enthralled me. Imagine the sight of two phantom armies, in the sky no less, clashing again and again down through the years, witnessed and recorded by plenty of reliable observers. Although there were no accounts of the visual apparitions being seen within living memory, there were a sufficient number of anecdotes reporting audible phenomena that I felt it would be worth a look.

As a young and enthusiastic ghost hunter, I took my first car (a battered old Ford Fiesta) up to the battlefield at Edge Hill in the last week of October and spent the night there. Although partly owned by the Ministry of Defence, certain parts of it could still be accessed as long as you stick to the public roads. Huddled and shivering in my sleeping bag, I lay with teeth chattering in the fully reclined driver's seat – October in England can be brutally cold, due in no small part to the wind chill factor.

A tape recorder with an external microphone hookup slowly unspooled on the seat beside me.

Periodically, I fired up the engine and ran warm air through the heating vents. Apart from the lights of an occasional passing car, everything remained dark and quiet. On the top of the hour, I would get up and walk around outside the car for ten minutes or so, keeping a camera and flashlight handy at my side but remaining lights-out in order to preserve my night vision. It felt strange to think that so much death and carnage had taken place on this very spot some hundreds of years before. There was certainly nothing spectral in the vicinity, and none of the reported groaning and sounds of bloodshed could be heard that night.

Edge Hill never felt anything other than tranquil to me, and I passed a peaceful (if uncomfortable) night there with nothing material to show for it except a series of audio tapes filled with the sound of howling wind, and some very strange dreams. But the investigation did teach me one very important lesson about the futility of investigating paranormal claims in the great outdoors. Although it *is* possible to conduct a productive outdoor investigation on a relatively windless evening, anything above a light breeze will render all of the audio evidence completely worthless. When the majority of activity reported at your location is sound based, it might be wise to check the local weather forecast before committing to an overnight vigil there.

Keep learning, Richard, I told myself. *Keep learning.*

CHAPTER SIX

THE TOWER OF LONDON

At least once each year, without fail, my wife and I return to my native England for a vacation. We spend several days in London, enjoying the life of a tourist and visiting some of the capital city's historic haunted spots. It is no exaggeration to say that we have both fallen in love with two of those locations: the Tower of London, and the charming Grenadier pub.

The history of England's ancient capital city is awash with blood and horror from one end of the city to another. By day, the streets are filled with the hustle and bustle of commuters heading to their place of work, while tourists throng the historic landmarks and side streets.

Big Ben chimes regularly, facing the colossal wheel of the London Eye across the banks of the river Thames. The Prime Minister attends to national business inside Number 10, Downing Street, or attends sessions of Parliament just a stone's throw away from the bones of Britain's deceased royalty buried beneath the stones of Westminster Abbey. Lord Nelson's stone effigy watches over the day to day life of London from atop a column in Trafalgar Square, while his body is interred alongside that of the Duke of Wellington in the crypt of St. Paul's Cathedral across the river. There is so much to see and do that Dr. Samuel Johnson's famous quote is proven to be true: "When a man is tired of London, he is tired of life."

But when darkness descends upon the city by the Thames, when the number famous red buses and black taxi cabs on the crowded roads thins out to a relative handful, London can take on a different character entirely.

London is a city with countless stories, and more than a few of those belong to its dead. For example, when her beloved consort Prince Albert died at the young age of 42 (with a diagnosed case of typhoid fever) in the year 1861, so great was Queen Victoria's grief that she ordered every single public railing in London to be painted black as an expression of mourning. They remain so to this day.

From an architectural point of view, the nation's capital is quite the anachronism. Crumbling old stone churches and graveyards sit side-by-side with glass and steel skyscrapers. Nowhere is this more apparent than in the region of Tower Hill, where can be found the infamous Tower of London. The centuries-old fortress sits directly across the Thames from the grey steel hulk of *HMS Belfast,* a decommissioned World War II Royal Navy battle cruiser, now operated as a floating museum.

London's Bloody Tower

The history of this forbidding royal prison is written in the blood, sweat, and screams of hundreds. King William the Conqueror set about construction of the Tower in 1066, following the Norman invasion of Britain. It was designed to be a base of power for the reigning monarch, and it has often been said that "whoever controls the Tower of London, controls all of England."

Although not intended to be a prison from the outset, the Tower has nevertheless served as a convenient place of incarceration and execution for those who were unfortunate enough to get on the bad side of British monarchs down through the ages. The last time prisoners were jailed in the Tower was during the 1950s, and the executions of convicted spies and saboteurs were still being carried out there by firing squad during the two World Wars. If you visit the one of the many Tower museums, it is still possible to see the bullet-riddled chair in which an unfortunate German spy met his grisly death during World War II.

Yeoman Warder "Bud" Abbott, author of several fascinating volumes detailing some of the Tower's more arcane secrets, relates a story from 1977 of a colleague, who witnessed the apparition of a man wearing 1940s-era clothing. The figure was seen by a Yeoman Warder, standing in the hallway of one of the on-site residences, and simply disappeared without a trace. Abbott relates that this ghost was scene mere yards away from the place in which the firing squad carried out their unpleasant duty. Coincidence...?

It is often thought that many people were put to death within the Tower's walls over the years. In fact, relatively few people were actually killed there. One person died during a suspected bomb detonation by terrorists in 1974 inside the White Tower, which wounded 41 others – the White Tower's mortar room was full of tourists at the time. But actual deaths inside the Tower are not the main source of the horror and the tragedy which are associated with the place, as we shall see. Public executions (the entertainment of their day) were really carried out on Tower Hill, located outside and to the north of the Tower of London itself.

Such executions could draw massive crowds, packing spectators together like sardines up on Tower Hill. The higher members of society would be decapitated. If they were lucky, the single stroke of a razor-sharp sword would end their life quickly and relatively cleanly. The alternative was having your head hacked off with an executioner's axe, which might take several blows to get the job done properly. The true unfortunates would die by hanging from the scaffold, or meet the grisly fate of death by fire, tied to a stake and burned alive.

When the corpse had finally stopped twitching and the crowds of ghoulish onlookers dispersed back to their homes and pubs, the prisoner's corpse would be carted back within the Tower walls and interred... unless the victim's crimes had been particularly offensive to the king or queen, in which case their body might be chopped into quarters and displayed on spikes throughout the City of London. Is it any surprised that so many of the ghost stories that are associated with the Tower of London today may be traced back to the victims whose lives were cruelly snuffed out on Tower Hill?

After buying our entrance tickets to the Tower, Laura and I sometimes stroll up to the small monument that now stands on the spot where the gallows once stood. The simple inscription on the memorial plaque is profoundly moving:

To commemorate the tragic history and in many cases the martyrdom of those who for the sake of their faith country or ideals staked their lives and lost. On this site more than 125 were put to death, the names of some of whom are recorded here.

It is a truly strange and melancholic feeling to stand on a spot where so many people died a violent and gruesome death, with the sights and sounds of modern London surrounding you.

Ghosts and the military seem to share a common affinity for one another, which makes complete sense when you think about it. After all, very few other professions experience death and trauma on the scale that the military does.

The Yeoman Warders of the Tower of London (not actually "Beefeaters", as the commonly used slang goes) are drawn from the British military's cream of the crop. All of them have achieved high rank, and served for over two decades with a virtually perfect service record to their credit. As such, the men and women drawn to this elite cadre tend to be extremely level-headed, down to Earth, and not given to flights of fancy. They are placed in a position of supreme trust by the nation, guarding its monarch and her jewels of state. It therefore seems reasonable that, when a Yeoman Warder speaks about experiencing the paranormal, even the most skeptical would be wise to listen.

Their tales of ghostly activity at the Tower span across several centuries, and often revolve around the various military regiments that serve as guard units there. Soldiers stationed at the Tower function as guards, standing watch at static posts and also patrolling the premises at all hours. As a former member of the British Territorial Army, I've spent more than a few nights on guard duty at various barracks...and having spoken with Yeoman Warders at the Tower, the boredom suddenly seems far preferable to the sheer terror that guards have experienced within those ancient stone walls.

A garrison soldier, standing watch at the base of Tower Hill during the Second World War, could not believe his eyes when he witnessed a ghostly parade of men (all wearing period clothing) descending the hill towards his post. As the column of figures drew closer, the guard made a horrifying discovery: they were carrying a corpse, freshly beheaded, with the decapitated head tucked in the crook of its arm. The soldier was able to get a good look at the historical clothing of the men, who disappeared into thin air before reaching his position.

This wild tale fits well with our knowledge of the way in which executions were carried out on Tower Hill. The body of the deceased, along with its newly severed head, was carried back down the hill into the Tower for burial. Did the sentry witness the replay of the aftermath of one of Tower Hill's many executions?

Some of the Tower's ghostly residents seem to take a positive delight in taunting, pranking, and sometimes plain terrifying the living guards.

Numerous sentries (particularly those working the night watch) have reported the sound of phantom footsteps seeming to follow them, pacing their own steps exactly. The experience is an eerie one, to say the least. Other guards have sighted dark, cowled figures as they make their rounds at night. When challenged by those sentries brave enough to do so, the figures simply disappear into thin air leaving no trace.

Other sentries have been pelted with stones whilst walking their beat. When the culprits are searched for, none are ever found.

A guard post outside the Queen's House (home to the Tower's senior officer) was the scene of a terrifying encounter one fog-shrouded night in 1864, when an infantryman standing at this post saw a glowing white figure approaching him. Gamely, the soldier thrust at the apparition with his rifle-mounted bayonet - and found out the hard way that bladed weapons do not work on ghosts! The soldier quite understandably fainted, and was found shortly after by his comrades. Being "asleep" at your guard post is an offence of the gravest magnitude in the British Army, and could have had serious repercussions for the young solder... but other soldiers stepped forward and testified to having encountered the same apparition. The petrified sentry was not to be the last soldier to encounter this nightmarish entity, as it has been reported several times since then.

Considering the number of spine-chilling tales that surround the Queen's House, it is a wonder that anybody can be found to stand guard there! The ghost hunter supreme, Peter Underwood, recounts a tale in his book *Haunted London*, in which a woman's form appeared out of the darkness surrounding the Queen's House, moving in the direction of Tower Green. The hapless soldier only then discovered that the woman had no head! It's hard to blame the man for fleeing into the night, even though it meant abandoning his assigned duty post.

Perhaps the most frightening military encounter in the Tower's history occurred in the year 1815, in the archway of the Martin Tower. This was the location of the Crown Jewels at the time, so unusual incidents occurring here underwent great scrutiny by the governing authorities. As the story goes, a sentry standing guard at the witching hour was pounced upon by the hulking form of a massive bear. With a surge of adrenaline, the terrified guard struck out at the bear with the only weapon close to hand – his bayoneted rifle. Much like the unfortunate soldier posted outside the Queen's House, the poor fellow discovered that a bayonet won't protect you against a ghost. The bayonet slammed into the tower door and stuck fast. Physically unharmed, the sentry nonetheless collapsed into a dead faint...and, two days later, died in his bed.

Strange sounds, disembodied voices, and blood-curdling screams have been persistently reported throughout much of the Tower's history. The cries of a baby are said to haunt a part of the resident housing quarters, for example. The Queen's House has been the site of mysterious chanting, said to be like that of monks at prayer, and accompanied by phantom music. Many of the screams originate from the execution site at Tower Green, but can also be heard from the areas of the White Tower in which torture used to be carried out.

Guy Fawkes, point man for the Gunpowder Plot which attempted to blow the Houses of Parliament, was brutally tortured in the White Tower, his body broken on the rack in an attempt to extract a confession.

Is it any wonder that the sentries who guard the Tower and walk the grounds throughout the hours of darkness tell stories of gut-wrenching screams emanating from the old dungeons?

• • • ● ● • ● ● • • •

Decapitation on Tower Green

Despite the vast majority of prisoners being executed on Tower Hill, a very privileged few were accorded the dubious luxury of meeting their death inside the walls of the Tower itself.

Tower Green is a deceptively tranquil green lawn located directly in front of the "Queen's House", the living quarters for Tower staff. History tells us of only seven people (all of them nobles of high rank, two being Queens) to have been executed there. That well-known advocate of the quickie divorce, King Henry VIII, had two "instant divorces" carried out on Tower Green, sending Queen Anne Boleyn (his second wife) to her death by sword and his fifth wife Queen Catherine Howard to the headsman's axe. Seconds after her decapitation, Anne's face continued to contort, as if in speech, when the Headsman displayed it to the crowd.

Since her execution in 1536, many witnesses have claimed to see the ghost of Anne Boleyn at various locations throughout the Tower of London, always making her way towards the site of her death. Her ghost has been seen leaning out of the window which opens onto her old room.

A building stood on Tower Green at that time in history, so this select few could at least spend their final moments without the yelling, jeering, and harassment that were characteristic of public executions on Tower Hill. Although cold comfort, it must have been preferable to ending one's life as entertainment for the masses.

Much like Tower Hill, the location of the execution scaffold on Tower Green has been replaced with a fenced-in memorial. The memorial takes the form of a circular table with a glass pillow set in the middle. The pillow is sculpted in such a way that the center of it is depressed, leaving the observer with the distinct impression of an invisible head and neck resting on the pillow and awaiting the Headsman's axe.

One of the unfortunate nobles who would fall victim to the anger of Henry VIII was the frail 67-year-old Margaret Pole, Countess of Salisbury. When Henry dissolved the monasteries and withdrew from the church, Margaret maintained her staunch Catholicism. Stripped of her lands and title by the King, Margaret was imprisoned in the Tower of London and executed in the year 1541. Jailers found the following inscription painstakingly scribed into the wall of her prison cell:

For traitors on the block should die;
I am no traitor, no, not I;
My faithfulness stands fast and so,
Towards the block I shall not go!
Nor make one step, as you shall see;
Christ in Thy Mercy, save Thou me!

Margaret was not to be saved. Defiant to the last, she maintained her innocence of any crime as the jailers hauled her protesting body to Tower Green. Struggling, Margaret would not place her head on the execution block when the Headsman requested her to do so. Jailers pinned her down forcefully.

Using an axe rather than the cleaner and more accurate sword, the supposedly young and poorly trained executioner hacked the axe blade into her shoulder. Contemporary accounts claim that Margaret then staggered to her feet and tried to flee, forcing the executioner to follow her and chop her blood-splattered body repeatedly until it fell to the ground and stopped moving.

Margaret was buried a short distance away, within the haunted Chapel of St. Peter ad Vincula. Pope Leo XIII later beatified her as a martyr in the year 1886.

Tower legend has it that every year on the anniversary of her death (Mary 27th) the grotesque execution is reenacted on Tower Green, with the bloody ghost of Lady Margaret being pursued round and round in circles by the hapless executioner, trying desperately (and unsuccessfully) to evade the swings of his axe.

Speaking to Tower historians and warders will leave one in no doubt that Tower Green and the area around it (including the chapel) is haunted. Although I could not locate anybody who has witnessed the ghostly execution scene, there are several reports of blood-curdling screams being heard from the vicinity of the Green. Could this be a case of an "anniversary recording" type haunting, which is slowly dwindling in energy as years pass by, until only the sounds remain? It's an intriguing possibility, and one which bears further scrutiny...

• • • • ● • ● • • •

A Queen Haunts Two Places

Lady Jane Grey. The tragic "Queen for Nine Days" was also axed to death here on Tower Green, on a charge of high treason. Her white form has been seen atop the Salt Tower, although the most recently reported sighting was over sixty years ago. February 12th is the anniversary of her death, and the apparition of this tragic lady is usually sighted around this time of year.

Sprawling across eight hundred and fifty acres of my native Leicestershire, Bradgate Park is a beautifully scenic stretch of public land appreciated by hikers, day trippers, and those who love to escape the hustle and bustle of city life for the day.

Although its recorded history goes back for many hundreds of years, the park belonged to the Grey family up until the year 1928, when it was generously gifted to the Leicestershire public. The second Marquess of Dorset, Sir Thomas Grey, constructed Bradgate House sometime around the year 1520, a huge manor house
that his family would go on to inhabit for the next two centuries.

Bradgate Park is most famous for its association with Lady Jane Grey, who many historians believe was born within the walls of Bradgate House in 1537. Jane could trace her royal lineage back to her great grandfather, King Henry VII, and would sit upon the throne of England herself...for just nine days. Through a bizarre and convoluted series of family connections and royal political maneuvering, Jane found herself crowned Queen of England after the death of King Edward VI in the year 1533. Jane relocated herself voluntarily to the Tower of London, but was quickly ousted by parliament and dethroned ten days later in favor of the dead King Edward's half-sister Mary. Jane rapidly went from being a guest resident of the Tower to one of its prisoners.

In short order, Mary was crowned, and wasted no time in declaring Jane and her husband traitors, charging them with high treason. A royal commission appointed to "study the issue" of what was to be done with Jane, unsurprisingly turned out to be a complete whitewash, recommending that she be put to death. Charitably, they allowed Queen Mary the option of either having Jane's head cut off, or burning her at the stake. Who says that politicians have no heart?

Jane and her husband Guildford remained prisoners at the Tower until the following February, when the wheels of execution finally reached the end of the line. Guildford went to the executioner's block one cold morning out on Tower Hill, and a distraught Jane watched his decapitated body being carried back inside the Tower walls afterwards for burial.

It was now Jane's turn. By all accounts, she recited the 51st Psalm, and was led to Tower Green, where the executioner rather touchingly begged her forgiveness. Jane graciously forgave him. She is said to have repeated the final words of Jesus Christ.

"Lord, into thy hands I commend my spirit."

The executioner's sword then swept off her head.

Jane's body was laid to rest alongside that of her husband Guildford, close to Tower Green in the very haunted Chapel of St Peter ad Vincula.

And there, the story might well have ended. But for hundreds of years, almost every Leicestershire child grows up knowing the story of Lady Jane's ghost haunting Bradgate Park.

Bradgate House is now little more than a brick ruin (and is usually referred to as "the ruins"), and it can be fascinating to explore the brick walls and below-ground corridors which are all the remains of this once grand manor house. Strange sounds are regularly heard there at night, but there is a decidedly natural explanation in the form of Bradgate's peacocks, which tend to be found strutting in an around the ruins most of the time.

For many years now, local legend has claimed that Lady Jane Grey's restless spirit still haunts the last place in which she was truly happy, her childhood home. The most colorful story, which used to terrify me as a young child, holds that Jane's ghost appears each Christmas Eve in a black coach drawn by four headless horses. This ghostly cavalcade gallops once around the park, before disappearing into the ruins of Bradgate House. Best of all, in most versions of the tale, Jane is said to be carrying her own head in her lap.

This story has now passed into the realm of folklore, because it has been impossible to locate any actual eyewitnesses. Bradgate Park does not lack for travelers on Christmas Eve, being used as a short cut to the pub for some local residents, who are interested in a different kind of spirit altogether.

Bradgate Park after dark *feels* haunted. Walking through the footpaths in the shade of overhanging trees can be a very eerie experience. The park was originally used for deer hunting, and many deer still inhabit the grounds today. In addition to the peacocks (which tend to stay close to the ruins), they are responsible for more than a few reports of moving shadows and strange noises at night.

I investigated the Bradgate ruins a number of times, in the company of Andrew, Tracey, and various others. During balmy summer evenings with fine weather, the park makes for a perfect training location, and we often used it as an introductory case for first-time investigators to get their feet wet. Experience taught us to avoid the area during deer mating season, as those were entirely the wrong type of "things that go bump in the night" to pick up on a tape recorder.

On one particular Saturday night, we were conducting EVP experiments in the ruins, when a sudden mist descended on the park. This is par for the course in Leicestershire, which is well known for unpredictable swings in the weather. Through clear patches in the mist, I could still see the stars shining brightly overhead. We continued to record, asking questions respectfully. The grey mist added to the general ambience of the evening, giving it a slightly spooky feeling which we all laughed about afterwards.

Four or five deer were milling about on the grass outside the ruins, while our small group was huddled in one of the dank towers. Suddenly, a brilliant electric white flash illuminated the scene, fading away as quickly as it had arrived. We were all startled. My first thought: "Who the hell is taking photographs at this time of night?" All of our team was accounted for. Stepping outside immediately, we heard the stampeding hooves of deer disappearing into the night, but nobody could be seen anywhere around us. It was close to midnight on a Saturday, and the park was deserted.

The flash had been an almost pure white in color, leaving an afterimage of the tower brickwork burned into both of my retinas. We immediately fanned out and quickly checked the remainder of the ruins, then the surrounding bushes. Nothing, and nobody, was to be found. We were absolutely alone.

We looked at one another, bemused, and more than a little creeped out. What had caused the flash? It definitely wasn't lightning, and the flash had appeared to be artificial. Certainly no human agent was lurking around with a camera and flashgun. It was hard to shake the feeling that we are in the presence of something unseen, though I freely admit that this could have been entirely psychological. All of us had seen the same thing, and the deer were highly spooked. And yet, the phenomenon also seemed to have been completely silent.

Walking through my front door at daybreak, I was excited to go over the tape recordings made during the investigation. Although the group's startled reaction to the flash was captured on tape, no EVPs or anomalous sounds turned up.

Bradgate Park is still a favorite amongst paranormal investigators today. You can see several videos concerning it on YouTube. I can't say for sure whether the ghost of Lady Jane Grey really does haunt the ruined manor house (the eyewitness testimony for her haunting the Tower of London is much stronger) but if you would like to test the theory for yourself, why not wrap yourself up warmly this next Christmas Eve, and take a trip out to the Bradgate ruins before it gets too dark...

• • • ● ● • ● • • •

St Peter Ad Vincula

During our last visit to the Tower, Laura and I were fortunate enough to pick a day on which the British weather was even stormier than usual. As the torrential rain came down in sheets, the Yeoman Warder conducting our guided tour apologized for the fact that the tour would have to be cut short because of it. I say that we were fortunate because the Yeoman Warder offered the tour group a very special consolation prize: we were to be given admittance to the chapel of St. Peter ad Vincula (*St. Peter in Chains*) which is not a part of the usual tour.

Stepping into the chapel, all men in the tour party were ordered to remove their hats as a mark of respect (ladies are allowed to retain theirs, though most also chose to take them off). The bodies of Anne Boleyn and Catherine Howard are buried beneath the altar of this small and unassuming little chapel. Once the informal show-and-tell was over, we were given a few minutes to look around the chapel interior. I took this opportunity to sidle up to our Yeoman Warder guide and ask him about any ghost stories that were attached to the chapel.

With the practiced air of a man who has told the same tale to dramatic perfection on countless occasions, the Yeoman Warder began to speak of one night many years ago, when a military officer stationed at the Tower happened to notice lights burning in the chapel window. Suspicious of a possible break-in, the officer approached the chapel and looked through the window. What he saw within took his breath away. A long line of medieval-era men and women were moving slowly towards the altar at the back wall of the chapel. Despite the ethereal lighting within, the officer insisted that the female figure leading this procession of the dead was none other than Anne Boleyn herself. Incredulously, the officer watched as the spectral lights darkened and went out, leaving the ghostly figures to dissipate and the chapel return to its usual despondent gloom.

As I looked around at the carved tombstones and ornate wood carvings in the light of a rainy twenty-first century morning, it required very little effort to put myself in the officer's quaking boots on that dark night so many years before, and a distinct chill ran down my spine.

The Princes in the Tower

Royal ghosts abound throughout the Tower of London, as one might expect from a facility used as a prison by so many Kings and Queens of England. Family feuds and struggles take on an entirely new level of viciousness when the "game of thrones" is being played.

The shade of King Henry VI is said to haunt the Wakefield Tower, scene of his bloody assassination.

Henry was stabbed multiple times while he was kneeling at prayer, and it is here that his sad apparition is said to walk, supposedly appearing always in the hour before midnight.

Perhaps the most famous ghosts associated with the Tower of London in the public's mind are the tragic "princes in the Tower". King Edward V was twelve years old, and his younger brother Richard was only nine. They were the only obstacle between the Duke of Gloucester (their uncle Richard) and the throne of England. Although there remains some disagreement over who ordered and carried out the heinous act, it is certain that on one night in 1483 the princes disappeared from their place of confinement in the Bloody Tower, never to be seen alive again.

Almost two hundred years later, workmen uncovered two small skeletons during reconstruction of the White Tower. The remains, believed to be those of the murdered princes, were interred with honors at Westminster Abbey, the traditional last resting place of British royalty. But despite their bodies being laid to rest, the mournful apparitions of both princes have been sighted by many occupants of the Tower throughout the years. The boys are always seen to be holding hands, and are seen most often in the Bloody Tower.

In his excellent book "The World's Most Haunted Places", author Jeff Belanger recounts an incident with a Yeoman Warder that takes place in the residential quarters. The Yeoman Warder's wife shook him awake in the middle of the night to ask about the two children who had appeared at the foot of their bed. Both were wearing long white nightgowns, and clinging to one another sadly. It is not a great stretch to associate these forlorn apparitions with the two princes who met such an untimely and brutal end.

I chatted with a Yeoman Warder in 2013 and asked him whether any new ghostly happenings had taken place since my last visit to the Tower (the year before). With a twinkle in his eye, he told me of a colleague that had been making his official rounds of the Bloody Tower one night and had taken his young son along with him for company. After making the necessary checks, the Yeoman Warder called to his son and told him that it was time for them to leave.

"Just a minute, Daddy," the boy was pointing to an empty corner of the room. "I haven't finished playing with the two boys!"

Needless to say, the somewhat shaken Yeoman Warder quickly gathered his equipment and his son, and made a fast exit.

The same Bloody Tower is also haunted by the noble Sir Walter Raleigh, most favored of Queen Elizabeth I but imprisoned for many years in the Bloody Tower by King James I. Raleigh was beheaded as an act of appeasement to the Spanish, who never forgave him for preying on their merchant shipping. Not only is Raleigh's ghost seen inside the Tower, but also drifting along the battlements at night along the path known as "Raleigh's Walk," startling many a sentry and Yeoman Warder as they patrolled the grounds after dark. Most of the accounts agree that this occurs on nights when the moon is shining full and bright, in the finest traditions of the classic ghost story!

CHAPTER SEVEN

MOVING TO AMERICA

Life took a series of twists and turns in 1999, both personally and professionally. In the summer of that year, I took a job in the city of Boulder, Colorado. I would ultimately relocate permanently to the United States. Along with a couple of suitcases, my passion for all things paranormal came with me.

It is no exaggeration to say that I was raised on a steady diet of Hollywood movies, TV shows, and books. There wasn't too much of a culture shock for me to overcome, and I found the American people to be a very warm and friendly bunch. Despite having been in the United States for fifteen years, one thing that has *never* quite adjusted to the change is my body clock, which still seems to think that it is running on Greenwich Mean Time.

One very pleasant surprise was my discovery that the Americans loved their ghost stories every bit as much as the British did. A little Internet research and browsing through some books on local folklore revealed a wide range of haunted places within driving distance of my newly adopted home.

Following the shocking and tragic events of 9/11, I signed up to be a volunteer firefighter, and after graduating from the fire academy enrolled straight away in an Emergency Medical Technician program at a local community college. I still volunteer for the same fire department, and now teach in that same EMT program.

It's safe to say that America has been more than good to me.

Last Goodbyes

We used to refer to the old firehouse as "the tin shed by the side of the highway." The department has since moved to newer and more modern quarters, but most of us firefighters still remember the creaky old place with great affection.

Late one Friday night, my buddy Trey and I were sitting in the crew lounge upstairs, watching TV and waiting for the tones to drop. Chores were all done, the rest of the crew had bedded down for the night, and we two night owls were up at two o'clock in the morning eating ice cream and enjoying Comedy Central.

Trey suddenly frowned and help up a hand. "There's somebody walking around downstairs in the bay. Listen."

I muted the TV and listened. Sure enough, the measured tread of footsteps could be heard on the concrete floor of the engine bay.

This is usually no big deal. Every member of the department has a code to get into the locked building, and sometimes they would drop by at night to pick up a piece of equipment, drop something off, leave a note, or whatever. But it was good safety practice to check it out just to make sure.

Trey and I walked downstairs. On the way down we heard the thump of a vehicle door closing inside the bay. Pushing through the swing door, we found the place in darkness. I brought up the lights and called out to whoever was messing around to quit it.

No answer.

Cautiously, Trey and I walked from vehicle to vehicle within the bay. We had two fire engines and a water tender parked in there, plus a wildland fire brush truck. Methodically we searched in and around them all, but nobody was anywhere to be found. The bay was absolutely silent and empty.

Getting annoyed now, we checked the rest of the ground floor. Nada. Went upstairs and looked around. Other than the sleeping forms of our brothers in the bunk rooms, nobody else was up there. This wasn't funny anymore.

We had all but turned the station upside down and found nobody to account for the footsteps. Bemused, we went back to the TV. About an hour later, Trey crashed out and I went to sleep on the couch (I snore like a chainsaw, so I'd sleep outside of the bunkroom as a mercy to the other firefighters). My alarm was set for six o'clock, but at a quarter past five I woke with a start. Somebody was tapping me on top of the head.

Throwing off my blanket, I leapt to my feet. *Crap! Did I sleep through a 911 call?*

The TV room was empty. To tell the truth, I was a little bit freaked out by then. The sensation of that hand touching my head felt totally real. In fact, I can still feel it with perfect clarity in my mind as I write about it ten years later. I even mentioned it to the rest of the firefighters at breakfast, which is almost a case of "sense of humor suicide" at a fire house because you know you're never going to hear the last of it! The captain, a salty old veteran with several decades of experience under his belt, was kind enough to not give me a hard time about it.

Shift changeover was uneventful at seven o'clock. I put all thoughts of the strange incident out of my mind as I drove home in the bright morning sunshine. It was a beautiful summer morning, with the sun climbing over the Rockies into a clear blue sky. It felt like I didn't have a care in the world.

When I walked in my front door, it was a shock to see my wife sitting at the kitchen table, crying. Her face was red and puffy with tears. Shaking and visibly distraught, she told me that her mother had died earlier that morning.

She had died at approximately the same time I was woken up by that invisible touch.

When I met the mother of a good friend while visiting her house, I was saddened to hear that she was terminally ill and did not have many months to live. We chanced upon the subject of the paranormal, and had a fascinating conversation about the afterlife and all things ghostly.

Although terminally ill, my friend's mom maintained a very upbeat attitude and an admirably positive outlook on life. She had lost none of her fighting spirit. Our chat concluded with an intriguing promise on her part.

"Keep a camera by your bed, just in case," she told me with a twinkle in her eye. "If there's any way I can manage it, I'll appear to you after I die."

We parted with those words, and I never saw her again. A few months down the road, I got a rather distraught phone call from my friend, telling me that her mom was on her deathbed and that footsteps were starting to be heard in empty rooms of the house. I assured her that this was actually not all that uncommon, and the paranormal case literature records numerous instances of this happening when a person is transitioning from this world into whatever comes next.

When she ultimately passed away, I kept my digital camera on the bedside table. Although she and I were not close at all, having met only once, it is not unheard of for apparitions of the dead to make an appearance immediately (or shortly after) their death. I had never before gotten one to agree to make the attempt!

Ten years later, she has not yet put in an appearance. My bedside digital camera has long since been replaced by a bedside phone with integrated camera. Numerous mediums have told me that either the concept of time does not exist in the spirit world, or that it is perceived in a very different way. So, I have not entirely given up hope that she and I may keep our appointment, and that I may capture the Holy Grail for all paranormal investigators: a truly high-definition image of apparition, caught on camera, and hopefully smiling.

My own beloved mother contracted lung cancer in 2003. After one last bittersweet Christmas spent together in Colorado, she entered hospice care in the spring of 2004 when the cancer spread to her brain. Doctors told me that if I wanted to see my mum again for one final time, then I needed to be on a plane within the week. I had an understanding employer, who let me have four weeks off so that I could fly back to England and spend some final quality time with her before the end.

Friends and family rallied around, and made my mother's last days as comfortable as possible. I was able to help her decide to not be resuscitated when her heart stopped beating, which is one of the kindest things I have ever been able to do for another human being. Mum didn't like to talk about the possibility of an afterlife too much. She was a very superstitious person, and I think that she didn't want to tempt fate in this regard. But she did tell me, and several other friends and family members, that she was very much looking forward to seeing her deceased parents again.

Tragically, I was not at her bedside when she died. Whether it was the prospect of spending some extra time with her son, or for some other reason of which I'm unaware, mum's health took a temporary upswing and she hung on to life for the month that I remained there. The day eventually came when I ran out of leave and had to return to the United States.

I will never forget that morning, typically cold and misty. Waking while it was still dark outside in order to make an early flight, I walked into my mum's room and kissed her goodbye for one final time, holding her hand and telling her how much I loved her. Despite her brain being affected by the cancerous tumors, she smiled back, and I knew that she understood me. We let go of one another in that moment, but only physically. She remains in my heart to this day, and always will. I was unashamed of the tears that streaked down my face as I stood in the doorway for one last look at the woman who had invested her heart and soul into raising me over the past thirty years.

Mum eventually passed away in the Leicester LOROS hospice. After making a few enquiries, I was not surprised to learn that in her final days of life, she began to see dead family members surrounding her bedside in the hospice. Although I wasn't able to get many specific details, the care providers did note that she was talking to somebody who did not seem to be in the room, somebody with whom she was apparently quite familiar. I was told specifically that she believed this to be her parents, both of whom had preceded her in death by many years.

The phenomenon of the death bed visitation has been with us throughout recorded history. If you speak with a palliative care professional today, such as a hospital doctor or nurse, they will tell you stories of the soon-to-die patient seeing and speaking to invisible people within their room. Meaningful conversations often take place, with the patient speaking their half and responses being silent to the ear of any listener within the room, as though they were catching only one half of a chat.

During my years as an emergency medical provider, I have dealt with a significant amount of death and dying. I have friends who work at the bedside of the terminally ill. All of them have told me stories of deathbed experiences similar to that which my mum underwent. Sometimes, physical and auditory phenomena such as footsteps and the movement of objects, is reported. Less frequently (but still common enough for us to sit up and take note) are deathbed apparitions, in which ghostly figures are reported in the company of the person who is about to die.

I was initially very skeptical of these accounts, until I actually did the research and spoke to the professionals who encounter this stuff on a regular basis. Another common symptom is that when a patient who is somehow mentally impaired (for example, one with a progressive cognitive disease such as Alzheimer's) is about to die, they sometimes experience a period of mental clarity and alertness in which they seem to see something which we cannot: a bright light, a distant place, or deceased people that have come to greet them.

The part of me that works as a paramedic and professional clinical educator would point out to you that the dying human brain is a very complex thing. In a physiologic sense, it is undergoing final structural and chemical changes that may induce bizarre side effects, such as auditory and visual hallucinations and a sense of an invisible person being in the room. The classic "bright tunnel of light" is often reported by military pilots who undergo brief periods of cerebral hypoxia - a temporary reduction of blood flow to the brain when experiencing high gravity maneuvers in a jet aircraft.

But the paranormal investigator in me would point out the wealth of cases documented over many hundreds of years, detailing experiences such as this with the dead and dying – and sometimes the phenomena are experienced by witnesses in the room with the dying person. The published works of Doctors Raymond Moody and Elizabeth Kubler-Ross are a great place to start, if you would like to learn more about this.

And finally, you might be wondering what I *personally* believe.

I like to think that, in her final moments of physical life, my grandmother and grandfather came back to escort my dear old mum into whatever world it is that comes after this one.

• • • ● • ● • • •

I have some fascinating experiences with psychic mediums over the years. Although I do not have one working for BCPRS, I am always willing to bring one in if the client requests it. Every so often I will learn something interesting from one of them that will cause me to raise an eyebrow.

During one investigation up in Central City, I was standing in the lobby of a deserted old theater with a lady who was a sensitive. We were waiting for fellow investigators to return from another building, and had about half an hour to kill, so I asked her if she would be averse to giving me a personal reading. I must profess to being a combination of curious, skeptical, and yet appropriately open-minded on the subject of psychic mediums. My research has led me to conclude that some may indeed be gathering information by apparently paranormal means, information that they could not otherwise have.

As we settled down to talk in the dark theater entranceway, I was more than a little curious as to what the psychic would report.

She began to tell me of a dead teenage boy (we'll call him "Michael"), who had committed suicide by hanging himself one night in a fit of depression. His spirit was said to have attached itself to me because he had seen me treating a patient during a medical emergency, and was drawn to my compassionate nature.

Michael was a fun and friendly spirit, I was told, that liked to hang out at my house and enjoyed the funny banter and interplay between my wife and I. Laura and I are both card carrying geeks, who can often be found enjoying something related to the worlds of science fiction and fantasy, and the psychic believed that Michael was particularly attracted to that aspect of our home life.

"He also *really* likes the way you swear." This was revealed in a slightly embarrassed manner. I do indeed swear more than I ought to, something I've been trying to cut back on doing.

The psychic told me that Michael was a harmless soul, not yet ready to move on to the next plane of existence, who was spending time in a comfortable and friendly environment until he was ready to take the next step.

Feeling ever so slightly embarrassed (have you ever tried talking to thin air?) I let Michael know that he was welcome to stick around me as long as he liked, unless

– ahem – the bedroom door was closed, at which point he was to make himself scarce. This was inspired by something I heard Dave Schrader, presenter on the excellent *Darkness Radio* paranormal talk show, said to the spirits that took up residence in his house. "Don't come near my kids, and don't bug me when I'm in the shower!"

CHAPTER EIGHT
THE HAMMER HOUSE MURDER

Sometimes the best service that my team can provide for a client is simply giving a home a clean bill of health. When they first contact us via email, some clients are more puzzled than afraid of the activity going on in their home. They want us to try and get to the bottom of the events and find out whether there is a mundane explanation, or something a little more unusual – they are looking for the truth, no matter what it might be, keeping a balanced and open mind on the subject until my team draws a conclusion based upon the evidence we've collected.

Another type of client hopes that we will find something paranormal going on, perhaps because they find the idea intriguing or exciting. In these cases, the hope seems to be that we will validate the client's belief that their house is haunted in some way. Sometimes this does indeed turn out to be the case, and sometimes it does not pan out that way.

Jimmy was the third type of client. He was rather hoping that the new investment property which he had just purchased in collaboration with a group of friends, was *not* haunted. Some people in the neighborhood already had their own idea about the building, and weren't shy in speaking about it.

I had worked with Jimmy for several years at the firehouse. He was a solid guy, not given to flights of fancy. The sort of solid firefighter you were happy to serve with.

After he moved on from the fire service, Jimmy reached out to me through a mutual friend with an intriguing proposition.

Jimmy had an entrepreneurial streak to him, and had decided to move into real estate. Purchasing what might politely be called a "fixer-upper" in the city of Denver, his plan was to convert it into multiple apartments and rent the place out to reliable professional tenants.

"The place is a 'fixer-upper' for sure," he told me over the phone. "But I got it for a song, so I'm not complaining."

It turned out that Jimmy had gotten the place cheaply for a very good reason. The former tenant, rumored to be a drug dealer in the local area, had been asleep in his bed one night when a person (or persons) unknown had broken in. The unidentified intruder had then bludgeoned the sleeping man to death with a claw hammer.

Understandably, the residence now had a bit of a reputation in the neighborhood as a possibly haunted house. Stories of a male apparition seen in an upstairs window bleeding from impact wounds to his skull and face, were circulating via the neighborhood grapevine. But having asked around, I soon found that there was no real substance to the spectral story. It was all "friend of a friend" testimony, and none of it was consistent. Equally, none of it came from adult eyewitnesses. It seemed like a simple case of local kids making up terrifying tales around a building which had been the scene of a genuinely brutal murder.

Jimmy was worried that potential renters would be put off by the property's violent history.

"Can you guys go in and investigate? And if you don't find anything, maybe give the building a clean bill of health..."

I wasn't against this in principle. Although there was nothing in the way of major ghostly activity reported about the place, it would be a chance to kill two birds with one stone: help out a friend, and also act as a training exercise for my team. And if we *did* collect evidence of the paranormal during the night, then that would be icing on the cake as far as I was concerned.

So, I wasted no time in arranging an overnight stay at the property for October 22nd. Five of us traveled down to Denver and met with Jimmy. As he enjoyed a glass of wine (and we clung to our policy of no alcohol on an investigation), Jimmy talked us through the background of the murder. I stopped him just as his tale reached the location of the murder itself.

"Don't tell us until tomorrow morning," I requested. "Let's see if we can figure it out for ourselves."

This little experiment had just suggested itself on the spot. The house was quite spacious, so could we "intuit" the murder location based on instinct alone? It wasn't going to be quite as easy as it sounded. Although we had been told that the victim was sleeping (and therefore probably in a bedroom) when he was murdered, the house had been completely gutted inside by construction workers. It was impossible to identify all of the former bedrooms by sight alone.

Construction crews had ripped out all the drywall throughout the property and were starting over, partitioning everything in such a way that a three-story house was converted into five single apartments. New walls were being put in, and old ones taken out. The interior was laid completely bare. The carpeting had been ripped up, leaving exposed floors to walk on.

Jimmy conducted us on a guided tour. I sketched a rough floor plan as we went, paying particular attention to the electrical outlets and newly installed wiring. We baselined EMF levels as we went along. The exposed wiring made it significantly easier to chase down the few spikes that were found.

No heating system was functioning yet. On the one hand, this could prove to be a benefit; no artificial air currents would be wafting about the place, creating cold spots that would have to be hunted down and explained away. But on the other, this was a night in *October*. Temperatures could, at best, be described as "chilly", but a more accurate description would be "teeth-chatteringly cold."

To an extent, the whole team had expected to be cold and prepared for it. We all wrapped up in lots of warm layers, finishing up with various knitted hats and caps. Flasks of hot tea and coffee would help too.

Having kindly fed us, Jimmy supplied us with keys to the building and left us to it for the night. Baselining complete, our team split up into two smaller groups and settled in for the night.

My overriding memory of this particular investigation is still the cold. Every surface, including the bare floors on which we sat, radiated the pervasive October chill. Long before midnight, we could see each other's breath misting in the air. Throw in a levitating bed and we'd be on the movie set of *The Exorcist!*

Midnight came and went without incident. As with so many investigations both before and since then, boredom began to set in. The occasional creak or groan of wood could be heard, emanating from the stairwell or one of the floors. Each one could be explained away by the natural settling of the house as temperatures dropped and construction materials contracted.

Suddenly, a thunderous *SLAM!* echoed throughout the house. We jerked bolt upright, fumbling for cameras and measuring equipment. The cold was making everybody sluggish.

It didn't take long to identify the source of the noise. Looking outside, Laura noticed that a couple of neighbors were loading lumber into the back of a pickup truck, and being less than gentle about it.

In an attempt to stir up some kind of activity, I hit upon the idea of placing control objects throughout the place. Control objects are items which should (theoretically) have some type of emotional link to a spirit that might be haunting a place. For example, when investigating haunted churches, it is common to use crucifixes as control (or "trigger") objects. When BCPRS investigated a haunted fire house, my firefighter helmet served as a control object.

The team scattered temporarily in our search for suitable objects. Considering the fact that construction workers were still renovating the building, it should have come as no surprise when Miranda returned with a trigger object that proved to be in remarkably bad taste.

"*What?*" she demanded, waving around a hefty-looking claw hammer.

All five of us had taken our best guess as to which room the murder had occurred in.

The house had four bedrooms, so statistically we each had a one in four chance of guessing correctly. To make things more interesting, our team agreed that the "winner" would be the person who guessed as closely as possible within the correct room, so two people might pick a bedroom but different corners or walls. One of the two would probably guess closer to the correct location than the other.

Luck was with me on this particular night. I took one look at the front bedroom on the top floor, pointed at the space next to a partially concealed attic entrance space, and declared "That's the spot!"

It turned out that I was right.

Much as I would love to ascribe this to some kind of psychic ability, there is actually a much more down-to-Earth explanation.

I've been in more than one scene in my emergency career where illegal drugs were a part of the equation. Looking at this particular room, my first thought was: *if I were keeping a stash of drugs in this house, where would I put them?*

Somewhere safe, secure, and concealed, was the obvious answer. A hidden space in the bedroom wall had been uncovered by the contractors when they started tearing down drywall. *The perfect spot.* And it followed that a person stashing their drugs somewhere like that would want to keep them close at hand, even when they were sleeping.

There was nothing more to it than simple suspicion and deduction.

We were all disappointed that nothing seemingly paranormal occurred during our stay.

The voice recorders which we had liberally scattered around the house picked up nothing abnormal when the playback was analyzed. A uniform coldness blanketed the place all night, with no significant temperature drops or peaks. And EMF levels stayed resolutely low throughout.

It is a well-documented phenomenon that hauntings which have lain dormant for a long time can be stirred up again by construction or renovation. Even something as simple as redecorating or moving the furniture around has been known to flare up paranormal activity.

Some have theorized that any spirits haunting a building take offence at things being changed in what they see as *their* home. One of the first questions a skilled paranormal investigator will ask is, "Have you recently made any changes within the property? Redecorated or renovated?" Ghosts seem to be resistant to change, and will often make their displeasure known to the living.

Stories of a ghostly and bleeding apparition are no longer being told about the hammer house in the local neighborhood, and the building's tenants seem to have no complaints of a paranormal nature. As a team, we learned a lot about the ways in which the quirks of building construction can mislead the aspiring ghost hunter, especially when the building is settling down at night.

CHAPTER NINE

THE RESTLESS FIREMEN

There are some opportunities in life that you just can't pass up.

A haunted and historic old fire house? Color me there.

Firefighters are exposed to death on a very regular basis, and I suspect that it is no coincidence that so many fire houses have their stories of a resident ghost or two. Although relatively few people end their life in a fire house (usually it is a heart attack or other life-threatening emergency following a high stress call), they do tend to be buildings that inspire deep feelings of love and affection in those who lived and worked there.

Travel south from Denver along Interstate 25, and you will soon end up in the industrial city of Pueblo, home to just over 100,000 people and known for its steel production. Impressively, no less than *four* recipients of the Congressional Medal of Honor came from Pueblo. During my visits there, I have found the people to be friendly and welcoming, and more than happy to talk about some of the city's ghost stories.

The Pueblo Fire Department, represented by Fire Inspector Gary Micheli and Fire Engineer Mark Pickerel, graciously allowed BCPRS to investigate the haunted Hose Company Number Three on several occasions. Our first visit with a small field research team (myself, Miranda, accompanied by Brad and

Randy from an associated group) took place in the March of 2008. This was a midweek visit, on a cool evening when the moon was full, and a light breeze stirred the treetops. We left early to avoid the gridlock of Denver traffic, pulling into the parking lot at four o'clock in the afternoon.

Surrounded by power and phone lines on all sides, the two-story firehouse is neighbor to a Masonic lodge building and a large mortuary. This should make for an interesting mix of energy, in more ways than one!

Mark (who pulls double duty as the museum curator) and Gary gave us a warm welcome, a place to drop off our equipment, and then a fascinating tour of the firehouse, accompanied by some of its historical background. The fire house dates back to 1895, when it was built by the Masons and offered to the City of Pueblo on a monthly lease until 1900, at which point it was sold to the city permanently...meaning that the City of Pueblo cannot sell the firehouse and land to anybody other than the Masons, and can *never* have alcohol on the property at any time. Still, not a bad deal for the five-hundred-dollar ticket price!

A horse-drawn hose company operated out of the fire house during those early years, and we would see many signs of the building's equestrian era as we were conducted on our tour by Gary and Mark. The second floor was originally used to store hay feed for the horses, and Mark pointed out a block and tackle mounted just above a second-floor door on the building's rear side. "They used that to haul hay bales up here for storage," he said.

What was once the hay loft was converted into a kitchen and dining area, after the Pueblo Fire Department transitioned over from horse-drawn fire engines to their mechanical equivalent, in 1915. We found the kitchen to have a very friendly atmosphere, not very different to that in my own firehouse. It took very little effort of the imagination to conjure up the picture of those nineteenth and twentieth century firefighters, congregated around the table with food and hot coffee, having just returned from an emergency "run" in the middle of the night. Gary told a macabre story of days in which the mortuary would be creating the bodies of their customers.

"When the wind was blowing a certain way, all of the ashes of those dead people would blow into the firehouse kitchen and stink up the food!" Note to self: never bitch about my firehouse kitchen ever again. At least it doesn't smell and taste like newly-cremated human remains.

At 4:18 on the morning of March 9th, 1979, the firefighters of Pueblo Engine Company Three were dispatched on their final 911 call. Three hours later, at what would normally be shift change, Engine Company Three closed up its doors and ceased to function as an active firehouse.

Walking through its corridors and rooms, it is easy to get overwhelmed with the almost tangible sense of historic tradition and service through adversity which permeates this beautiful place. On all sides, you are surrounded by artifacts from a bygone era of firefighting history, most of it stored carefully inside glass display cases for protection. I was like a kid in a candy store, drawn first to axes and pike poles, before my eye was caught by an antique fireman's truck belt or helmet, and then on to another piece of memorabilia such as a brass extinguisher or a speaking bugle.

Mark was justifiably proud of the fact that his father was a Pueblo firefighter before him, joining the department in the early 1960s. Along with fascinating pieces of trivia from the station's past, Mark's dad would also tell stories concerning its ghostly activity. One of the more chilling involves the window located at the top of the main staircase. According to Mark's father, a handprint would frequently appear and disappear on the glass windowpane. The fire service has always been a stickler for cleanliness and neatness (it tends to save lives in our line of work) and so the duty officer would order the hand print to be washed off, but it would always reappear sooner or later in the same spot on the window.

To be fair, the fire service is also well known for its sense of humor. Some of the pranks that take place in firehouses, particularly if they are slower stations and the firefighters have a little more time on their hands, have become the stuff of legend. But in this case, the activity went on and on for months, with no culprit stepping forward or being caught in the act. With what one imagines would be a sense of exasperation, the department admitted defeat and had the glass replaced.

Needless to say, the handprint wasted no time in coming back. But the handprint began to appear less often, with appearances finally trailing off into nothingness. The window now sits directly adjacent to the wall of fallen firefighters, containing photographs of those Pueblo firefighters who have died while in service to the department.

Vehicular issues seem to abound at Hose Company Number Three, with two crashes standing out as particularly bizarre. During the early hours of one morning in the 1960s, while the firefighters slept upstairs in the crew quarters, the fire engine started itself up of its own accord, plowing through the closed engine bay doors. Fortunately, nobody was hurt. The fire engine came to a halt in the road outside the firehouse, and was soon surrounded by bleary-eyed, confused firefighters.

Was there a mechanical explanation for this bizarre episode? The firefighters theorized that the truck was left in gear when it was parked after their last 911 call, which was a few hours prior to the crash, and that a residual charge left in the magneto may have sparked the vehicle to life and caused it to burst out into the street. Certainly, *something* put the truck into gear, though whether it was left that way by the driver or something rather more unusual took place is something to which we shall never know the answer. But it is worth pointing out that the driver must also have neglected to set the parking brake *in addition to leaving the truck in gear,* which seems uncharacteristically sloppy for the operator of a fire engine.

A single occurrence such as this, with a single fire truck, might be dismissed as merely an odd chain of events, and written off as a fun fireside story. But it isn't an isolated case. Mark and Gary told us of an even stranger situation dating to 2006, which occurred with the "Chief's Car," a historic Model T Ford that has been lovingly restored to its former glory.

Three firefighter museum staff were moving equipment around inside the building in preparation for transport to the Firefighters Banquet later that day. The Chief's Car was one of the larger exhibits that had to be moved, so that other items could be accessed more easily. On trying to start the car, they found that the battery was almost dead. Somebody hit upon the idea of driving the Model T out to the parking lot behind the firehouse and letting it idle, allowing the battery to charge up a little.

A few minutes later, firefighters loading museum exhibits onto a flatbed parked at the front firehouse doors witnessed a streak of red and were shocked when something slammed into the flatbed with great force. As you will probably have guessed, it was the Chief's Car, which was now sporting a smashed front end from its collision with the flatbed. Fortunately, Gary and his two colleagues were unharmed.

This second mysterious incident concerning a fire department vehicle turned out to be significantly more peculiar when two witnesses came forward to fill in some of the gaps in this tale. A couple living nearby said that they were looking down from their apartment window and saw the Model T suddenly accelerate from its parking spot, heading straight for Evans Avenue where their own van happened to be parked. Just before it would have hit the van, the Model T swerved sharply to avoid it. The couple initially thought that the car was been remotely driven, because even without a visible driver, *the*

Chief's Car appeared to be under complete control at all times.

As the couple watched in amazement, the Model T threaded the needle through a six-foot gap and took a right turn onto Evans Avenue, made *a second sharp right turn* onto Broadway (blowing through a stop sign in the process!) and began to gather momentum. More witnesses enter the story at this point, as patrons of the tavern which sits directly across from the fire house reported seeing the car picking up speed as it hurtled straight down Broadway towards the front of Hose Company Number Three. They were very clear about the fact that the Model T turned *for a third time,* swerving towards the open bay doors of the firehouse and crashing into the flatbed trailer which the firefighters were loading.

"She must have been doing twenty miles an hour," Gary said. "Busted the front end up pretty badly. But she's been restored to her proper condition since."

Take a moment to compare these two vehicle crashes. It's one thing to attribute a fire engine starting itself up in the middle of the night and driving into the street through a closed bay door, to mechanical failure. The charged magneto/truck left in gear theory has at least some degree of plausibility. But how does the fire chief's car make *three ninety-degree turns,* without hitting anything along the way, and basically "home in" on the front door of its own garage, in plain sight of several witnesses? The couple who watched the Model T start its journey firmly believed that it was under the control of an invisible driver, such was the precision with which it turned corners and avoided obstacles. Simple mechanical failure does not explain three sharply executed ninety degree turns. In fact, I can think of no convincing rational explanation that does explain it satisfactorily.

We were soon joined by a reporter from the local newspaper, the *Pueblo Chieftain,* who wanted to shadow us during our investigation. Continuing our guided tour through the structure, we arrived next at the sleeping quarters. A polished brass pole dropped away through the floor to the engine bay below, allowing the firefighters rapid access to their fire engine when bells sounded in the middle of the night. A metal grille cover had been placed over the pole for safety reasons. During the 1970s, a child fell through the opening surrounding the pole. Although seriously injured, the child did not die.

One thing that struck me immediately on entering the sleeping quarters was the close proximity of power lines to the upstairs windows, and I made a mental note to check the EMF levels carefully during the baselining process. We soon discovered that background levels of up to six milligauss were common in the sleeping quarters, being highest at the point where the bed frames and pillows came close to the outer walls. While not dangerously high, sleeping in an elevated EMF zone might cause unpredictable cognitive side effects over several hours.

An EMF hot spot of fifteen milligauss was picked up in the engine bay, seeming to originate with an old telegraph machine...which was not plugged in or powered on. We were never able to account for the source of this artificial EMF spike, but the most reasonable conclusion is that it was an underground source such as a power line.

Daylight was fading. We took the opportunity of taking some establishing photographs on all sides of the building, for future reference. Gary and Mark handed over a master key to the property and promised to return at daybreak the next day. The team got to work sealing doors and windows with surgical tape, leaving just one door unsealed to allow us out for dinner later that night. Baseline readings were unremarkable. So far, so good.

Placing the remote cameras was to be the next challenge. We had a number of thermal cameras (capable of detecting heat rather than just light) and made sure that they covered the entire engine bay, most of the crew quarters, the kitchen, and the corridors. Due to the size of the fire station, we had almost complete camera coverage, an unusual luxury for us.

Control objects – items having some sort of significance for any entity haunting a location – are an underused tool of paranormal investigation. At Hose Company Number Three, I employed a bunch of fire service equipment such as my helmet, an axe, firefighting glove, and suchlike. Placing them carefully on sheets of white paper, I used a thick black permanent marker pen to draw a border all the way around the object. In some cases, control objects have been moved by apparently unseen forces.

It was now getting dark, and before getting down to the business of the evening, our team needed to be fed. We headed across the street to eat at the friendly tavern, locking the door behind us and securing it from the outside with surgical tape to prevent tampering. A lone digital voice recorder was left running at the top of the staircase.

The tavern was bustling and boisterous, and it stood to reason that the noise would cause some problems for our EVP recording experiments later that night as the drinks continued to flow for its patrons. On the other hand, we could probably count on the morticians building staying quiet...

• • • ● • ● ● • •

The tamper seals were intact when we returned, with full bellies (but no booze) on board. In a break with our normal procedure, Randy wanted to conduct an EVP session alone in the engine bay, and so the remaining three of us experimented as a group in both the sleeping quarters and the kitchen. Sitting in the darkened sleeping quarters, Miranda, Brad, and I noticed a metallic clicking noise which we soon traced to the bedsprings that we were sitting on.

In a break from our typical routine, a friend named Robbin (who believes she has psychic abilities) kindly offered to phone in during the night, trying to gather some information regarding our location. This was a first for our team, using a different method of gathering information. It would yield some very interesting results.

Listening over the phone, here's what I was told:

"I'm getting the sense of an angry man attached to the firehouse. Very angry."

I nodded. "Is he visible to you? Can you tell me what he looks like?"

She described him as being tall and square jawed, with a mean set to his face. The man was uniformed in blue station pants and a blue shirt.

When pressed for a name, there was a pause as Robbin considered. A name tag was visible on his uniform shirt, which the man was trying to show her deliberately. She believed the name to be 'Lawrence' or 'Laurence', although he said that his friends called him "Larry" or just "Larr."

It seemed that Larry was not a nice man. Based upon what our on-call psychic had to say, that may not even have been his true name. She described him as being a very deceitful character, a compulsive liar.

"I don't trust anything he's telling me, and I get the impression that he's trying to conceal something from me...something big. I couldn't swear that he was even a fireman there in Pueblo, he might be deceiving me about that. I don't know exactly what his attachment is."

I asked about the presence of bars or bugles – rank insignia – on his uniform, and was told that there were none visible. So, probably not a lieutenant, captain, or chief, then. However, even line firefighters tend to wear some form of collar insignia. Could Robbin tell me a little about his personality?

She was unflinching in her condemnation of Larry.

"This man is angry, bitter, and resentful. He's mad at the world. He's so hateful, Richard. In fact, I think we might be looking at something like clinical depression or bipolar disorder. He's capable of outbursts of explosive anger. You might want to be careful."

Outbursts of explosive anger...might that translate into physical activity of some kind?

I thanked Robbin for the warning, and asked if she could pick up on the years when Larry was involved with the Pueblo Fire Department. I wanted to try and pin down a timeframe. Were we talking about an 1800s-era old-school fireman, depression years, World War II, or more recent? Assuming we were dealing with a real entity here (which was by no means certain) then his era would color the way in which I wanted to approach him.

Robbin placed Larry with the department in the years leading up to the mid-nineties, stating that he was forced to leave the fire service because of ill health. He was a very heavy smoker, which ultimately ended his career as a fireman.

I thanked Robbin for her help, and hung up, turning over the possibilities in my mind.

• • • ● ● • ● ● • •

A comfortable hush pervaded the firehouse, broken only by the distant sounds of Randy asking questions in the engine bay below as his EVP experiment unfolded. We sat in companionable quiet, digital voice recorders running, attempting to get a discarnate entity to answer our questions.

I kicked things off by respectfully asking Larry (or any other entity present) to please make a noise, shine a light, or touch one of us to indicate his presence.

Nothing stirred. I set down a Tri-Field EMF meter in the doorway and continued to speak, a little self-consciously, to thin air.

"I'm a fireman, just like you used to be. Come on and help a brother out, will ya? Talk to me, if you can."

Silence. I persevered.

I asked Larry what he did for the fire department, trying to place him in the hierarchy. Was he a fireman? A chauffeur (fire truck driver)? An officer, or perhaps an administrator?

"Did you serve here at Threes?

"Did you like this place? Was it home to you?

"When did you last run on a structure fire?"

I carried on this vein for ten minutes, without any positive results. The EMF meter didn't so much as flicker. Sighing in frustration, I turned things over to Randy, who stepped in with enthusiasm. Right out of the gate, he hit it out of the park.

"Were you married, Larry? How about divorced?"

WHAM.

The EMF meter's needle flew to thirty milligauss, and then began to fluctuate violently. We seemed to have touched a nerve: marriage and divorce.

Randy asked if Larry's wife had left him. This generated some massive EMF spikes, the needles swinging wildly from high to low and back again.

Keeping with this theme (and hoping to touch a nerve) I asked Larry how he felt about women being in the fire service. The response was unequivocal. Now, the needle's movement was flying through irregular cycles of peaks and troughs in a crazy way that seemed almost angry to me. Robbin had warned us that Larry had an angry personality – were we seeing that particular aspect manifest on our EMF meters?

The existence of female firefighters goes back only a few decades, and it is fair to say that those first pioneers were not always treated fairly or kindly at some firehouses. I was working on the theory that, if "Larry" actually existed and turned out to be an angry fireman from several decades ago, he might have a few prejudices that would work as "hot buttons" when we tried to communicate with him. It was only when our team was asking questions about females in general, and the presence of female firefighters in particular, that we got anything approaching meaningful activity on our EMF meter.

Back on the phone, Robbin said, "He likes you, Richard. You're bonding. I think he's following you around now." I wasn't convinced, but nonetheless a chill ran down my spine and I couldn't help taking an involuntary peek over my shoulder, just in case.

Robbin interjected that somebody else was coming through to her now, a male whose name is either "Arnell" or "Darnell."

Organizational charts of the Pueblo Fire Department going back for over thirty years were available to us on the night. Poring over them carefully, we couldn't find any mention of an Arnell or Darnell. Shrugging, I made a note of the names and moved on, writing it off as a probable miss from our guest sensitive. But I'd check with Gary and Mark the next morning.

A few hours afterwards, I happened to be wandering through a corridor to the restroom, and caught sight of something remarkable. A plaque mounted on the wall, dating back to 1910, was inscribed with a list of firefighter names. The first name on the list.

Darnell.

• • • ● ● • ● ● • •

It wasn't long before Robbin began to sense a third spirit.

"He's attached to this fire house, either because he died there or was brought there and then died somewhere else. I get the sense that he was rescued from a body of water, a lake or a pond, something like that."

It didn't track with anything we had been able to find out about the firehouse and its history, and neither did the woman in period costume that Robbin believed was sometimes seen gazing from an upstairs window. On the other hand, before the days of ambulance-based emergency medical services, victims (both living and dead) were sometimes taken to the nearest firehouse.

Larry and Darnell seemed to have disappeared, and in the early hours before dawn, the EMF meters returned to their quiet resting state.

Brad pointed out that we had a long drive home ahead of us at daybreak, and floated the idea of getting some safety naps going for those team members who would be acting as driver. This made perfect sense to me, and it would also provide an opportunity to conduct another experiment. There were beds made up in the sleeping quarters, and I have always been an advocate of the old soldier's saying that "any idiot can be uncomfortable." Why rack out on the floor when we could take advantage of ready-made beds, and also see what happened when one of our team slept in a relatively heavy EMF field?

Miranda gamely volunteered to go first, choosing the steel-framed bed furthest from the pole. Within a few minutes of dimming the lights, she was softly snoring. The three of us who were still awake waited in the doorway, chatting quietly and monitoring temperature and EMF levels. Everything stayed flat. We'd locked off a night vision camera, centering her bed in the middle of its field of view.

An hour after bedding down, Miranda woke up and stretched. Daylight was streaming through the windows. How well had she slept?

"I heard breathing, male sounding, from over there," she yawned, pointing to the fire pole in the corner. Instinctively, we all looked. Nothing. None of our equipment had registered any abnormality. None of our control objects had been disturbed.

It was a sleepy bunch of investigators that wandered around the station, winding up cables and packing away gear. Optimistically checking my control objects, I was a little deflated to find that none of them had been moved during the night. You win some, you lose some.

Gary and Mark let themselves in, instantly twice as popular because they had brought us coffee. We turned the keys over to them and shook hands, thanking them for the opportunity to investigate this wonderful historic firehouse.

"How was your night?" they wanted to know."Intriguing," I smiled. "We'll be back, if that's alright. And we'll bring reinforcements!"

The Pueblo Fire Department adopted blue station uniforms in 1988, which might be consistent with "Larry" (if he existed) appearing that way to the sensitive. If his term of service did indeed end in the mid-Nineties, station blues would have been standard attire by then.

The name "Lawrence" or "Laurence" raised an interesting question when viewed in the light of his name badge. Fire service convention usually dictates that *last* names are put on name tags, not first names. A check of the Pueblo Fire Department's human resources records revealed no firefighters of any rank with the last name of "Lawrence" or "Lawrence" had been employed there since the 1940s (it was much more difficult to check records pre-dating this). *However...* one of the framed documents located on the wall of the sleeping quarters near the pole does mention a former Captain of the department with the first name of

Larry. Additionally, when the Pueblo Fire Department wanted to design and institute a departmental patch, one of the bids was tendered by a man called...you guessed it, Larry.

Coincidence? The time frames are hazy, so it is hard to say. You be the judge...

Round Two

Just as we had promised, we came back with three times as many investigators the second time around.

Along with the core team from BCPRS (myself; Joey; Kira, with her husband Seth; and telecommunications specialist Kathleen) we had contingents from several other trusted teams. Brad was the sole representative from The Other Side Investigations, returning for a second night at Hose Company Number Three. Representing The American Association of Paranormal Investigators were ordained minister Stephen Weidner and his friend Lisa, a no-nonsense Army veteran with a talent for paranormal research. Dave and Sharon Kirby, a husband-and-wife team operating a group called River Bears Investigations, completed our line-up. I was thrilled to have tripled the number of personnel this time around, knowing that we could more than adequately cover every nook and cranny of the firehouse.

Coordinating the arrival of four groups felt a little bit like herding cats! Personnel arrived at various times between seven and ten o'clock that evening (it was a Friday night, so most people were driving down at the end of their working day). Mark Pickerel joined us for the first part of our investigation, accompanied by his girlfriend Terri. Both of them had developed a keen interest in the haunting of Hose Company Number Three, and were eager to see what developments the night's vigil would bring.

I have always been a firm believer in mixing up the members of various research groups during the course of an investigation. This not only prevents cliques from forming, but exposes everybody involved to new and different ways of doing things. It's difficult to count the number of techniques and fresh ideas that I've picked up from working with investigators from fellow teams over the years, and hopefully I've taught some useful methods in return. Everybody wins.

Dividing the enthusiastic investigators into three groups, we established a central coordination point in the firehouse kitchen. Team One consisted of Joey, Lisa, and Sharon; Team Two of Dave, Stephen, and Connie; and Team Three was composed of Kira, Seth, and Brad. Radios were distributed, and the entire crew pitched in to take care of baselining, which was completed before midnight. A massive EMF spike in the basement was tracked down to a transformer, and nothing significantly different turned up from the first investigation.

EVP experimentation kicked off slightly past midnight, with the three teams rotating through each of the three floors. Some excitement occurred in the sleeping quarters when it seemed that the K2 EMF meters were responding to our questioning, but we were never able to get any consistent and coherent results during this session. Recalling Miranda's experience with disembodied breathing when she slept on one of the beds, Joey and I gamely picked a bed each (I like the guy, but not *that* much) and took a nap while our colleagues monitored us. I was reliably informed that my snoring remains the most horrific thing that occurred on this particular investigation; certainly, there were no nightmares or disembodied breathing felt by either Joey or myself.

Despite our very best efforts, the second investigation was a bust. We tried to get a response from Larry and Darnell, but neither of them seemed to be in a talkative mood that night. It was a disconsolate bunch of ghost hunters that exited the building the following morning, swapping theories regarding why things had been so much quieter this time around. I could not shake the feeling that this might be my fault...had I brought in *too many* people? Ten investigators and two guests didn't seem excessive on paper, but the paranormal case literature is rife with cases in which smaller teams of people produce impressive results where larger groups have failed miserably.

• • • ● ● • ● ● • • •

Haunted Collector

The Sci-Fi Channel (or "SyFy" as it is now called) contacted me because they needed haunted locations to feature on a TV show called *Haunted Collector*. If you haven't seen the show, the basic idea is that John Zaffis, a collector of allegedly haunted objects for the past forty years, travels to a haunted location, finds an object that has an entity attached to it, and removes the object in order to calm down the paranormal activity.

After seeking permission first, I put the TV production company in contact with the owners of the Millsite Inn and also Pueblo Hose Company Number Three, which is the location they finally chose to go with. The show is episode four in the first season, titled "Firehouse Phantom".

The physical findings of John Zaffis and his team (such as the EMF spikes due to power lines) mirrored our own, though they also believed that their natural tri-field meter might have picked up anomalous readings from a cabinet. They used the "ghost box" device, which gave the name "William", answered that a book might be tying an entity to the building, and asked for "John".

Meanwhile, John and a fellow investigator were experimenting with EVPs inside the Seagrave fire truck which had started on its own all those years ago. Getting involved in the ghost box experiment himself, John found that the word "William" occurred again, and said that it was here because of "blaze." John voices the opinion that most paranormal investigators don't give the ghost box much credence, and upon reflection I tend to agree with him with him. The vocabulary size on most devices such as this is too small to provide much in the way of real meaning, and on the cases in which I have seen it used, the output tends to be garbage. But an interesting counter argument is offered in this episode, as John and his colleagues discover the name and photograph of

William A. DeLong (1892-1949) mounted on the wall at Hose Company Number Three.

DeLong died in a collision with a first aid truck while responding to a call. The name "William" *did* appear twice, but William DeLong did *not* die in a blaze, as the box suggested.

More EVP experiments follow with John and his tech team, targeted specifically at contacting "William." No EVPs turn up on the digital voice recorder. Research conducted by John's daughter Aimee turns up reports of the same Model T Ford being prone to spontaneously releasing its emergency brakes when left idling, which might explain why the Chief's Car started driving on its own during its "phantom ride" – but John and his team are ignoring the fact that the vehicle was *seen* to make three sharp ninety-degree turns out of the parking lot and completely around to the front of the building. "Mechanical issues" doesn't begin to explain that.

A cabinet door is found to be open in the captain's office, which was closed before. Gary Micheli later verifies that this particular cabinet has been closed and locked for many years, being used to store historic memorabilia and keepsakes. A brooch is found within the cabinet, which appears to spike the natural tri-Field EMF meter. The episode focuses on this particular object from this point forward. An antiques expert identifies it as a Victorian-era mourning brooch, and is made of human hair. It is theorized that it could have belonged to the widow of a fallen firefighter, though this is never proven, I do believe it is a reasonable theory. John tells Gary that "hair does hold on to energy" and with Gary's permission, John takes the brooch with him when he leaves, in the hopes of calming down the paranormal activity inside the firehouse. A coda, spoken over the episode's end credits, states that this did indeed turn out to be the case.

I met with John Zaffis in September of 2014 at a paranormal convention in Kentucky, where we both happened to be guest speakers. When I mentioned that Hose Company Number Three was going to be covered in this book, he smiled and said enigmatically, "I remember that episode well. We didn't have time to show you even *half* the evidence!"

For my money, the episode still leaves a number of key questions unanswered. Was "William" a genuine contact attempt made by the spirit of William DeLong, a completely different William, or nothing more than random chance appearing to be meaningful? Who was the owner of the mourning brooch, and how did it end up in a cabinet at the firehouse? How did the cabinet get to be open after being locked and untouched for many years?

Plainly, Hose Company Number Three has yet to give up all of its secrets, and BCPRS will be returning there in the near future to try and unearth more of them.

CHAPTER TEN

THE FACE AT THE KITCHEN DOOR

An intriguing email arrived in the BCPRS help case inbox on Halloween night of 2010. A lady called Carol, along with her husband and brother in law, own a secluded inn called the Millsite, up on Colorado's scenic Peak to Peak highway.

If you've never driven it, the Peak to Peak is a fifty-five-mile road that takes somewhere around three hours to cross. Follow it eastward through some of Colorado's historic mining towns, and you will ultimately end up in the picturesque town of Estes Park.

The drive offers some spectacularly beautiful sites, and is beloved of tourists and those who just want to get away from it all for a while. Passing through dilapidated old ghost towns such as Caribou, it is still possible to get a taste of frontier life. Trailheads snake off from both sides along the way. Despite its natural beauty, once darkness falls, a sense of definite isolation arrives along with it.

"Most of us have seen or heard the ghost who lives in the restaurant," Carol went on to say. *"Despite the sage burnings, and suggestions that he 'go into the light', he continues to stay."*

It took me no time at all to make a decision on this particular case. Where better to investigate our next ghost story than an isolated highway leading up to a haunted inn? Needless to say, I jumped at the chance.

Assembling a team of BCPRS investigators was a good start. I also invited representatives from several trusted local paranormal research teams.

The folks I invited to attend an initial overnight investigation were people I knew that I could count on and trust implicitly.

Brad, an affable I.T. professional by day and experienced paranormal investigator by night, represented "The Other Side Investigations", a team with whom we had worked very often. Apart from being one of life's genuinely nice guys, Brad brought a wealth of equipment and experience to each case that he worked on.

On the more spiritual end of the spectrum, Stephen (representing the American Association of Paranormal Investigators) is an accomplished professional cellist and also an ordained minister. For years, he has been my "go-to guy" for clients who require a cleansing or more metaphysical approach to their case – so much so that I have him on speed dial. Stephen graciously accepts my phone calls at shockingly early hours of the morning, something for which I will always be grateful!

From the BCPRS side of things, three married couples made up the bulk of our staffing. My wife Laura and I were spending yet another date night in yet another haunted building. Jeff and Miranda Metzger are both highly skilled IT engineers who were colleagues of mine, and somehow picked up on my passion for the paranormal. Kira Woodmansee, an outstanding artist who is our best drawer of floor plans, brought along her husband Seth, a licensed massage therapist and all-round great guy. Seth now trains our new recruits, a critical task for which he has a natural aptitude.

And last but by no means least, our wisecracking radio communications expert Joey was along to make sure that we could all talk to one another over the course of the evening. Joey is effectively my right-hand man on the team, combining a hard-nosed east coast practical sensibility with some wicked technical skills and a box of gadgets that would bankrupt a small country.

A light dusting of snow covered the landscape as our convoy headed eastwards from the town lights of Nederland and turning north onto the darkened Highway 72. I was in a significant amount of pain, wincing every time we hit a pothole in the road. On September 11, I had joined hundreds of my fellow firefighters in climbing 110 storeys of a Denver skyscraper while wearing full protective firefighter bunker gear, carrying an air pack on my back, and fifty feet of hose. Unlike them, I blew out my back pretty badly, to the point of needing surgery.

The surgery was scheduled for six weeks later, but until then I was surviving on pain killers and gritted teeth. And because it isn't safe to drive whilst heavily medicated for pain, I was left with "suck it up" until we reached our destination.

The Millsite Inn is a welcoming place, a little oasis of light and friendliness located in a sparse area of western Boulder County in Colorado. Stepping out a nicely heated car, the cold hit us like a slap in the face. It was already close to freezing, with ice beginning to form on the roads. Breath misted the air in front of our faces, important to remember when taking (and assessing) photographs at this location. I've lost count of the number of outdoor "ghost photos" that have been sent to us, which later turned out to be breath misting the air in front of the camera lens.

At over 9,300 feet (nearly two miles) above sea level, the Millsite may be the highest place that I ever get to investigate!

Taking up seats and relaxing into companionable conversation, it wasn't long before a distinct *thud-THUD* was heard from above our heads. Eyes rolled towards the ceiling.

"There's nobody up there," Carol assured us.

The thudding had sounded a lot like two heavy footsteps. Joey happened to be watching the bar at the time, and believed that the tapping happened immediately after one of the drinkers stopped shaking his leg. We tested this theory out later in the evening, using the same barstool in the same position, and could not make the thuds repeat.

Ten o'clock was just rolling around as we settled in to enjoy some hot pizza from the kitchen, some non-alcoholic beverages, and gathered to hear a little history of the Millsite and its resident specter from Carol and bartender David.

"We've gotten used to him being around for years now," Carol began, referring to the male spirit that she believes continues to haunt the Millsite Inn. "You'd think you saw something out of the corner of your eye, but when you turn around, nobody's there. Every so often, he'll knock on the ceiling or walls, tap you on the shoulder, things like that."

She went on to relate the story of Sunday evening when her husband, Scott, was standing behind the bar while counting up the evening's take. The building was locked up securely, so there is little possibly of an intruder having gotten in without his noticing. As Carol told it, Scott experienced that sudden sensation of somebody being in the same room with him, watching him. Turning around, Scott was shocked to encounter the figure of an old man, staring back at him through a hole in the kitchen door.

The old man had an expression of surprise on his face, as though stunned to find that Scott could see him. Scott noticed that the old man was wearing brown or tan-colored dungarees, beneath which was a plaid shirt covered with suspenders. Disheveled grey hair and hollowed, sunken cheeks also stuck in Scott's mind.

"Scott thought we were being robbed! He pushed through into the kitchen and called out for me to come quick. But when he got in there, the kitchen was empty."

One of the first things an investigator will question when somebody reports the possible sighting of an apparition, as unpleasant as it may be to contemplate, is the possibility of a fanciful imagination or other more mundane reason for seeing something that isn't physically present. Carol soon set us straight on that score. Scott was an engineer by profession, not a believer in ghosts and the non-tangible. Scott was adamant that he had seen a real, live, physical person. Enlisting Carol, the pair of them searched the Millsite Inn inch by inch from top to bottom.

There is a basement accessed via a hatch in the kitchen floor, nobody was found hiding down there. All locks on the ground floor doors and windows were in place, securely fastened. Again, no intruders were hiding away on the ground floor. The upstairs attic space, used as a storage room for items such as Christmas decorations, was also devoid of life.

"I've got goose bumps the size of Long's Peak!" Scott told Carol, finally calling off the search with great reluctance. He had just come face to face with a ghost.

This incident came to be known as "the ghost in the doorway", and neither Scott nor Carol were averse to sharing it with friends or customers. After recounting the experience to some friends one night, an older gentleman seemed able to shed light on the nature of this mysterious figure.

This particular listener had grown up locally, and he remembered the days in which the Millsite was first built. Back then it was known as the Aspen Grove Inn. Two brothers had pooled their resources and built the inn together, running it jointly for a time until (for some unknown reason) a feud developed between the two men.

Carol recounted that one of the brothers was of large build, but the other (somewhat fitting the description of the ghost in the doorway) was smaller and less burly. His name was Carl. Fascinated with this unusual situation, Carol decided to conduct a little background research of her own, in the hopes of finding out about Carl and his estranged brother. More will be revealed about this later on in this chapter.

Scott is not the only witness to paranormal phenomena at the Millsite Inn. Carol herself saw the

full-body apparition of a man, once again matching
the description given of Carl, walking *through* the
closed front door as if no physical barrier existed,
before taking a sharp right turn towards the pool table
section of the bar and then disappearing into thin air.

Other members of staff have noted the sensation of
being watched whilst behind the bar, which fits with
Scott's sighting of the apparition (he first sensed that
somebody seemed to be behind him) but without the
accompanying visual appearance. It is of course
possible that the crop of ghost stories associated with
the Millsite have simply primed the staff and
customers to feel that they are being watched
whenever a cold chill goes through them – we cannot
really consider this subjective sensation to be
anything other than circumstantial supporting
evidence at best.

On the more objective end of the spectrum, both
staff *and* customers have reported the heavy tread of
what sounds like male footsteps on the ceiling above
the bar (which would equate to the wooden floor of
the attic). Carol told us a particularly satisfying
account of two visitors to the inn who were being told
of the stories surrounding Carl's ghost, and who both
voiced skepticism about the truth of those stories.
Before the doubtful pair had finished speaking, a
series of sharply distinct raps were heard on the
ceiling above their heads.

Fascinated and perturbed in equal measure, the
visitors entered a "conversation" of knocking with
whatever it was that had seemed to take offence to
their skepticism. Carol then took the visitors upstairs
in order to prove that the attic space was completely
empty. They left in a state of puzzlement.

And lest it seem that Carl's ghost is the only resident
spook at the Millsite, other witnesses claim to have
seen a female figure in nineteenth century period
dress, forlornly peering out of the attic window facing
the highway. Who she might be, and why she appears
to be so sad, are not yet known.

We toured all three floors of the property (including the surrounding grounds) after our chat with Carol and David, and then got down to the business of the evening. It was noted that a side basement window had been broken out and not replaced during a recent burglary, sending a significant icy cold draught throughout the basement level. This break in had occurred after Scott's sighting of the ghost in the doorway.

One major concern was to be my role in the investigation. As a practicing paramedic, I always insist upon knowing the medical history of every one of BCPRS' clients, including a full list of any medications that they may be taking. While a deeply personal and private thing (and something that we retain in absolute secrecy) I have always taken the view that paranormal accounts reported by individuals taking certain types of medications, or with certain types of behavioral disorders, must be treated with extreme skepticism and usually dismissed as evidence.

For example, a person who is drinking alcohol, or taking medications that may cause hallucinations or other sensory distortions, would have their testimony strongly questioned in a court of law. With that being the case, why would we give any more slack to such reports if they involve events that call into question the very laws of physics themselves and the bedrock of the entire scientific model?

Therefore, as I squirmed in my chair before taking a pain-killing dose of Vicodin, I had to be intellectually honest about the fact that my role as an observer was basically useless tonight. A parade of headless horsemen could have come galloping past on the highway, and my word wouldn't have meant squat because of the medications I was popping. The same went for our colleague Stephen, who was taking pain medication for another medical condition. How could we be useful without working as observers?

The solution turned out to be one of command and coordination. Stephen and I would work to coordinate the investigation, manning the radios and logging reports from each team whenever something of significance occurred. That way, all we had to do was talk, type, and stay awake. We set up our command center (the grandiose name for a table, laptops, and a bunch of radios) next to the pool tables. This gave us a good view of the bar and the kitchen door through which Carl's apparition had been seen – we placed a tripod-mounted video camera to shoot down the long axis of the bar from our location, so anything anomalous that we might see would hopefully show up on the hard drive when we reviewed the files later.

At a quarter till midnight, Stephen and I had divided the teams up into working task groups, and they were hustling and bustling around the Millsite, getting down to business. Factory fresh batteries were unsealed and loaded into all pieces of equipment that were not plugged into a mains power supply. Joey and Kira were deploying Gauss Master and Tri-field EMF meters in a grid pattern, base-lining the background EMF levels throughout the building. They were backed up by Brad and Seth, who were doing the same thing with temperature levels. Miranda and Jeff worked to identify the causes for several artificial (alternating current) EMF spikes that had been located, by locating the utility lines into the building, the wireless Internet router, and some other common sources. The air compressor in the basement, for example, was emanating a massive EMF field for a radius of two-and-a-half feet.

This led to a moment of excitement when the Tri-field EMF meters began to detect fluctuations with no apparent source. As the team huddled round the EMF meter curiously, Joey soon pointed out that the spikes were apparently bunched together in groups...ten EMF spikes, then twelve, followed by ten EMF spikes, then twelve. The loop repeated itself over and over again.

"That's got to be something artificial, a device," Joey insisted. We looked all around us but could see nothing plugged in that would account for the spikes. "Everybody check your phones."

I don't embarrass easily, as a rule. But this time, I was blushing a very deep crimson. My cell phone, up here in the wilderness with no cell towers within communications range, was repeatedly searching for a signal. Everybody else had the foresight to turn their phones off. Mine was turned on, a rookie mistake that I still blame on the drugs to this day...with a completely straight face.

Temperature levels had come back at a steady sixty through sixty-four degrees Fahrenheit on the ground floor (slightly warmer in the kitchen), sixty-one degrees upstairs, and a chillier forty-two to fifty degrees in the basement (consistent with the broken out window). Nothing to write home about there.

Midnight came and went uneventfully. Shortly afterwards, the investigators split up into teams of two, deploying one team per floor. We conducted a series of knocking and rapping experiments, using Carol to duplicate the methods she had gotten to work in the past. We were sadly out of luck on this particular night. Four of the investigators reported hearing a faint, music-like noise from outside of the building somewhere. Stepping outside into the bitter cold, Stephen and I confirmed that the Millsite's one neighbor (living in a house perhaps one hundred feet away, set back from the road) did appear to be home, as the lights were on in the downstairs windows. However, no noise from a TV or radio was heard coming from that direction. A hurried walk of the perimeter (hey, we were shivering!) yielded no other noises either.

Teeth chattering, we went back inside for a hot drink. A couple of investigators went through the Millsite and made sure that all TVs and radios were turned off. Warming up with a hot cup of tea, I reflected that the most reasonable explanation for the music was a car off in the distance with a loud sound system playing. Sound travels much further at night, particularly when the air is cold and still, and fewer things are moving about to mask noise. A later review of our digital recording equipment showed that the music was not picked up on any microphones.

After a break for refreshments, Carol dimmed the lights throughout the Millsite and our teams spent some time in silent observation and listening. Once again, all three floors were covered (I pity Miranda and Jeff, freezing away in the basement).

At twenty minutes past one, what sounded like a miniature avalanche from the dark recesses of the bar area. Laura and Brad were on it, as quick as a flash, storming towards the sound with cameras shooting photo after photo.

Which is why we have several photographs of an ice machine that has just disgorged a significant quantity of ice. Laura and Brad emptied the machine of ice and unplugged it.

The investigation continued in very much this same vein, without any tangible results. We packed up our equipment shortly after three o'clock, based on the fact that nothing anomalous seemed to have occurred. Carol took this in good cheer, and we promised to review the evidence as soon as we had gotten some sleep, and get a report back to her before we returned for a longer all-night investigation at a later date.

I received an email from Stephen a few days later, explaining that he had gone over his voice and video data several times and *might* have a possible EVP. He kindly sent an attached sound clip. You can plainly hear an investigator asking, "Is there a woman present, who might have something to say to us?"

I couldn't hear much of anything answering the question. Stephen thought that an *extremely* faint voice could be heard, saying either "*Who's that?*" or possibly "*What's that?*" Even having heard his opinion,

I couldn't quite agree with Stephen that there was any intelligible answer to his question on the audio recording.

The analysis results of our own audio and video data was unremarkable.

Christmas of 2010 came and went, occupied mainly with rehab from my back surgery. Although I was back on my feet almost immediately, a regime of stretching and physiotherapy was needed to get me back into proper working order. It felt terrific to be free of pain, and able to conduct investigations without the impediment of pain medications.

Once the New Year was in full swing, I started to think about a return visit to the Millsite. After making contact with Carol again, I learned that her research had yielded some interesting results. Carol had tracked down Carl's full name, and various other documents including his obituary. Carl had died of a heart attack in a nursing home back in the 1970s, survived by his brother...and yet, when asked about his brother during his lifetime, Carl always claimed that his brother was dead. Clearly their rift ran deep.

The soonest we could get a team back up to the Millsite was to be the first Friday in March. A much smaller team went up this time: me, Jeff, Joey, Kate (a former telecommunications specialist, now retired) and a rookie, Jenna. Although snow was in the forecast, we luckily dodged that particular bullet. A magnificently clear night sky festooned with stars hung over the Millsite as we pulled up. Yet again, the weather was icily cold and the wind almost non-existent. One change from our last visit was that the highway was significantly busier, which made sense when Carol pointed out that the Frozen Dead Guy Days festival was starting that weekend.

Frozen Dead Guy Days is a celebration of the town of Nederland's resident cadaver icicle, a Norwegian citizen who died here and whose corpse is still maintained in packed ice by volunteers. With a fine sense of macabre black humor, town residents host coffin races through the streets of Nederland over the course of a long weekend. This illustrates the reason for planning your time and date for an investigation with great care, and I was kicking myself for not knowing about the increased traffic beforehand. I was to blame for scheduling this badly. The constant hum of engines passing by within only a few feet was going to contaminate much of our audio recording data, and there was nothing much we could do about it.

The team got down to business shortly after nine o'clock. One of the nice things about a return visit to a haunted location is that much of the initial heavy lifting has already been done: floor plans already exist from the prior investigation, and you are familiar with most of the nooks and crannies (including EMF hotspots). After a quick consultation, we elected to ignore the basement this time around – it was hardly a hotbed of paranormal activity, in fact it wasn't a "hot" *anything*. All that could be heard down there was chattering teeth and shivering.

Setting up equipment and establishing communications proceeded smoothly (I made sure to turn my phone *off* this time) and just over an hour later, we were getting ready to baseline the place again, when Joey let out a startled shout. All eyes were on him. He was pointing animatedly towards the windows on the south side.

"There was a man's face outside the window," he said. "Right. There."

Whoever or whatever it was must have come and gone again in an instant, because there was nothing visible outside the window now except darkness. We burst through the door into the deserted parking lot, searching for anybody that might be lurking out there, in the dark on a freezing cold night, in the middle of nowhere...it sounds quiet ridiculous to me even as I write it! Shining my flashlight on the snow beneath the window, I found it to be completely undisturbed – whoever had peered in at us seemed to have left no footprints.

Our team protocol for the rare instances in which somebody witnesses an apparition is very specific. If there are multiple witnesses, we separate them immediately and have them write down what they saw – this avoids the accidental contamination of eyewitness testimony by having one person's story influence the other. It quickly became apparent that nobody but Joey had seen the man's face, so that wasn't going to be a problem here.

"It was a male, a Caucasian male," Joey told us excitedly, "looking straight in through the window at us."

"Could you tell his age?" I asked.

Joey shook his head. "He was just there for a second and then gone."

Not even enough time to fire up a camera and take a picture. Because nobody else witnessed the apparition, we couldn't corroborate it, and therefore couldn't call it evidence. It's dispiriting (pun very much intended) but that's where the bar has to be set.

The incident reminded me very much of the "ghost in the doorway" episode, where a curious male face was once again seen peeping in at somebody. Could this be Carl's standard *modus operandi?* Was it worthwhile paying more attention to the windows than to the building interior?

Of course, the first priority was to try and find a mundane explanation for whatever it was that Joey saw. To this end, every effort was made to duplicate his sighting. Putting a real person's face at the window and backlighting it with flashlights didn't produce the same effect, and without additional lighting the face was barely visible at all. Joey was adamant that the face he had seen was illuminated somehow.

We carried out a number of drive-bys, gauging the effect of car headlights as they splashed through the windows before turning the corner and disappearing. Not remotely the same effect, Joey insisted. Attempts were then made to reproduce the face by tinkering with light sources *inside t*he Millsite, even though none of us had been using flashlights or any type of artificial lighting at the time. It would have been quite a trick of smoke and mirrors to cast the reflection of a face on the window from the inside, for a fleeting moment, and to do so without being noticed by at least one of the team.

As we split off into two small teams, I fired up my camera to take a few photographs of the windows in question, before heading upstairs to stake out the attic. I soon found myself puzzled to discover that the camera batteries appeared to be dead. I frowned. The batteries had been factory fresh, as per our standard operating procedure, and only placed an hour ago. I had gotten just five digital shots out of them before the camera shut down and died. The dead battery LED glared at me. It refused to power back up again once I had let it stay shut off for a minute, even after I employed the tried and tested method of hitting it repeatedly with the flat of my hand and swearing at it.

I went back downstairs to the ground floor, with the aim of grabbing a fresh set of batteries. The camera immediately powered itself up again without prompting from me.

"Maybe bad batteries?" theorized Joey. I popped the two AAs out of the camera housing and handed them to him. According to his battery tester, they were both charged to fifty percent capacity. So why had the power level seemed dead upstairs in the attic?

We settled in to conduct some EVP experimentation. Carol was making a real effort to try and contact the spirit of Carl, but if he was there, he wasn't cooperating so far. No raps, knocks, or bangs answered her spoken enquiries. EMF and temperature levels remained flatly unremarkable as the witching hour came and went without any activity. Both teams reconvened in the bar at one-thirty to talk strategy. The bar area was dimly lit by a couple of table lamps, and rather creepily atmospheric.

As the team broke open sodas, we began to discuss the events of the night so far in hushed tones. The relative quiet was suddenly broken yet again by Joey, jabbing a finger excitedly at the couch which sat directly next to the front door.

Joey was convinced that he had seen a shadow, moving across the curtains above the couch. It was hard to believe that he wasn't seeing things due to the dim lighting and the suggestive effect that this semi-darkened state was having on all of us to some degree. Joey is a level-headed and pragmatic guy, the quintessential east-coaster, and isn't prone to flights of fancy. Could tiredness be playing tricks on his eyes... or was something paranormal really going on here?

And then a third sighting, which he described as a faint shadow glimpsed in the mirror near the bathroom. The shape flashed across his field of vision for a second and then vanished. Joey reported seeing this first from the bar stool, and a second time within the bar while sitting down on the couch. Frustratingly, all of these sightings were restricted to Joey. There were transitory EMF spikes, but these measured completely within normal parameters for background EMF – in other words, they were statistically insignificant.

Joey was also fatigued after a busy week at work, so the smart thing to do was for him to crash out in his sleeping back for some rest while the rest of us kept vigil over the Millsite. In no time at all, he was gently snoring away. I wish that I could say my motives for encouraging him to sleep were purely altruistic, but I had been told by Carol that some guests who have spent a night at the Millsite have suffered terrible nightmares. She informed me that the residents during the 1970s always felt very freaked out and uncomfortable at night.

True to his nature, Joey bucked the trend and woke up two hours later with no recollection of any dreams. It was now going on three o'clock, and our friend the mysterious music was back. Jeff could hear it off in the distance, just as he had on our previous visit. Partnered up with him, Joey confirmed that he could hear faint music too. Once more I went outside, listening for music reaching me across the chilly night air – nothing. At the same time, my team searched the Millsite from top to bottom yet again, and also drew a blank. The music has never been caught on our digital voice recorders, and remains a mystery.

Our overnight watch went on through till dawn. As the sun rose in the east, it was a weary bunch of paranormal investigators that packed up our gear and shuffled out to the parking lot. The night's investigation had added more questions than it had answered. Was Joey hallucinating? If not, who had been the face at the window?

The Millsite has subsequently been put up for sale. We still keep in touch with Carol and the good folks there, and every so often we'll hear about further bizarre occurrences at the inn. Activity seems to be strongest in the fall months. Disembodied footsteps are still heard in the deserted attic, and on one memorable occasion, Carol tells me, the sounds of furniture being moved around upstairs were heard. Needless to say, nothing was out of place when the attic was checked. Just a few weeks ago from the time of writing, Carol happened to be buffing up the floor downstairs when she heard the distinct sound of a ball bouncing around on the floor upstairs.

It appears as if Carl may now be indulging in temperature shenanigans, as the kitchen thermostat has physically turned itself off on several occasions when nobody else was present in the building.

One of the great "what might have been" questions involves John Zaffis, and the crew of *Haunted Collector.* This was one of two locations that I had referred the producers to, as a possible venue for investigation. They turned up some intriguing evidence at Hose Company Number Three in Pueblo, and I cannot help but wonder what story would have come to light if they had instead chosen to investigate the Millsite.

One thing is for sure: *something* unusual is happening at the Millsite Inn. If you should happen to be in the area one night in the fall, I can heartily recommend a visit.

CHAPTER ELEVEN

HOUSE OF ANGELS AND DARKNESS: A PRIVATE HELP CASE

Of the many potential cases that cross my desk each month, the highest priority is given to those in which people are living in fear within their own home. Helping those who are afraid is the primary reason for the existence of BCPRS...even research takes a back seat to helping out our clients.

The help cases range from "I'm getting creeped out by footsteps, cold spots, a sense of being watched", all the way up to "I'm being attacked." Two types of cry for help are guaranteed to fly straight to the top of our case list. One is any situation in which children are involved. And the other involves either actual violence, or at least the threat of physical force. We take both types of situation so seriously that the client will usually receive a call from us the same day we receive their email.

Help cases can therefore be very rewarding, but they can also be challenging when the client does not much care for the end result.

"It Knows You're Here..."
"Samantha", a single retiree in her mid-sixties, contacted us by email and requested an urgent phone

call. She insisted that she was under attack by a dark and malevolent force. Having spoken with one of our investigators and outlined her present situation, the case came to my attention and shot directly to the "next investigation" slot. Days later, I found myself sitting on Samantha's couch, accompanied by Joey, Lucilla, Kate, our hard-nosed journalist Gene, and probationary member Anna, listening to an incredible story unfold.

Samantha was utterly certain that she was being haunted by a demonic entity, she told us without meeting any of our eyes. She felt physically threatened, convinced that the entity wanted to hurt very badly, if not kill her in order to satisfy some kind of twisted pleasure.

Worst of all, she told us that the entity was molesting her sexually.

With tears in her eyes, Samantha went on to explain that these incidents of abuse happen when she is laying bed at night. She reported feeling an invisible and evil, malicious presence pushing down upon her with a great deal of weight. It would then squeeze her breasts violently, causing sharp pain. Samantha would be pinned down, incapable of moving or struggling, no matter how badly she wanted to fight back.

"This...*thing* is taking pleasure in making me afraid, I can tell. It wants me to be frightened."

I was taking down notes as Samantha talked. Of particular interest was the way in which she referred to the entity as "it", rather than as "he" or "she".

Lucilla asked whether Samantha had ever seen this entity, either inside the house or somewhere else.

"I've seen it inside the house. I've seen it for my entire life."

She went on to describe an extremely tall and thin humanoid figure, cloaked and hooded with some kind of dark colors. Her description reminded me of the Dementor characters from the *Harry Potter* series of books and films. Interestingly enough, the Dementors were also engaged in tormenting human beings, but not in a sexual way. Samantha went on to say that she had observed this dark, hooded figure in every home she had ever lived in, going back to the age of five or six. She wasn't sure whether it was the same entity, or just something very similar, but Samantha was adamant about having seen it.

"It knows you're here, and it's hiding right now."

Samantha fixed her gaze on each of us in turn. I was sure that, no matter the truth of her claims, *she* utterly believed the truth of what she was saying to us. She did not strike me as being deceptive, simply frightened and confused.

Samantha continued to expand on the details of her case. The entity was active at all times of the day and night and throughout the house, but the worst of the activity tended to focus on the bedroom (and to a lesser extent, the living room) during the hours of darkness. She could hear banging and pounding on the living room walls, then knocking sounds like knuckles rapping on them. The disturbances would progressively worsen up until Samantha's bedtime, around ten or eleven o'clock each night, and they would then tail off as she started to drift off to sleep.

After a short period of time (sometimes just minutes, at other times an hour or two) a different set of noises would jolt her awake again.

Samantha would start out hearing clicking and scratching noises, starting under her pillow and then working their way into the walls. She described it as being like the noise a huge insect might make if it were trying to communicate, or the tail of an angry rattlesnake. She was convinced that these sounds were the entity's attempts to communicate with her.

To her great credit, Samantha had acknowledged the need for professional health, and proactively sought out a licensed therapist. One excellent suggestion that arose from those meetings was for Samantha to keep a journal of the unusual events that were taking place in her home, to see whether they fit a specific pattern.

For example, Samantha logged hearing the sound of a doorknob rattling violently, for a prolonged period of time, in the early hours of the morning. This was logged on lots of different nights. She would often be awakened by the sound of deep breathing, and the feeling of some invisible presence surrounding her – once again, late at night or early in the morning. Disembodied breathing and muffled voices were reported throughout the house with regular consistency. As weeks passed, the doorknob sounds grew longer in duration and much louder.

The perception of a malevolent "something" that wanted to wake her up became a constant preoccupation. More objectively, the lights were seen to be flickering in her master bathroom at about 2:00 a.m. on several occasions. Samantha was sleeping with the lights on at this point, in an attempt to claw back some sense of security.

And the auditory phenomena continued. Samantha wrote of hearing a loud "chomping" sound while she was working in her office, which sounded as though somebody was standing directly behind her. Turning immediately, she found herself alone in the room. This happened in broad daylight, and not after dark.

There were multiple episodes of pillow scratching, followed by the feeling of "an animal" of some sort pouncing upon her right shoulder. Again, this occurred at around 2:00 a.m., seemingly the trigger time for activity in Samantha's household.

Apparently, Samantha has been hearing the scratching noises since childhood as well. In fact, as I listened to her speak it became apparent just how much of the stated activity seemed to originate from sixty years into her past. Gathering some background history would be of vital importance in getting to the heart of the matter.

Samantha's home was immaculately kept and a beautiful place, a huge sprawling structure with a sizeable basement. But as we walked around it on a guided tour, it became obvious that she had chosen a less than conventional décor scheme. She was obviously a big, big fan of angels. Everywhere I looked, as far as the eye could see, were angels.

Cherubim and seraphim sculpted statuettes, paintings, dolls, and all manner of angelic ornamentation covered every square inch of shelf and wall space. There was no privacy from them even in the restroom! It's a little disconcerting to answer the call of nature while being watched from on high by a heavenly host.

While my teammates set about baselining the house and drawing up floor plans, I met with Samantha in her office for a closed-door interview. As a medical professional, I needed to gather some more information about Samantha's current and prior health history – both physical and mental.

It's important for me to stress that I was not taking the approach that this was all in her mind. But ask any reputable paranormal investigator, and they will tell you that a significant number of the individuals who claim to be haunted (particularly those claiming to be physically attacked or sexually assaulted) have a background of mental illness. One can speculate as to the nature of the apparent link between those two factors, but the link does arise again and again. Am I saying that all people who believe they are being attacked by disembodied entities are delusional? Absolutely not. But it is something that must be carefully assessed before we approach any kind of paranormal explanation.

We sat down in the calm and quiet room, with late afternoon sunlight streaming in through the open window blinds. Samantha was visibly nervous and trembling, but responded to my gently prodding questions with admirable candor. As her personal back story unfolded, I found myself deeply moved by not only the tragic events that made up her life, but also by the courage with which she had faced them.

Samantha was raised in a heavily religious background. Not one of the mainstream Christian denominations, but rather a less conventional branch that I will not name in order to avoid compromising her anonymity. Her father, whom she described as a monstrous bully of a man, regularly abused her sexually from the time of her first memories, right up until the age of fourteen.

"He stopped when I turned fourteen," she said in a flat monotone. "I think it's because I underwent puberty and stopped looking like a little girl and started to look like a grown woman. He was a pedophile, plain and simple."

I was starting to get angry and had to work hard to maintain a professional demeanor. What kind of monster would do that to a little girl?

Samantha hadn't had contact with him since she left home, and didn't know whether he was alive or dead. She really didn't care which of the two applied. She was married to a man from the same church. Her new husband was also both physically and emotionally abusive. She received regular beatings, sometimes severe enough to break bones. Samantha stayed with him for the sake of the children and family unity, but slowly began to lose her faith and just couldn't take any more.

When Samantha left home, roughly twenty years prior to our investigation, her family disowned her. Right on the heels of the family breakup, Samantha's church excommunicated her. Two decades later, Samantha's family was not involved in her life in any significant way. Although they did keep in touch, it was not what could be termed a close or truly familial relationship.

Samantha was crying now. I patted her hand in an awkward attempt at reassurance, and asked gently where her spiritual beliefs currently stood.

"Oh, I still *believe*." She dabbed at her moist eyes with a corner of one sleeve. "I still pray to Jesus. I'm a Christian! But I don't go to church. It can get very lonely, but I know that the Lord understands. He sees all."

"Have you tried talking to them about your experiences with the entity?"

She shook her head vigorously. "Goodness, no! They won't tolerate any talk about ghosts or demons or anything like that. They'll just think I'm a crazy old lady..."

I also learned the sad news that Samantha's mother had recently died, and that Samantha had been her primary caregiver throughout her terminal illness. This placed a significant burden upon her both physically and emotionally. Many people are unaware of the struggles that occur in countless homes every day, as people struggle to care for extremely unwell loved ones, picking up where the healthcare system leaves off. I spent a few weeks caring for my own mother prior to her death from lung cancer, and have nothing but respect and admiration for those who do this on a long-term basis. The demands are high, and the pressure is constant. It was inconceivable to me that caring for her mother had not taken a toll on Samantha's physical health and on her emotional wellbeing.

Things became even more complex when I gathered more information regarding Samantha's own medical state. The list of medications that Samantha was prescribed all had potentially serious side effects. She was taking a medication for bipolar disorder, high blood pressure, a skeletal muscle relaxant, and a benzodiazepine (used to treat severe anxiety). The ability to interpret this list of medications accurately was one benefit of having a paramedic working on the team.

Some of the side effects of Samantha's medications are: headaches, blurred vision, dizziness, insomnia, worsened depression and anxiety, suicidal thoughts and feelings, confusion, mood changes and changed mental states, severe feelings of nervousness and trembling, and plain old drowsiness.

Some of these side effects actually contradict one another - for example, insomnia and drowsiness. A "side effect" is the term used by medical professionals to describe actions caused by a drug that are undesirable, and also somewhat unpredictable. When multiple drugs are taken together regularly, the interactions between those drugs become even less

predictable. Take a look at the number of side effects listed for Samantha's medications that involve altering the state of consciousness in some way. Pretty much all of them! I was seriously considering the role that her health issues and pharmacological treatments were playing when it came down to her experiencing "paranormal
assaults."

Having browsed Samantha's DVD shelf, it was obvious that she was a fan of the *Ghost Hunters* genre of paranormal TV reality show. She had purchased a digital voice recorder and left it running overnight several times, in an attempt to capture objective evidence of her haunting. Yet again, she was ahead of the curve in terms of what we would have advised her to do. But when she eagerly played back the sound files for us (which supposedly captured the clicking and scratching noises), along with what she thought might possibly have been EVPs, the BCPRS team members could hear nothing out of the ordinary on them.

Was Samantha hallucinating the sounds, or were they undetectable by digital recording equipment?

Baselining had gone smoothly, with the only abnormal EMF spike occurring in Samantha's bedroom, more specifically on the bed itself. We soon figured out that this was caused by the electrical vibrating mattress, which generated high electromagnetic levels even when plugged in but not powered on. This meant that Samantha was sleeping in a perpetually elevated electromagnetic environment, and who knows precisely what effects that might have been having on her perceptions? Joey wisely recommended that Samantha should sleep in the guest bedroom for a few nights and see whether activity diminished or not.

One intriguing event described by Samantha had taken place down in the basement. She told us that a plastic ball had begun moving on its own, rolling as if manipulated by invisible hands until it finally came to a stop in the middle of the basement floor. Intrigued, the team trooped downstairs to inspect the ball and the area of floor in question. One of the most frequently overlooked measuring parameters is the *grade* of a floor, the angle at which it slopes over a given distance. We quickly discovered that the basement floor sloped gently, and was also subject to a definite breeze coming from the ventilation system. Some rapid experimentation with the ball confirmed my suspicions: the plastic exercise ball was easily pushed by even a light wind, which in turned pushed it in a spiraling motion towards a drain in the center of the floor, where it came to a stop spontaneously. One mystery, at least, had been solved.

Our EVP experiments went smoothly, and we were unable to provoke any kind of anomalous activity during those sessions. Samantha was convinced that the entity fixated upon females rather than males. Based upon this, and her report that the activity occurred mostly at night when she was sleeping, I asked her to go and change for bed. This time, however, there would be a twist. I arranged for Kathleen and Anna to spend time on the bed with her, to see if this would draw anything out of the woodwork, so to speak.

While the ladies settled down for the evening, Joey, Gene, and I remained in the kitchen to discuss events so far. We were all under the impression that Samantha was perfectly sincere, but we had not seen a single piece of objective evidence to support her belief of being under attack by some kind of disembodied entity.

I was also deeply concerned by the tragic and traumatic events of Samantha's early life, particularly the many forms of abuse she had suffered at the hands of two despicable men. It was becoming increasingly difficult to escape the conclusion that her experiences of being held down and molested were very similar to those she reported at the hands of her abusive father. Was the hooded and cloaked black figure which Samantha had seen for most of her life (and in every place she had lived) a mental construct, resulting from her childhood trauma?

Having looked through Samantha's bookshelves, it was also apparent that she was having a crisis of faith. The vast majority of her reading material was on the subject of her former religion, the church from which she had been excommunicated. They spanned many decades of publishing, dating from the 1950s right up to the present day. And these were interspersed with books covering practically the entire range of the paranormal, with a special emphasis on ghosts, hauntings, and the demonic. Coupled with her love for paranormal reality TV, was it really so unreasonable to conclude that her frightening experiences were being fueled by a mixture of her reading and watching habits, along with the residual emotional issues arising from her childhood abuse, were combining to produce a kind of psychosis?

Samantha has been subjected to a terribly difficult and trying life. She has done an admirable job in coping with very tough circumstances to the very best of her ability, but it should come as no surprise that her fascination with all things paranormal is manifesting itself in this way – as a contributory factor to a larger problem. She lives on her own in a large house, full of religious iconography. By her own admission, Samantha's evenings are long and very lonely. She is cut off to a great extent from family and has few friends, and since her excommunication from the church, the solace of a faith-based support system has also been denied to her.

Gene, Joey, and I also discussed the probability of her "ghostly assaults" being a form of hypnagogic or hypnopompic experience. Both of these are a form of "threshold consciousness", in which the human mind is drifting somewhere on the borderland between sleeping and waking. Experiences of sleep paralysis (being unable to move for a short time after wakening) may occur during this period, and vivid hallucinations are not uncommon. This paralysis can occur for several minutes, as the neurochemicals which keep the body paralyzed may not wear off immediately upon awakening.

A common component of the sleep paralysis experience is a definition and unnerving sensation of there being an unseen presence in the room, often one with a sinister or harmful intent. Historically this has been referred to as the "old hag" or the "night hag", or more recently, "the intruder." There are complex physiological reasons for the way in which the human body perceives this as a type of threat and reacts to it with great fear, but a sensation of being touched, strangled, or otherwise harmed are not unusual. Researchers are still investigating the specific biological reasons behind this frightening experience, but it is already clearly a realistic explanation for why some people report sleeping/waking experiences such as Samantha's, and also the nighttime alien abductions that we hear so much about. I am not saying that this is the *only* possible explanation, but it must certainly be high on a list of reasons to be considered.

While the three ladies were trying (without success) to provoke a response from Samantha's demonic entity, I phoned my "spiritual go-to guy" Stephen Weidner. As an ordained priest and generally all-round smart guy, he serves as a great sounding board for cases such as this. After listening carefully and posing a few pointed questions, Stephen agreed that we were probably all on the same page. He offered to make contact with Samantha in his dual capacity as a paranormal investigator and spiritual minister, a fact which reassured her greatly.

As two o'clock in the morning rolled by, the only noises coming from Samantha's bedroom were some light snoring and occasional hushed conversation between Anna and Kate. They confirmed that nothing unusual had taken place: no scratching, clicking, no electromagnetic or temperature anomalies. All three ladies had joined for EVP sessions, neither of which turned up anything unusual (and, as we had anticipated, nor did those conducted by Joey, Gene, and I). Samantha was definitely more relaxed, and as the BCPRS team packed up our equipment to head home for the night, we left her in the capable hands of Stephen and his colleagues at the American Association of Paranormal Investigators.

True to his word, they met with Samantha and addressed her fears from both a scientific and spiritual perspective.

Can we say for certain whether any of Samantha's experiences were paranormal in nature? It is impossible to say definitively, but I lean towards the interpretation that they were not. But I would point out that just because a client may have emotional and medical difficulties, does not necessarily mean that they are not experiencing what they say they are. One colleague who consulted on this case, pointed out to me that Samantha's emotional vulnerability, coupled with her extensive medical history and medications list, may simply have made her an attractive target for a malevolent entity of some kind.

It is now several years since we investigated Samantha's case, and Stephen stills meets with her on a regular basis for an informal chat over coffee. He tells me that she is doing better, with her terrifying nocturnal experiences diminishing in both frequency and intensity. As she gets out into the everyday world more often, and as her family and social situation improves over time, she is being bothered less and less by the terrifying experiences.

It was encouraging to note that Samantha was never a passive victim in all this. My first piece of advice (which she had followed long before every consulting my team) would have been to seek help from a mental health professional. It impressed me greatly that Samantha was not only open to the possibility of her physical and emotional condition playing a role in all this, but also that she was brave enough to reach out to a counselor. She deserves a lot of credit for that.

Speaking for myself and the BCPRS team, we are simply glad that she got the help and support that was so desperately needed. Samantha continues to face her struggle with great courage and with as open a mind as she can manage, given the circumstances. It's good to know that her life is starting to turn around for the better.

CHAPTER TWELVE
A HISTORIC HOTEL HAUNTING

I have a soft spot in my heart for the historic Hotel Boulderado, located in the heart of downtown Boulder: after conducting an investigation of the place and its many reported ghost sightings, I ended up marrying my wife Laura there on the grand mezzanine staircase.

Located in downtown Boulder, the Hotel Boulderado has a colorful and fascinating background. I refer interested readers to Sylvia Pettem's highly readable *Legends of a Landmark* as the definitive history guide to this remarkable building. Many of the rich and famous have chosen to stay there when visiting Boulder and the surrounding area.

Robert Frost, the world-renowned poet, would stay there during the 1930s when visiting his daughter in Boulder's sanitarium where she was a tuberculosis sufferer. Musicians Duke Ellington and Louis Armstrong also stayed there, as during the racially segregated years of the 1960s, most Boulder hotels would not accept black guests.

Room 205 was the temporary home of Helen Keller in both 1914 and 1923, along with her teacher Anne Sullivan. Swashbuckling actor Douglas Fairbanks also checked in for a stay.

The Boulderado's haunted history is well known to the hotel staff, who tend to take it all in their stride. Guest reactions, on the other hand, can be mixed.

Some (like my wife and I) deliberately seek out a haunted room when checking in. Others, sometimes unaware of the deaths that have taken place inside this grand old hotel, experience such a fright that they vow never to return.

It wasn't difficult to research the ghostly goings-on at the hotel. Staff proved very helpful and forthcoming, obviously fond of their workplace and intrigued by some of the bizarre experiences that had taken place there. Much of the paranormal activity tends to center around two rooms, 302 and 304.

In one of these rooms, a double suicide attempt went horribly wrong back in 1924. While his wife was bathing, the husband administered a fatal dose of chloroform to himself while lying on the bed. The wife became understandably unhinged upon discovering his dead body, and tried to kill herself using the same method...but failed. The poor distraught woman under-dosed herself on the inadequate amount of chloroform left in the bottle, and fled the hotel to buy more. She attempted suicide a second time, failed again, and ended up in a Denver hospital.

One hotel manager, Beverly Silva, has spoken to the *Denver Post* about her paranormal experiences at the Hotel Boulderado in a 2007 article, and singles out Room 302 and 304 specifically. As a young housekeeper during the 1980s, she was cleaning Room 302 and changing the bed linens when the television set suddenly turned itself on.

A grandfather clock in Room 304 was seen on two separate occasions to spin its hands wildly, as if the clock was being wound by some unseen force. Even more strangely, according to the manager who witnessed both events, the clock hands would stop at precisely the correct time of day.

One staff member told me during the pre-investigation interview that a Native American guest had checked in but flat refused to enter room 304. "There's something supernatural in there," he told desk staff, refusing even to open the door. The guest would not be drawn further on what exactly the supernatural "something" was. This incident took place at two o'clock in the morning, and 304 was the only available room in the hotel...yet the gentleman left to find another hotel.

Whatever it is that haunts the third floor seems to have spread its influence to nearby Room 306. When a female staff member was spending the night in that particular room, she awoke terrified and paralyzed by an invisible force that pressed her down helplessly into the mattress.

One common thread of complaint that has arisen again and again over the course of the Boulderado's century of operation, is the sound of scratching noises emanating from deep within the walls. I heard this from several staff members myself during my interviews.

The *Denver Post* article also references a group of six women who, while enjoying the atmosphere in the hotel bar, all witnessed a heavy window lift itself halfway up the wall.

Some of the staff members we talked to believe that the dead man's spirit is responsible for much of the ghostly activity at the Boulderado. But I'm not so sure, because another apparition is also reported by staff members and guests alike. The grey lady was the spirit that I was most hoping to encounter during the course of our investigation.

Since 2006, I have taught EMT students at a local community college. Most of the instructional staff members are fellow firefighters, EMTs, and paramedics. Jesse was a local firefighter-paramedic who was aware of my paranormal interests, and when he heard that I was investigating the Boulderado could not wait to tell me about his personal sighting of the grey lady. He used to be a security guard in a building located directly across the street from the hotel. One night, after making his uneventful rounds, Jesse happened to look up at the hotel's upper floor...and his jaw dropped in disbelief.

An unusual-looking lady was looking right back at him from an upper window. Jesse maintained that the lady was definitely not of our era. Her dress and hat appeared to be of nineteenth century vintage. We talked briefly about the theory that some ghosts are not aware of their environment, but are impressed or "recorded" on their surroundings in much the same way as an image is recorded on film or magnetic tape. Jesse was not impressed with this idea.

"She looked *right at me*. She definitely *saw* me. She was *aware* of my presence. You couldn't pay me to spend the night in that hotel."

Needless to say, I was thrilled.

Some guests have reported the lady wearing white instead of grey, others that she looks like an old monochrome photograph. But she is most frequently reported on the upper floors of the building, and appears to be searching for something.

In the older part of the Boulderado, the ghostly figure of a dark clad man with a bandanna covering his nose and mouth has been reported. Who this might be is unknown, as there is no obvious tie between such a figure and the hotels history.

Every hotel sees its share of death, both natural and intentional. The Boulderado has seen multiple suicides (staff told me of two self-inflicted gunshot deaths, one taking place on the fire escape) and the usual number of "died in the night" type deaths from natural causes over the years. One former manager and owner of the hotel died of a heart attack while eating there (nothing to do with the food, which was excellent!)

Talking to the kitchen staff, I was told of pots and pans that would swing on their hooks without apparent cause, or ring as if rapped upon by unseen knuckles. Porters told me that the elevators have a habit of moving between floors without any guests inside, and no call buttons being pushed...something that I have seen while investigating a number of haunted buildings, such as the Weld County

Courthouse in Greeley, Colorado, and the Dickens Opera House in Longmont.

BCPRS was in its second year and still finding its feet somewhat when we investigated the Boulderado on the night before Halloween in 2007, in conjunction with some guests from our friends over at Colorado Paranormal Research.

The Hotel Boulderado management kindly gave us the run of the hotel, within reason. We were not able to shut anything down, but could go pretty much wherever we please as long as we did not disrupt hotel operations or interfere with the guests. Room 302 was available, so we made that our base of operations for the night. I slept in during the day and awoke refreshed and ready to tackle this grand old dame of the Boulder hotel industry.

Our investigative team of seven people checked into room 302 after eating on-site at the excellent Q's restaurant. Seven people isn't a very large number to cover such a large hotel, so my strategy was very simple: focus on the supposedly haunted room 302 until after midnight, when we could be reasonably sure that most guests would be in their beds, and then rove the upper floors and staircases in search of the mysterious ghostly lady.

You always find yourself wishing for more personnel or more technical resources when investigating any building larger than a single-family residence. That's simply human nature. I watch guilty pleasure TV shows like *Ghost Hunters* and practically drool at the equipment budget T.A.P.S. has, and the sheer number of investigators they can deploy into the field.

But life is all about doing the best you can with the resources you have. I like to remind myself that the very first true ghost hunters – men like Sir Arthur Conan Doyle and Sir Oliver Lodge, to name just two – worked in very small groups, and sometimes alone. Their primary tools were a pencil, notepad, two eyes, and a keen deductive mind. Everything else is nice to have, but secondary. All the flashy tools and toys in the world won't compensate for a weak investigator.

Setting up our equipment was becoming a familiar and comforting ritual by now. Factory-fresh batteries were removed from their wrapping and inserted into equipment, then tested. On some cases, I've seen brand new batteries run down to zero charge in less than five minutes. This didn't happen at the Boulderado.

As our resident artist, Kira tends to wind up with the job of drawing an accurately scaled sketch floor plan of whatever building we happen to be investigating. As teams fan out and begin to take baseline readings, any anomalies in temperature, EMF, air ionization or even background radiation levels will be logged on the floor plan by the team leader.

Room 302 didn't yield any such anomalies, so baselining was a relatively quick and painless process. My colleagues zipped through the process, checking the room from floor to ceiling in less than ten minutes.

My good friend and colleague Randy Schneider is a big fan of paranormal gadgetry. It certainly has its place on an investigation, and the distinct lack of activity at the Boulderado overnight case suggested that now might be a good time to try something new. "Frank's Box" is gaining more and more interest in the paranormal research field, and has polarized opinions of the investigators who use it. Designed by the inventor Frank Sumption back in 2002, the box was still relatively new to the scene in 2007 when we were investigating the Boulderado. Randy had brought a working Box along with him, and we decided to try it out.

The Box is basically a frequency-hopping AM radio receiver, paired up with a white noise generator. When you turn the box on, it cycles through radio frequencies at a very rapid rate and presents audio snippets from each frequency through a speaker. Supporters of the Box claim that this can allow spirit voices to manifest more easily through the constant stream of static that is generated. Detractors insist that the gullible will mistake random patterns in the white noise for voices of the dead.

I'm on the fence in this debate, but I do tend to side with the latter party in this debate. I have seen and used Frank's Box on a number of cases, and never found the results to be particular impressive or conclusive. There are those who swear that the Box has produced spectacular results, but I have yet to see evidence to back up those claims.

At any rate, Frank's Box was a dead bust for us on this particular night. We sat through what seemed like hours of hissing, squawking static. No "spirit voices" came through for us, or anything remotely intelligible for that matter. I was disappointed but not surprised, though I do applaud Randy's willingness to bring a new tool to the table and give it a shot.

Feeling the need for some air, I went out onto the balcony and leaned over the busy street below. The balcony was shared between rooms 302 and 304, and I soon found myself chatting with the gentleman who was staying in the room next door. He and his wife had stayed there for the past couple of uneventful nights. After some gentle and circumspect questioning, I told him about the history of his room. He found the story to be pretty cool, and after eliciting a promise from me not to discuss it with his wife ("in case you scare the crap out of her!") he took my business card and said he'd let me know if anything unusual happened overnight.

Unfortunately, I never heard back from him. I hope that his night was an uneventful one.

It was getting on for eleven o'clock at night. The volume of traffic on the roads outside had dwindled to the point where I felt that an EVP session would be a good idea, and we shouldn't have to worry about too much extraneous background noise.

Our questions were specifically targeted towards the history of rooms 302 and 304.

"Did you die in this room?"

"Did you take chloroform?"

"Did you commit suicide?"

"What happened to your wife? Where is she?"

"Are you aware that you are dead?"

"Do you mean to disturb the people who stay here?"

Nothing anomalous turned up from this EVP session when we scrutinized the output files a few days later. Neither Frank's Box or our standard EVP recording protocols had produced anything in the way of results.

Fortunately, we wouldn't leave the Boulderado entirely empty-handed, though our result would come from an unforeseen location.

The Witching Hour came and went without incident. Seven weary ghost hunters loaded up on caffeine and sugar to help see us through until daylight.

We re-checked the temperature and EVP levels several times, with no cause for suspicion. Room 302 was looking like a dead loss for the night.

With the lobby and staircases now empty, and most of the guests asleep in their rooms, it was time to roam the hotel. I divided us up into two groups of two and one of three, with myself being the command element that was integrated into one of the groups of two.

If you anticipate a busy investigation, then the team leader really needs to be static in a central location and free of distractions, so that he or she can focus on running the show and coordinating teams by radio. In the emergency services, it's a golden rule that command's role is to *command* – to run things, not to do anything hands-on or practical. The team leader's focus needs to be on the big picture.

I felt comfortable with breaking that rule at the Boulderado. For starters, things were extremely quiet and this was shaping up to be an undemanding case. If something happened to one of the teams that meant they needed to call for backup, all they had to do was get on the radio and holler for help over the common frequency we all shared. It didn't take a dedicated team leader to do that for them.

Laura and I spent the next few hours roaming the upper floors, including the mezzanine and grand staircase. The third floor got a lot of attention, a deliberate choice that I made based upon the haunted histories of rooms 302, 304, and 306. Other teams focused on the lobby and the kitchens, with only the guest rooms being off-limits to us. We took breaks on the hour, to give ourselves a bit of a rest and to chat with staff members and our fellow team members. The atmosphere was mellow and low-key.

We all secretly harbored a desire to run into the ghostly grey lady on one of the upper floors. I had a digital camera slung around my neck, ready for just such an eventuality. If she made an appearance tonight, I would rapid-fire a bunch of photographs and then adopt the classic plan devised by Bill Murray's character in *Ghostbusters* – "Get her!"

EMF and temperature levels stayed within normal limits on the upper floors and staircases. Laura and I diligently monitored them throughout the night, and snapped random pictures with the uncertain hope of picking up the spectral lady. Luck was not with us, sad to say.

At the top of the stairs there is hung an oil painting of a dark-haired woman, wearing a cream-colored period dress and posing next to a large vase of purple flowers. We both took photographs of this picture, and hung out on the landing beneath it for a while to record an impromptu EVP session.

As the sun crested the Rocky Mountains and began to flood the hotel with daylight, it was a sleepy and slightly dejected bunch of investigators who packed up our equipment and headed for home. Sleep and shower were all I could think of at the time, as I bid the hotel staff a fond farewell and turned in the room key at the main desk.

All that remained was to go through the hours of digital audio recordings and hundreds of photographs taken that night. But all that could wait. My bed was calling.

Wading through the digital sound recordings using Audacity software, something quite extraordinary occurred. I played it back several times to make sure that I was hearing what I thought I was hearing. Then I had my colleagues check it again for me.

According to the timestamp (04:27 a.m.) and my notes, Laura and I had been standing on the staircase landing at the time, directly underneath the painting of the lady with her flowers. My notes said that a radio was playing music in the lobby down below, but this was not audible on the rest of the recording.

A male voice can quite clearly be heard to say the word – *Careful.*

Only Laura and I were present at the time. She definitely does not sound like a man, and I have a pronounced English accent despite my years of residence here in the United States. Neither of us said the word "careful", and neither of us was responsible for the voice picked up on the digital voice recorder.

There were no cleaners present within earshot, no other residents, and no other source of a human voice that we could identify. It's also interesting to note that the voice was picked up on Laura's recorder but was noticeably absent from mine.

I encourage you to listen to the EVP clip yourself and make up your own mind. You can find it under the Hotel Boulderado investigation page at our website. www.bouldercountyparanormal.org.

● ● ● ● ● ● ● ● ● ●

The story of the "careful" EVP has one last twist. Shortly after our investigation was concluded, I was contacted by a Boulderado staff member, who does not wish to be named. She had been working at the hotel for just under a year, and had gotten a copy of the EVP from the hotel management after I emailed it to them. Shortly after hearing about my EVP, she was standing on the grand staircase at precisely the same spot where I unwittingly recorded the male voice.

The employee was relating the story of my EVP to a friend, and no sooner were the words out of her mouth, she suddenly pitched face first down the staircase,
landing on her back and looking back up at the painting in question.

Fortunately, she wasn't injured by the fall. You might think that her friend would show some sympathy at her plight, but the reaction was instead a rather snarkily voiced: "Careful!"

She went on to relate that during her year at the Hotel Boulderado, she had experienced many inexplicable and seemingly paranormal incidents.

Upon reflection, this casts the EVP story in a very interesting light. It could, of course, be pure coincidence. Note that the staff member doesn't claim to have been pushed, or felt any outside force acting upon her when she stumbled.

On the other hand, perhaps something invisible was lurking on the grand staircase that didn't want to be talked about. Much depends upon your own personal beliefs about the nature of coincidence. What is the likelihood of somebody standing in the exact same spot, relating the specific story about the "careful" incident, spontaneously falling down the flight of stairs?

Once the investigative report was published on the BCPRS website, I was contacted by another recent hotel resident. This lady ("Nancy") was less than happy with her experience there, and vowed never to return.

Nancy and her family were in town for her daughter's wedding, and the families involved stayed at the Hotel Boulderado. Nancy had specifically requested the two suites that opened onto the balcony, and was subsequently assigned to rooms 302 and 304. The balcony was made into a "private" balcony used only by Nancy and her family members.

All went flawlessly with the wedding, and after an utterly exhausting day, Nancy and her husband returned to their room and retired for the night. Nancy told me that her husband always sleeps like a rock, and coupled with the celebratory wine from the wedding reception, was out like a light.

Nancy was lying awake in the dark, and suddenly heard the main door in the living area of the suite open. In a state of self-described shock, she jumped out of bed, dashed into the main room – and found the door is closed and tightly locked.

Quite frightened now, Nancy turned on the lights and gave the room a thorough looking over. Nothing was found to be out of place, and all doors and windows were sealed tightly. Nancy nervously went back to bed.

Through the rest of the night, she could hear a squeaky door opening and closing numerous times. The room temperature became unnaturally cold, and Nancy sensed movement in the room just beyond the edges of her vision. The atmosphere was pervaded by an uncomfortable feeling, which led Nancy to the coping strategy of finally just pulling the covers up over her head and waiting for sleep to come. Beside her, Nancy's husband slept through everything.

Nancy played detective the following morning. After opening and closing each and every door in the room in an unsuccessful attempt to duplicate the sounds she had heard, Nancy gave up and put it down to the room being haunted.

The following three nights passed uneventfully, with no further nocturnal disturbances. It was only when she arrived home that her husband dropped a bombshell. Both Nancy and her husband have a routine of double-checking all door locks, and they did this at the Boulderado before going to bed each night. This includes the door leading out to the balcony, which was found to be securely locked. On the morning after her frightening experience, Nancy's husband had found the balcony door unlocked and standing open behind the heavy curtain.

Nancy signed off on her email to me with an unequivocal, *Best Wishes (won't be back to the Boulderado)*.

I must confess to being more than a little jealous of Nancy's experience in the room we had also stayed in. But our doors remained stubbornly closed and locked throughout the course of our stay.

In the summer of 2013, I received the following email from Barbara, a recent Boulderado guest who had loved the hotel itself but was less than happy with the ghosts that haunt it! Barbara makes it clear in her message that her husband didn't tell her about room 302 being haunted until after her brush with the paranormal.

Barbara was startled awake one night to see a man walking past the end of the bed. The apparition was wearing a bandanna across his nose and mouth. Petrified, and thinking that this could be an intruder who was intent upon robbing them, she watched as the dark figure circled the end of the bed and walked around to the side where her husband was sleeping.

The man stood staring at the nightstand, not moving. Barbara knew by this point that she was looking at a ghost, not an actual physical person. Closing her eyes and opening them again, the figure had vanished into thin air.

The following morning, Barbara asked the concierge about the hotel being haunted. She was told that yes, the figure of a man wearing a bandanna across his face had indeed been seen before. Interestingly, nobody knew who he was or why he should haunt the Boulderado, but that this ghost was usually seen in the older wing of the hotel. Barbara's room was in the newer side of the hotel, and the concierge told her that this was the first reported sighting of him to occur on the new side.

Despite being very happy with the customer service and friendliness of the staff, Barbara also closed out with: *It's a nice hotel but I'll never stay there again.*

It always saddens me to hear that people have been scared away from a place as beautiful and charming as the Boulderado. Although potentially frightening (particularly when the guests were unaware of the hotel's haunted history) there is nothing to suggest that the ghosts might be malicious or harmful in any way.

At most, they appear to be seekers of attention, as if some of the hotels former residents or staff still bear some form of fond attachment to the place, and occasionally like to make their presence to known to their modern-day counterparts.

If you should find yourself visiting Boulder, a decidedly Bohemian and charming city in the foothills of the Rocky Mountains, I wholeheartedly recommend the

warm welcome and ghostly companionship of this magnificent, haunted hotel. Be sure to ask for room 302, 304, or 306. And don't necessarily expect a good night's sleep.

CHAPTER THIRTEEN

THE LADY ON THE LAWN

One of the most curious pieces of evidence that BCPRS has ever gathered, took place on the lawn of a Victorian style home in the city of Longmont, Colorado. To this day, it divides opinion between the members of our team.

The great businessman and philanthropist T.M. Callahan moved to Longmont with his wife Alice in the year 1889, opening a small store on Main Street for the sale of dry goods. The store, named "The Golden Rule", flourished to such an extent that before long, it was a national concern. "Golden Rule" store openings exploded throughout the states.

One of Callahan's employees was a failed butcher whom you may well be familiar with. J.C. Penney ran a "Golden Rule" store in Longmont, and when it was time for him to branch out into his own business concerns, J.C. Penney opened his first store in the city of Longmont too.

The Callahan house was built in 1892. This two-story (plus basement) sandstone house was purchased by T.M. Callahan in 1896. Callahan was an extremely wealthy man, and lavished both money and attention on his new home. He installed central heating, hot and cold running water, a complete electrical system, and the luxurious concept of indoor plumbing.

After residing there for ten years, Mr. Callahan instituted an aggressive construction project that basically doubled the square footage within the home. Servants' quarters were expanded upon, business and personal space was increased, and a garage for an automobile and driver were also included. In fact, it is believed that the Callahan family were the very first automobile owners in the city of Longmont.

A visitor to the Callahan house would have been left in no doubt as to the owner's financial means.

The Callahans graciously deeded the house in trust to the city of Longmont, who still retain custodianship of the house and grounds to this day. It was therefore a genuine privilege for BCPRS to be invited in to conduct a paranormal investigation of the building, accompanied by a number of city employees.

We were informed by the property manager that the security system of the house seems to malfunction on occasion, sending false alarm signals out when the house is empty at night. City maintenance workers find no evidence of faults in the alarm circuitry when checks are performed. On some of these instances, the front door has been found unlocked and swinging open.

More fascinating than this are the reports of a female apparition being sighted in the second-floor windows. The ghost is believed to be that of Mrs. Alice Callahan, though nobody is sure why she appears. Because there are no overtly negative stories surrounding the house, it would be more reasonable to assume that Mrs. Callahan would haunt the place because she loved it so much during her lifetime.

BCPRS arrived at the Callahan House on a clear and cold night in March, with a full moon rising in the sky. A light breeze stirred the trees gently, but soon died down as darkness began to fall. Walking through the garden of the Callahan House after dark is a somewhat surreal experience, because it feels a little bit like being in a graveyard. There are numerous stone carvings and statues scattered around, including those of several mythical characters such as Pan, Artemis, and Baccus, all of which seemed to be staring at me when I was passing by.

For a fairly large location, we had scheduled a more than adequate number of personnel. Joey and I shared command and coordination of the investigation. We split our experienced investigators up into three teams, so that we could cover each floor of the house simultaneously.

Our trusted senior investigators Seth and Kira formed the backbone of team one. They were to be training our two newest probationary members: Sean, a mechanic by profession who was also one of the most enthusiastic probies we have ever encountered, and Catlyn, a professor of Women's Studies who brings a very analytical slant to our interactions with witnesses. They were both on their first investigation, and eager to start learning the ropes. I couldn't have placed them with two better teachers.

While new to *us,* Jason and Linda Fellon were experienced paranormal investigators who had joined our team after getting a look at our research methods and deciding that they quite liked what they saw. They turned out to be a good fit for our team, being of similar mind and bringing some great skills to the table. The Fellons are the only people I know who have a large bumper sticker that reads: I'D RATHER BE GHOST HUNTING.

The Fellons joined with experienced BCPRS investigator Anna, to form Team Two.

Our final team was comprised of another two married couples, but this time guests from a neighboring team. Randy and Robbin have accompanied us on many overnights, and they brought along Eric and Mindy, with whom we had also worked before. I trusted all of them implicitly, and had a high confidence level in their abilities.

Sprinkled in amongst our three teams were a handful of interested city employees, all enthusiastically giving up their Saturday night off to participate in this ghost hunt. Joey distributed radios to all teams and made sure that we could all communicate with one another, before sending everybody off to baseline their assigned parts of the structure. There was just enough daylight left to allow Joey and I to take reference photographs of the building exterior and of the grounds.

Part way through, I was interrupted by a radio call from the second floor. Randy wanted to get my opinion on something. Poking my head around the door of the front bedroom, he directed my attention to a framed black and white photograph located on a shelf inside a locked cabinet. Did I see anything odd about it, he wanted to know.

Squinting, my eyes roved across the surface of the photo. It contained the front side of the Callahan House, an early Twentieth Century automobile, and the Callahan family posing. And then...

In the upper window, a form was visible. It looked to me like the figure of a woman with long dark hair, flowing down to her shoulders, wearing a white nightgown or dress of some sort. The picture was taking during the daytime, and at first I wondered whether this could be the reflection of a cloud in the windowpane. But none of the other windows facing in the same direction had anything reflected in them, despite being lit by the same source (the Sun) from the same angle.

"It looks like a woman in the window," I told Randy. He nodded enthusiastically.

This called for a spot of experimentation.

Anna happens to have dark shoulder-length hair. She isn't exactly in the habit of wearing long white dresses or nightgowns on paranormal investigations, however, so we had to improvise. I dashed downstairs and grabbed a pristine white tablecloth from the dining room, then asked her to wrap it around her neck and shoulders like a shawl or gown.

What followed was a series of trial-and-error photographs, as we attempted to duplicate the framed photograph by having Anna appear at various distances from the same upstairs window as the mysterious lady. Sometimes she would be in direct contact with the glass, and on other shots she would be standing a few feet backwards. Investigators standing in the front garden snapped off a long sequence of shots as Anna changed position relative to the window, using multiple cameras and slightly varying angles.

The window had an inner sill or ledge, large enough for a child to stand on if they were pressing their nose against the glass, or for an adult to kneel on. When we reviewed the photos a few minutes later, it was unanimously decided that the shots which looked most similar to the old monochrome image were those in which she had been pressing directly against the glass, in actual physical contact with it. The photos where Anna was standing back a foot or so all appeared much blurrier and less distinct.

The team debated this for a while. If the figure in the old photograph were a child, they would have to be standing on the windowsill in order to be that distinct. If an adult, they would have to be leaning forwards and pushing their face against the glass. Either way, they would have to be in almost direct contact with the glass in order to replicate the images we had taken.

Another small detail to be explained was that of the apparition's identity. The figure of the woman in the window (if a ghost it actually was) could not be Mrs. Callahan, because Mrs. Callahan was alive and well, and standing in the photograph next to the car!

As a quick aside, phantoms of the living are not unheard of. There are plenty of documented cases in the paranormal case literature that detail apparitions of people who are not actually dead. But they rarely appear within sight of the physical person themselves, and certainly not at the same time.

Now that it was full dark outside, Linda had stepped out into the front yard and was busily snapping photographs with her full spectrum camera. Becoming increasingly affordable as the price of the technology drops, the full spectrum camera sees a little further into the light spectrum than a normal camera does.

The hope amongst paranormal investigators is that this technology might be capable of seeing something paranormal that is visible at a slightly different wavelength than normal light. The jury is still out on just how effective this new tool can be, but it would certainly yield interesting results at the Callahan House.

While Linda was shooting, Joey and I were delivering the obligatory safety and investigative etiquette briefing to our colleagues and guests. This is where the rules of good behavior are outlined for newcomers (for example, always say "flash!" before taking a flash photograph) so that we are all on the same page about how to do things.

Just as we were finishing up the briefing, Linda came inside and told us that she had something on her camera. Gathering around, we peered at the tiny screen. Eyes widened.

"We need to blow that image up," I said. It took just a minute to copy the image files across from Linda's full spectrum camera hard drive onto my laptop, and then zoom the image in on the seventeen-inch screen. There was a most definite "wow" moment.

The two images that fascinated us were the frames numbered 555 and 556. Both were taken in the middle of the front yard, near to the large ornamental stone fountain. Linda was taking pictures of the front wall of the Callahan House.

What looks to be my outline can be seen in the ground floor window, obviously conducting the briefing with Joey and the assembled investigative team. The interesting thing is a light anomaly, purple in hue, which appears as a smear in front of the window and part of the yard. Anomalies like this turn up from time to time on investigations, and usually cause little more than a raised eyebrow. What made us all sit up and pay attention in this particular instance is the next frame, number 556, taken exactly one second later.

The purple shape in frame 556 bears a striking similarity to the figure of a woman wearing an old fashioned hooped-type skirt, and what may be a bonnet on her head. The form obscures my form, indicating that whatever it happens to be, it is located in front of me (in relation to the camera) and is outside the house, not inside. It just so happens that this particular window is located beneath the window in which the ghostly apparition presumed to be Mrs. Alice Callahan has been seen to appear.

I sat back and blew out a long, slow breath. Then the debate began, and it hasn't really stopped since. Some of us believe that it does look like the transparent figure of a woman in a dress, whereas others are convinced that this is simply a case of lens flare. Attempts to debunk the anomaly by returning to the same spot and shooting a string of photos of the same area did not succeed in replicating the strange form. This may be because the figure was no longer there to be photographed in the IR spectrum, or alternatively the lighting conditions (primarily the angle of the moon) were never exactly the same again because the moon had risen higher in the sky, and therefore did not enter the camera lens at the same angle.

Bottom line: it's impossible to say. I showed it to my buddy Chris Balassone, a fellow paramedic who investigates with Tri-City Paranormal out East. I respect Chris' opinion enormously, and he is unequivocally convinced that this is a simple case of lens flare. Personally though, I am not so sure. Had it been lens flare, I still think that we should have seen similar effects in later photographs taken in the same spot, even accounting for the changed angle of the moon. The fact that the anomaly begins to the left of the window in frame 555 and then continues to the right and then obscures the window in frame 556, suggests to me the motion of some form of anomaly passing from left to right in front of the house at that time. By frame 557, taken one second later, all is back to normal again.

The photographic evidence can be read either way. My own mind is divided on the cause, but leans more towards a paranormal explanation simply due to our inability to duplicate the effect later on.

All three teams were dispatched to their respective floors by nine thirty. Unsurprisingly, three sets of batteries failed in cameras and flashlights, despite having been factory fresh at the beginning of the investigation. Our old friend, the paranormal power drain, was still alive and kicking.

Some interesting subjective experiences followed. Anna felt uncharacteristically weak and dizzy, though this soon passed. She and Linda also heard what they believed to be an indistinct male voice, though it was not caught on our digital voice recorders. Nor were the scattered clicking noises which plagued this particular investigation, appearing at random times and intervals throughout the Callahan House. No explanation was ever found for them, so I tend to go with the mundane idea of it being the old house settling down for the night.

The Rem Pod (an EMF detector with a telescoping antenna) alarmed several times throughout the night, for no apparent reason. Randy was also busily employing his Ovilus, a word-generating device that some believe will ask as a mouthpiece of disembodied entities.

When asked what the spirit's favorite part of the house was, the Ovilus answered with *Outside*. It also came up with the name *Steven*. An engraved mirror upstairs was dedicated to a former house manager: *In loving memory of Steven*.

And just as Joey's voice came over the airwaves to call a ten-minute break between sessions, the Ovilus pre-empted him by saying *"break"*.

I was sitting at the command table with Joey and the banks of radios, quietly entering data points into the investigation journal on my laptop. Joey was quietly daydreaming. As the clock struck ten, the heavy tread of footsteps sounded directly above our head, followed by the sound of something heavy being dragged across the floor. Joey and I looked at one another. That would place the footsteps in team three's location, and it was pretty bad form if they were stomping around during the middle of a designated EVP session.

Taking another caffeine break, we enquired about the footsteps and dragging. Nobody had been dragging anything heavy at that time, and nobody assigned to team three had heard the noises which had been so loud to Joey and I. Excitedly, we dispatched Robbin and Seth upstairs to walk across the floor and drag something. It sounded nothing like the cacophony we had heard earlier, being much quieter and harder to hear.

It should come as no surprise to you by now that, when Joey and I downloaded and analyzed the data from our digital voice recorders, nothing unusual could be heard during that timeframe. And yet we are both certain of what we heard, logging it in specific detail at the moment it took place. Yet another unsolved mystery from inside the Callahan House, and the inability of our equipment to capture anything of a seemingly paranormal nature was fast becoming a running theme.

Shortly after eleven o'clock, Mindy and two city employees heard footsteps on the staircase which leads down to the basement from the dining room. The footsteps were also accompanied by an indistinct whispering. No team was assigned to the basement at the time, but this was something I wanted to remedy immediately in case the basement or its staircase were becoming active areas.

In the meantime, Randy's team had elected to investigate the carriage house. It was a very cool old structure, which had contained the turntable used by the Callahans' first car because it had no reverse gear! The chauffer lived and slept in there during his time off.

A growl emanating from the space right next to Randy was witnessed by both himself and a city employee named Donna, though they differed on their interpretation of the sound. Whereas Randy thought it was a deep male voice, Donna believed it to be the sound of a growling stomach. Evidence on the digital voice recorders? Zilch, frustratingly enough. And the same is true for the female voice which Eric and Robbin believed they heard say the word "saw", which happened immediately after a request for a spirit to do something to an investigator.

Fighting through a stomach bug, Joey left just before the stroke of midnight. Robbin was dispatched to the basement, accompanied by a female city employee, to follow up on the whispers and footsteps reported there, while Randy remained in the dining room to cover the head of the stairs. At around twenty minutes past one, both women described encountering a small, nebulous black cloud in the basement, the appearance of which froze them on the spot just long enough that they did not get off a photograph. The cloud passed through a basement wall and disappeared.

Meanwhile, Randy saw what he believed to be a shadow moving down the staircase through the open doorway – it was gone far too quickly for him to take a photograph, despite having a camera with him at the time.

Was the shadow on the staircase related to the black cloud seen downstairs? The two incidents occurred at around the same time, and were independently witnessed by three observers. EMF meters and thermometers remained in the normal range throughout, and no EVPs were successfully recorded from anywhere in the house during this investigation.

The team packed up its equipment and left the house shortly after four o'clock. To this day, we still debate whether Linda's camera captured a truly impressive slice of paranormal energy or a mundane instance of lens flare. Nothing similar has appeared on any other investigations on which she has used this same camera, taking hundreds of pictures with it under similar low-light conditions.

Could it have been a tantalizing glimpse of the female figure, whoever it is, that appears in the framed period photograph? And does that person, in turn, bear any relation to the female apparition reported in the upstairs front window by several witnesses over the years?

The black cloud reported in the basement and the shadow seen on the stairs, remain entirely unexplained. The jury is still out on whether one should best attribute this to tired eyes and too much caffeine, or if it was a genuine paranormal manifestation. All three investigators stick to their guns regarding what they saw, and their testimony has not changed one iota.

As far as I am concerned, the wonderfully atmospheric Callahan House has not given up all of its secrets just yet. My intention is for BCPRS to return there again in future. At the very least, I would like to find out once and for all whether there truly is a ghostly lady on the lawn.

CHAPTER FOURTEEN
THROWN IN THE CLINK

We all know what it means to be "thrown in the clink," but have you ever given thought to where that particular term comes from?

The answer is medieval London, and the United Kingdom's oldest jail.

Few people today would relish the idea of building a prison in their own back yard. And yet this is exactly what Bishop of Winchester Henry of Blois did during the twelfth century. It served not only as a place of incarceration for London's undesirables, but also provided an extra influx of cash for the Bishops coffers. Being located in a part of London renowned for its prostitution and gambling didn't hurt the flow of business either.

Life in the Clink was brutal, hard, and miserable... unless you had money. Guards were paid a subsistence wage at best, but in the grand tradition of enterprising civil servants throughout history, they wasted no time in devising ways to make more cash. Bribes of either goods or sexual favors were also commonplace. The guards indulged in a little pimping on the side, running a prostitution ring inside The Clink walls and pocketing most of the profits themselves.

The worst scum of medieval London were tossed into the prison alongside everyday working folk who were guilty of nothing more than being down on their luck. Professional thieves, highwaymen, murderers, and rapists, were able to prey upon a constantly growing pool of helpless victims who passed within the prison walls. Violent death was an unremarkable fact of everyday life inside the Clink. If one survived the horrors within the prison walls, their only escape might be the snap of their neck and dancing the "Tyburn Jig" of death at the end of a hangman's rope. Those prisoners with a higher profile often ended up decapitated by the headsman's axe at Tower Green.

Conditions inside the prison were either roasting hot or ice cold, depending upon the time of year. For those inmates who were poor of pocket and lacking in friends and family on the outside who could help support them financially, this meant either boiling or freezing. Death could be caused by either extreme of temperature. To those with a ready supply of money, the guards would be happy to sell fresh water, warm clothing, and wood to burn for heat and lighting.

The only option for poorer inmates was begging. Metal grates were the only connection between many of the beggars and the outside world, linking the prison cells to the street above. If you were lucky, a passer-by might take pity on you and donate some money or food. But it was more likely that you would be treated as a source of cruel amusement, and it was not unknown for unsympathetic Londoners to pause at the prison grates in order to empty bladders and bowels onto the unfortunates clamoring for help below. Small wonder, then, that disease was rife in the Clink, claiming hundreds of deaths over the centuries.

Even in the days before sanitation, hygiene within the Clink left much to be desired. There were no privies (toilets) for the inmates, so feces and urine would simply pool around their feet and ankles. We can only imagine how much worse this must have felt when the prison flooded, as it often did. Those miserable prisoners who could not afford their own private room (with an elevated bed) would have been awash in a lake of sewage.

Do we know why the prison came to be nicknamed "the Clink"? I spoke with a local historian, who advanced several possible explanations. The most obvious theory is that the clinking referred to comes from the manacles which bound the arms and legs of prisoners. As the resident blacksmith pounded an iron pin through the manacles of each hapless inmate, the hammering *clink clink clink* noise sounded the death knell of their freedom...sometimes forever. Even in this regard, the prisoners were unequal when it came down to money...those who could afford it were shackled into lighter, less uncomfortable chains than the paupers and debtors.

Another theory is that the "clink" in question is the sound of metal door latches slamming closed at the hands of its jailers. Whichever explanation is true, "the Clink" has now become a universal term for being incarcerated.

Throughout recorded history, Londoners have often indulged in the traditional pastime of rioting, which dates back to ancient times. In more than one civil revolt and uprising over the years, rioters broke into The Clink, butchered such guards as did not flee, and released the prisoners into the streets. In the ensuing merriment, the Clink was usually burned to the ground. The prison has been razed and rebuilt several times over the course of its lifetime, eventually falling into disrepair before being burned down one final time in 1780. It was never rebuilt, but the site of The Clink is now home to the Clink Prison Museum, a faithful reproduction that serves as a piece of living history for tourists from around the world. One of the original prison walls is still standing, and one can't help but wonder what horrific stories it would tell us if it could only speak.

Reviewing the prison records allows us a glimpse of the torments inflicted upon generations of poor souls kept imprisoned within The Clink. There is one Laurence Vaux, starved to death. The 1586 Babington Plot, intended to assassinate Queen Elizabeth I and replace her with Mary, Queen of Scots, resulted in a number of convicted traitors being consigned to the Clink. Many were subsequently hung, drawn, and quartered, dying in agony after enduring a slower form of suffering inside the prison.

Suicide seems to have been a popular escape option, such as a priest known only as "Saxy" who hanged himself sometime in the sixteenth century in order to beat the torturers to their mark.

Marriages took place inside The Clink on a fairly regular basis...after all, there was no shortage of imprisoned priests to carry out the ceremony! And entire generations of family were born, raised, and died within its walls. And just like any other prison, the Clink was not completely secure and impregnable. Some of those who escaped were Puritans, who fled England to start a new life in the fledgling colonies of America. Such a man was the Reverend Lorthorpp, a heretic who made it to the New World after fleeing The Clink in 1634.

Considering the centuries of misery and horror that took place within its walls, it should come as no surprise at all that The Clink boasts a number of ghost stories. In October of 2009, national newspaper *The Daily Mirror* dispatched an enterprising reporter to the Clink. Andy Rudd documented his experiences in an online article at www.mirror.co.uk entitled "Ghost hunting at haunted prison the Clink" that makes for fascinating reading.

Rudd mentions a murderer with a predilection for blonds, who latches onto a blonde reporter and keeps mentioning her "pretty golden hair", according to a sensitive that is accompanying his group. The same sensitive also experiences a vision of one man being whipped inside a doorway, and two guards brutally stabbing an inmate to death.

The medium then made contact with the ghost of a physician called Alexander whose main occupation was checking prisoners for signs and symptoms of the plague. My own heartbeat picked up a little when I read that Alexander caused chest pressure and throat pain to build up in the medium and a fellow investigator that night. Would I experience anything similar?

A simple Internet search turns up wealth of information regarding paranormal activity at the Clink. One review from March of 2014 stated that a man and his girlfriend visited the museum and took a number of photographs inside. When looking at the pictures closely, they noticed a pair of ghostly figures lurking in the background. Staff at The Clink examined the photographs and confirmed that the figures were not any of the mannequins which dot the museum interior in order to provide atmosphere.

Located in the fashionable district of Southwark, not far from the banks of the River Thames, the Clink Prison Museum is easy to miss if you don't know what you are looking for. It is situated on Clink Street, home to office buildings, bars, restaurants, and hotels. The museum is something of an anachronism, a slice of medieval history buried within the heart of modern London.

It was a balmy summer evening when the taxi dropped me off on the corner of Clink Street. I had flown in from the United States the day before, having packed lightly – passport, a couple of changes of clothes, and my kit bag of ghost hunting equipment. The streets of London were full of revelers enjoying the summer air, laughing and chatting the night away. I spotted the huge Rose Window, inset within the standing wall of Winchester Palace (traditional home of the Bishop of Winchester). A short stroll along the cobblestones brought me to the prison entrance, comprised of a flight of steps leading down below street level and topped off by a leering skeleton encased in a replica wrought iron gibbet.

As I grow older, I find myself to be opening up to more alternative methods of research and investigation. When the opportunity arose to spend a Saturday night investigating ghostly activity within the Clink, I naturally jumped at the chance. One of the aspects which I found most intriguing was that the group that I would be accompanying happened to be firm believers in the use of Ouija boards, table tipping, glassing moving, and various similar methods of research.

Oddly enough, in almost two decades of researching the paranormal and hunting ghosts, I have never been part of a séance or used a Ouija board. I lack experience with the techniques involved, and the opportunity had never really arisen before. As the start time crept closer, I found myself getting increasingly excited at the prospect of broadening my horizons as an investigator. This would hearken back to the origins of attempting to communicate with the dead that became popular behind the closed parlor doors of the Victorian séance room. I was starting to feellike a kid on Christmas morning!

A gaggle of enthusiastic investigators clustered outside the museum entrance, talking animatedly to one another and occasionally stepping aside to allow tourists and diners to pass by. I introduced myself to some of my new teammates, learning about their diverse backgrounds and past experiences with the paranormal. My companions for the evening were a diverse bunch, most of them being veterans of previous overnight investigations. What some may have lacked in experience, they more than made up for with enthusiasm.

A freelance reporter named Matt was taking copious notes as he interviewed various attendees. He was writing an article on ghost hunting at the Clink for an airline in-flight magazine, and was completely new to the paranormal field. I was impressed with his level-headed and balanced approach throughout the investigation, as he was to be an objective devil's advocate amongst a crowd made up primarily of believers.

The sunlight was just starting to fade when our group descended into the warm darkness of the Clink. We had been warned that it would be T-shirt weather inside, which was quite the understatement. Packing over twenty people into a confined and somewhat claustrophobic subterranean space was a recipe for generating heat, especially with the very minimal airflow to be found inside. In no time at all, we were all sweating. The stout wooden main door closed with a disappointingly mundane click (no ominous creak or thud) and we all found ourselves in the dimly lit main entrance hall, where a skilled local historian treated us to a theatrical and entertaining half hour of the Clink's historical background.

After some suitably gruesome explanations of the various torture devices and methods employed when The Clink was still in operation, our guide led us on a behind-the-scenes tour of the building. It was a great opportunity to draw up a sketch floor plan and assess the lie of the land.

Grotesque, misshapen mannequins can be found scattered throughout the building, representing both the jailers and the inmates alike. The waxwork dummies were used to illustrate the dreadful toll exacted upon the prisoners by their living conditions. Bulging eyeballs, screaming mouths, and assorted ghastly wounds made it quite clear to the visitor that hardship and torture would have been a common thing during the Clink's heyday. There was also a pack of rubber rats distributed throughout the place, peering out at us from nooks and crannies. I set about forming a mental map of the building, fixing the location of each dummy in my mind's eye. It would be pretty bad form for me to glimpse one of these latex denizens of the darkness at some point during the night and get an inadvertent scare!

Splitting into three groups, we would cycle through three different areas of the prison and use a different investigative method each time. Right out of the gate, my group was attached to a sensitive, who would lead us in a session of table tipping (also known as table *tilting*). This particular technique of paranormal communication dates back to the Victorian era, and I was excited to give it a try. This was something totally new to me. Some claim that table tippers are making direct contact with the spirits of dead strangers who are local to the place you are investigating, restless ghosts who are trapped between planes of existence and desperately trying to attract the attention of the living. If this is the case, one might expect there to be many such restless souls residing at the Clink. Other mediums offer the opinion that table tipping is actually a means of conversing with the spirit guide of one of those touching the table, in order to obtain guidance and answers.

Our medium addressed any spirits who might be present with great respect, requesting that they offer make use of the energies assembled in the room in order to manifest physically and tip up a small table around which our group was gathered.

Table tipping can appear a little embarrassing at first. At our medium's direction, several members of my group placed our hands lightly on the edge of the wooden table and began entreating the discarnate entities to tilt it.

It took a while for any energy to build in the room, and several false starts, but after a quarter of an hour things began to pick up.

"Move the table," we asked. Following instructions, our polite request grew to a vigorous shout as the table began to slowly tip up onto two legs. "Move the table. Move the table! *MOVE THE TABLE!*"

I'll be the first to admit to feeling a little self-conscious, standing in a darkened room beneath a London city street, huddled with seven other people and yelling at a table. I placed both a standard and a natural tri-field EMF meter beneath the table, although neither of them spiked significantly. Immediately before the table tilting session began, some water dripped onto Matt's hand. Sweeping the ceiling above him with lights, we could find no obvious source for it. No damp patches or leaks were visible.

Could it have been sweat from Matt's own brow? No, because we confirmed that his forehead was dry. The group filed this under "puzzling," and moved on to some experimentation with Frank's Box. The frequency hopping radio scanner filled our ears with a mixture of white noise and fractions of radio transmissions.

Our medium for the evening invited any spirits present to make their presence known by speaking to us, and preferably giving their name. Team members then took it in turns to fire off questions in a round robin fashion, following our circle of investigators clustered around the central wooden table.

Were you a prisoner in this prison?
Did you die here?
What's it like where you are?

Nothing of note came through the wall of white noise. The medium switched off the Frank's Box. Suddenly, a member of the group exclaimed that she had just seen a big face looming in the darkness. She described it as the face of a bald man, whose appearance was scaring her deeply. We all noticed that the air in the room had turned a little bit colder.

Although none of the rest of us had seen the intimidating male face, our sensitive guide said that she was sensing the presence of children in our midst.

"Let's split up and go to the corners of the room and try calling out," she suggested.

Shuffling into our own separate spaces, we all watched in fascination as the medium attempted to establish contact with these childlike spirits. She began to make a game of it, clapping her hands and inviting a response.

Thud. Dull and faint, but an apparent response, nonetheless. I couldn't pin down the origin of this banging noise, and the obvious explanation is that we had heard a natural sound generated at random somewhere in the building.

Two members of the team heard a cackling laugh, and also couldn't identify the source.

"That sounded like an old witch's laugh," one of the ladies said with a visible shudder.

Unfortunately, neither sound was caught on my digital voice recorders when I reviewed the evidence afterwards. I did not hear either of the sounds myself, but things were about to take a definite turn towards the unusual deep within the bowels of the Clink.

• • • ● ●• ● ● • • •

Table tipping got off to a flying start. My own all-male group worked up quite a sweat, exhorting the table to move. Fingertips pressed to the tabletop in a circle, it did indeed appear that the table was beginning to sway and become slightly lighter. I was starting to become intrigued.

The men stopped to take a short break. As we removed our fingers from the table and took a step back, our guide told us that she had witnessed a female form walk past us in the gloomy background. This figure had been wearing some type of headdress, such as that of a nun or nurse. I peered into the darkness, trying to pick the figure out, but could see nothing. A level-headed female observer said that she had also seen the figure pass from left to right behind us.

One of the male investigators' flashlights began to flicker and die. Its owner looked at it in bemusement. He had put fresh batteries into it just an hour before our investigation had begun. The all-too-common problem of battery drain was starting to plague us.

Now it was the ladies' turn to try their hands at table tipping. They put quite a bit more effort into it than we men had done, showing us up with their lack of self consciousness. As energy built in the room, they began to coordinate their efforts verbally across the table.

"Tip the table over! Tip it towards me! This way! Over here! Thank you!"

The table tilted up onto first two legs, and then finally onto one single leg tip. There was definitely a charged atmosphere building up the room. I squatted down on my haunches, eyes at the level of the tabletop and watching the girls' fingers like a hawk.

The fingertips were all resting lightly on the wooden surface, and I saw no signs of pressure being exerted, such as blanching in and around the nail beds that would lead me to suspect deliberate force was being applied. I also eyed the participants' forearms, looking for tensing and bunching of the muscles. This was tee shirt weather due to the London summer warmth, and I could see no sign of the tilters exerting their arm muscles.

Building to a crescendo, the cries of "Move the table!" stopped abruptly as the table fell onto the stone floor with a loud crack.

This really got me thinking. I remain convinced that there was no conscious fraud was involved here. It would be easy to dismiss this table tilting exercise as simple ideomotor movements of the participants' muscles, but I find it difficult to believe that it completely explains what I saw in the Clink that night. I have since tried to replicate this experiment with friends, and it is blatantly obvious when the table is being tilted by direct physical force.

Matt the reporter had also been keeping a careful eye on things, and seemed equally puzzled by the cause of the table tilting. He was keeping an open mind, describing himself being "interested but skeptical."

What with men being men, we couldn't leave it at that. We wanted to try again, to see if we could better the ladies' results. We put a lot more effort into it this time out, and in just a few minutes the table was tilting up and rocking back and forth before dropping to the floor with a loud clatter. I know for sure that I was not intentionally moving the table, having kept my arms relaxed and loosely resting my fingertips on the tabletop. Having also observed my teammates during the tilting, I saw no signs of them using their muscles to tip the table either. If this was not a paranormal phenomenon, it would have to be at the very least a subconscious one.

It is also worth pointing out that our hands were sweating after just a short period of time, which would have made the contact between skin and wood more slippery.

A number of the investigators present had recently spent the night researching the London Tombs, and told us that the table tipping session which they had conducted on that night had resulted in the wooden table literally bouncing and flipping. Ours was said to be quite tame by comparison.

Morale was high in the wake of the table tipping experiments. A ten-minute break was in order, giving everybody the chance to drink, smoke, and use the restrooms. I chatted with Matt about what we had experienced so far. Because the rest of our companions were pretty firmly in the hardcore believer camp, I was curious to see what he was making of events thus far.

He seemed ambivalent about the table tipping, not willing to concede that it was necessarily paranormal in nature, and yet also uncertain that it *wasn't*. The drops of water on his hand impressed him a little more, especially as we had been unable to track down a water source above him that would account for it.

As the evening was wearing on, it became apparent that many of the local revelers used Clink Street as a means of transit between the various pubs and bars. Two extremely well-lubricated young guys stopped at the brick wall directly facing our building, and proceeded to empty their bladders into the gutter with loud sighs of relief. Hopefully we hadn't found the explanation for Matt's wet hand! But all joking aside, any liquid trickling down from the street outside should still have left a visible trail on the ceiling and walls. The water droplets were not that easily explainable.

After finishing up a soda, I followed the rest of my group back downstairs. Our next port of call was to be the "coffin room", so called because the centerpiece museum display in here was a replica coffin. Various screaming mannequin replicas of former Clink inmates stared back at us as we shuffled in, taking up positions among age-old implements of torture such as the stocks and hanging hooks.

My second new tool for experimentation was introduced to me in the coffin room, that of dowsing. I had read about dowsing in many paranormal books over the years, but had never felt the urge to try it out for myself. Dowsing involves using two metal sticks or rods, which can supposedly be manipulated by external forces or entities to answer questions or to point the dowser in a specific direction.

Our psychic guide handed out some dowsing rods to each investigator, and we were invited to find our "yes" and "no" positions. This entailed holding the rods loosely in each hand and allowing them to pivot about their central axis until they came to a rest in a specific position.

A brief period of trial and error followed, as we were coached on getting answers from the dowsing rods about the location of certain hidden objects around the room. This culminated in a very interesting test of the dowsing process. A young lady named Linda volunteered to be the test subject, taking a pair of dowsing rods and being led out of the room. The psychic then gave me Linda's phone, which went into my pocket and completely covered up. Linda was then invited back into the room and told to dowse for the location of her phone.

"Please find my phone," Linda asked respectfully, repeating this at roughly twenty second intervals as the dowsing rod tips began to drift across one another.

"Point to my phone."

Linda was slowly and unerringly advancing in my specific direction, stepping tentatively towards me. When she got to within ten feet away, I stepped towards her with my tri-field EMF meter −ostensibly to take measurements around the dowsing rods, but my actual intent was to test this process in a more rigorous way. The rods crossed more visibly as I stepped towards Linda, her phone still in my side pocket. I then cut across Linda's front and stepped around to her side, moving to a position against the back wall some fifteen feet away.

"Just getting out of your way," I grinned in the politest manner possible. Would the rods pick up on my change of position?

Unbelievably, they did. Linda's dowsing rods pivoted in her hands ever so slowly, leading her in my general direction again. I made sure not to move a single muscle, not wanting to give away my guilt with subliminal cues such as body language – not that this was much of a danger in the semi-darkness in the coffin room, but I wanted to make this as fair a test as possible under the circumstances.

Closer and closer she came, dowsing rod tips creeping nearer to one another with every step Linda took. Finally, she was standing directly in front of me with a puzzled look on her face. Looking down, I saw my natural tri-field EMF meter needle bury itself briefly (for the first time all evening) and then dropped back into dormancy. I couldn't keep a straight face any longer and burst out laughing, taking her phone out of my pocket and handing it over.

How could she have known? It would be very easy to claim that somebody on the investigative team had told her the location of her phone, but it had been given to me after Linda had left the coffin room, and nobody had gone to fetch her when she returned – she was simply called out for.

My first impression of the dowsing technique was a favorable one, and I remain very interested to use this particular tool on future investigations. Dowsing has been used to locate underground sources of oil and water, according to its many devotees, and to follow the flow of mystical energy lines known as "ley lines" in the United Kingdom. The rods had done a surprisingly good job of locating Linda's phone when she did not know where it was hidden, even zeroing in on me when I changed position. My curiosity was most definitely piqued.

Glass moving came next. This is another technique of purported spirit communication that was new and unfamiliar to me. With six or seven participants placing a single fingertip on the upended base of an ordinary glass, the idea is to generate sufficient energy to enable spirit entities to manifest and deliver messages.

Our medium guide placed the glass atop the coffin lid, and several of us placed a fingertip atop it as directed. No sooner had she politely asked for spirit energy to begin moving the glass, than an investigator named Lucy reported feeling a light touch upon her back. Needless to say, nobody was there.

I was shortly due for my own encounter, as the medium looked me squarely in the eye and asked if I could feel a presence of some kind behind me. Shaking my head, I asked her why. She was sensing the presence of a religious male spirit directly behind me, somebody she believed to be a monk or friar. He was quite a bit shorter than me, and apparently peeking around my shoulder.

"I hate to tempt fate, but would this religious gentleman like to touch me somewhere, to make his presence known?"

When it appeared that no physical touch would be forthcoming, Matt invited the religious man to move our glass instead. Our psychic joined in, exhorting him to either touch me or to move the glass. As a last-ditch effort to provoke some kind of response, I volunteered to be placed into the wooden stocks as a prisoner. But results were still not to be forthcoming, so we shifted gears and broke up into sub-groups in order to conduct some EVP sessions.

Breaking my cardinal rule of paranormal scene investigation, I decided to take a once in a lifetime opportunity of spending an hour alone inside part of this ancient historic jail. While my group mates congregated in a next-door room, I found a comfortable spot in the oubliette. In mediaeval times, an oubliette was the equivalent of solitary confinement – the term means "place of forgetting". Prisoners were cast into the oubliette, locked in, and forgotten. Sometimes, they would starve to death without ever seeing daylight again.

I parked myself on a wooden bench next to a kneeling medieval peasant mannequin that appeared to be deep in prayer. The lights were dimmed to a very comfortable low level, and with my digital voice recorder running, I settled in to wait.

Peaceful silence descended upon the prison. After twenty minutes, the hushed tones of each group asking respectful questions into their digital voice recorders could be heard. A loud and distinct *pop* jerked everybody's heads up, but despite our repeated requests for it to happen again, the clear popping sound never returned and was not detected on my digital voice recorders. It remains unexplained as of the time of writing.

I stood up to stretch my stiff legs and back for a second. Two ear-piercing screams cut the air, within a split second of each other. I charged through into the adjacent room, where the rest of my group had been sitting.

"What happened?"

One of the ladies had seen a man's face at the open window separating our two rooms. Chuckling, I pointed out that this had almost certainly been my ugly mug. The first scream had occurred almost immediately after I stood up, so the chances were that my profile had caught the dim light and appeared to be an apparition.

But the reason for the *second* scream wasn't so easily explained.

"Somebody bloody well grabbed me," insisted a lady who was standing at the back of the room. "Somebody, or some*thing*."

Rolling up her sleeve, there did indeed appear to be a red mark visible on the back of her arm. She claimed to have felt a strong hand grip her momentarily, at almost the same time as the first lady had spotted my face through the open window across the room. Yet another coincidence...

As the investigation started to draw to a close, we arrived at the section that I was most eagerly anticipating. We were going to be conducting a séance using a Ouija board. I have always steered clear of such boards in the past, having heard a number of deeply concerning stories about them having nasty side effects. Some mediums liken the use of a Ouija board to leaving your front door unlocked at night and inviting anybody passing by in to visit!

We were cautioned by our guide that we should not expect good spelling and grammar from any entity that had been dead for more than a hundred years. This concept started to fascinate me. Following it through to its logical conclusion, wouldn't most of the older spirits who might be attached to the Clink, speak an entirely different form of the English language – one barely recognizable to people from modern times?

After our team gathered around the board, our guide requested that we announce our names to any discarnate entities present one by one. A glass was substituted for the more traditional planchette as a pointing device, and Laura entreated the spirits to speak through the glass.

Things took less than ten minutes to develop. Following our guide's gentle promptings, the glass quickly progressed from moving in a slow and hesitant manner, to speeding around in a figure eight on the board. Shortly after that, meaningful messages began to appear that seemed to relate to the older lady who had spotted the face of a big man earlier that night.

Although she would not identify the spirit with whom she believed she was communicating, the lady stated that she was very satisfied of its true identity. This was based upon the spirit having a specific number of dogs (six) and being able to spell out its name on the board. So far, so good. But when the lady graciously offered the opportunity for other spirits present to come forward and communicate with somebody at the board, none of us were prepared for what happened next.

Following a hesitant series of questions, a young lady who was attending with her husband began to quietly weep as she became convinced that the spirits of her dead mother and father were speaking to her through the Ouija board. The answer to each question validated her belief further and further, and there seemed to be no "misses."

I must confess to being a little disappointed that no messages came through the board for me. Truth be told, I was hoping that my dear old mum would snatch this opportunity to visit and nag me a little, as she did when I was growing up! But I'm not quite selfish enough to wish the opportunity to get emotional closure out of somebody else's hands in order to satisfy my own desires.

With each successive "hit", the skeptical part of my brain was screaming that this lady and her husband must be a plant. But if that was the case (and I do not think that it was) then she must have been a professional grade actress.

"Where you been, Mum?" she sobbed. "You'd promised you'd be back long before now. Let me talk to Dad."

The English football team had suffered a pretty brutal defeat a few days beforehand. Although I'm not much of a sports fan, there was no way to avoid this news because it was splashed all over the newspapers, the Internet, and television news. This loss was a big deal.

"Dad, did you see the football?" she asked. The Ouija board began to slowly spell out the letters S—H —I—

Just as the glass hit the letter "T", the entire group exploded in a fit of laughter that must have been heard on the other side of the River Thames. Best of all, the female investigator's tears had transformed from those of sadness to tears of absolute joy.

"That's *exactly* what he would have said!"

The atmosphere instantly lightened, no longer feeling oppressive and dark. Communication between the girl and her parents wrapped up just five minutes later, as if all the energy in the room had suddenly drained away. We all felt *tired,* and not just because it was coming up on three o'clock in the morning.

As the crew all congregated in the coffin room for one final wrap up, I found my mind picking over the Ouija episode. On the one hand, the simplest explanation would be that the two ladies were acting for an audience, for a motive known only to themselves. But I pride myself on having become a pretty good judge of character over the years. Paramedics get lied to *a lot,* and so tend to develop finely honed BS detectors. And mine *wasn't* going off. Either these ladies were terrific actresses, or they genuinely believed in the validity of their experiences.

Could they have perhaps been delusional? Possibly. And yet, the specificity of some of the hits argued against this explanation, to my mind. Six is a very specific and somewhat unusual number of dogs to have, for example. Who on Earth would accurately guess that somebody had *six* dogs? Why not four, five, or seven? They're all equally large numbers in terms that most people would consider normal. Anything above two or three would make for an unusual and unlikely guess.

As our exhausted and yet strangely exhilarated group trooped out into the warm darkness of a gray London Sunday morning, we cheerily said our farewells and thank-yous. I hailed a black cab to take me back to my hotel, across the city at Heathrow Airport. As the historic landmarks of this much-loved capital city flashed by in the light of sunrise, my brain just would not switch off.

In retrospect, the events of that Saturday night spent inside England's oldest prison still fascinate me.

Looking back in the cold light of day, some of the experiences and phenomena raise more questions than answers.

Table tipping, glass spelling, and Ouija boards are believed by many to be an effective means of communicating with the dead, whether it is the spirit of a dead stranger or that of a guide or guardian. One only has to review the literature of the paranormal dating back to the Nineteenth Century, in order to find some compelling anecdotal evidence that supports this position.

On the other hand, skeptics believe that they have found a more mundane explanation. Ideomotor muscular activity – the capability of a person's muscles to move apparently of their own accord, without signals being *consciously* sent from the brain – is said to be the cause. The electrical pioneer Michael Faraday was one of the first scientists to discover this phenomenon, when investigating table tipping in 1852. Modern day skeptics attribute the messages delivered by Ouija boards and glasses, plus the tipping of tables, to this fascinating physiologic effect.

Personally, I'm not so sure. I think that the jury is still out. I can state with absolute certainty that I was not consciously tilting the table or helping to spell out messages on the boards we used. Nor do I have reason to question the integrity of my fellow prisoners in The Clink. Not the slightest hint of suspicious activity or trickery reared its head during the night, and believe me, I was *looking* for it.

Perhaps most intriguing of all is the final séance, during which the spirit of a lady's father seemed to come through and manifest several meaningful messages on the Ouija board. The lady absolutely believed that she was in the presence of her dead father, as the tears streaming down her face would attest. When the board spelled out the word "SHIT" in response to her question about the recent football game, she told us joyfully that this was *exactly* what her dad would have said under the circumstances. So, she and her husband were both utterly convinced by the Ouija session. I found it to be a very moving experience, and I must confess to a little disappointment that none of my own dead friends and relatives made an appearance.

Being jailed in the Clink for the evening had raised more questions than it answered.

CHAPTER FIFTEEN

AFTERWORD

I do hope that you have enjoyed these case files from my two decades of hunting ghosts and trying to separate fact from folklore. You will probably have noticed that, contrary to some of the popular reality TV shows out there, not every case ends with a spectacular piece of evidence for me to reveal to the client. The reality of paranormal investigation is similar to that of my professional field of emergency work in one regard: ninety percent boredom, ten percent sheer adrenaline!

The BCPRS casebook is continuing to fill up, accruing new files with each passing month. Our workload is busier than ever. Having just reached forty years of age, I am hopeful that the next twenty years will allow me the opportunity of investigating even more intriguing cases on both sides of the Atlantic. Although it has been said that the British and the Americans are two peoples separated by a common language, it has been my experience that they are united in a mutual love for a great ghost story.

I began my journey as an avowed skeptic. Looking back with the benefit of twenty/twenty hindsight, I believe that I was being unreasonably closed minded. "Skeptic" is a word that gets a bad rap in the paranormal community these days, precisely because it *is* associated with individuals who simply refuse to entertain the possibility that the paranormal might exist, no matter what testimony is presented before them.

I can see both sides of this debate. On the one hand is the very reasonable concept that "extraordinary claims require extraordinary evidence." If even a fraction of the paranormal encounters that are reported around the world on a daily basis should turn out to be true, the scientific applecart is going to be upset and a whole lot of textbooks will have to be rewritten.

But on the other hand, the sheer volume of eyewitness testimony leads any remotely dispassionate observer to conclude that *something* bizarre is going on, and has been doing so since the dawn of recorded human history. No less a distinguished source than the Roman scholars gave us a blood curdling ghost story regarding a murdered man and the villa which he haunted. If *just one* of the ghostly encounters you have ever read about (or personally experienced, perhaps) happens out to be real, then the scientific community has been ignoring or scoffing at one of the most important human experiences that we could possibly imagine.

In the truest sense of the word (the one that I have embraced) the term *skeptic* simply means "show me the evidence." Police officers and scientists alike will freely tell you that human eyewitness accounts are often the least reliable form of evidence found during a criminal prosecution. What the human eye *thinks* that it sees is not always the same as what it actually does see, and the same is true of memory recall. Numerous cases exist in the records of law enforcement in which eyewitness testimony from multiple credible observers is contradicted by camera footage. The eye and the memory can both lie, it is true.

But are we truly to believe that every recorded instance of a ghostly encounter, which now run into the hundreds of thousands (if not millions) is a mistake, a self-delusion, or outright fraud on the part of the observer? If so, we must include Abraham Lincoln and Winston Churchill to the list of those who suffered from such flights of fancy. Leaving his own ghostly experiences aside, Lincoln's shade appeared to Churchill when the British Prime Minister was enjoying a bath while guesting at the White House. The great president was said to have met Churchill's gaze, before slowly fading away into nothingness.

I do sometimes wonder whether I might have dedicated the last eighteen years of my ghost hunting career to a wild goose chase. But if that should turn out to be the case, there are millions of good people who have shared that same boat with me over the years. This is not a doubt that I seriously entertain, however. My encounters with the paranormal have led me to believe that there is indeed a realm beyond that of the ordinary human senses, some kind of area in which the dead and disembodied can occasionally interact and communicate with us if the circumstances allow.

As I grow older, I find my approach to paranormal investigation becoming a little less hidebound. My experiences at The Clink prison museum have sparked an interest in alternative research techniques that I would like to pursue on future cases.

At the heart of it all, though, is the mission of the Boulder County Paranormal Research Society to help those who are afraid inside their own homes. For as long as we are able, my team of enthusiastic and dedicated investigators will stand ready to go into those places where people live in fear.

CHAPTER SIXTEEN

BREATHLESS AT WAVERLY HILLS

Some haunted buildings have permeated the public consciousness so thoroughly that even their shape, outline, or silhouette has become instantly recognizable. Stop a random passer-by in the street to show them a photograph of the infamous "Amityville Horror" house, for example, and their eyes will more likely than not widen in instant recognition at the glowing windows which look so much like a malevolent pair of eyes. (This is the main reason why a past owner of the house took those windows out).

The twenty-first century equivalent of the Amityville House could easily be the foreboding edifice of the Waverly Hills Sanatorium, nestled out of sight in the Kentucky countryside. Nowadays, one can hardly switch on a paranormal TV show without there being an episode filmed at Waverly Hills. More than one visitor has described the sanatorium's wings stretching out from the central building like two grasping arms, as if to enfold the unwary visitor in their clutches.

Waverly Hills may appear run-down and derelict today, but during its heyday, the sanatorium was praised for being the very model of medical modernity (try saying that three times in a row!), a state-of-the-art facility designed to cope with Kentucky's huge and expanding population of tuberculosis patients. The sheer volume of sufferers had overwhelmed the smaller facility which once occupied the same site.

Built in 1910, the original sanatorium could handle just forty patients, and its capacity was soon swamped. Contrast this with the building which replaced it: what we still call Waverly Hills Sanatorium was completed in 1926 and came equipped with 435 beds – a more than tenfold increase in capacity. That capacity was sorely needed, for the county was hit brutally hard by the tuberculosis outbreak – most likely because of the swampy nature of the land, which makes it an ideal breeding ground in which the insidious bacterial infection could hide and fester.

Pulmonary tuberculosis is capable of sneaking up on a sufferer like few other diseases. Night sweats and chills come first, often accompanied by a lethargic weakness and general malaise, all of which the infected patient often tended to write off to whichever current nondescript seasonal sickness happened to be making the rounds. Coughing up phlegm suggested some sort of chest infection, but still wasn't necessarily a cause for the patient to visit the doctor — especially if they couldn't afford it.

The unexplained weight loss could be a little more concerning, but what could definitely not be ignored was when the afflicted individual began to hack up blood from fulminating, frothy lungs. At this point, the disease was firmly entrenched within the chest, and the prognosis was often grim.

Tuberculosis patients, it was decided by the local health authorities, needed to be segregated from the general patient population and given care which addressed their specific needs.

Treatment boiled down to one major thing: fresh air, and lots of it. Bitingly cold winds were allowed to howl through the facility during the winter months. Patients were left either outside or with windows wide open, to suffer the indignities of the elements such as rain, snow, and frost, in the hopes of curing their lungs with regular infusions of fresh, clean air. At Waverly Hills, their beds were often pulled out onto a balcony known as a solarium. Not such a bad thing during the summer months, but extremely unpleasant once the weather turned cold.

Bed rest was mandatory, often for months at a time. Death from hypothermia was a common and predictable result of being exposed to the outdoors, although the nurses at Waverly Hills kept a close eye on their patients in order to minimize the likelihood of this happening.

Other attempted cures were a little more exotic in nature. If the tuberculosis had progressed into the patient's larynx, doctors attempted to combat it by reflecting the rays of the sun onto their throat with mirrors. Although we tend to think of tuberculosis as being a pulmonary disease (restricted to the lungs and the respiratory system) it can also infect the bowel and gastrointestinal tract, not to mention the brain and other bodily organs. Physicians at Waverly Hills dealt with such cases by using mercury-powered ultraviolet lights, focusing the UV rays against the abdomen, in conjunction with still more high-dose fresh air and sunlight.

Advanced cases of tuberculosis received more aggressive treatment. Patients were made to lie on the most infected side, the idea being to prevent the lung from expanding too far, and therefore allow it to rest. A similar goal was behind the "shot bag method," where a pound of buckshot was put in a bag and hung over the patient's clavicles. A few ounces were added each week, until the unfortunate patient was walking around with up to ten pounds of iron shot pushing down on his or her chest. One can only imagine how uncomfortable this must have felt. If all else failed, there was one final resort: invasive surgery. One such method was to induce an artificial pneumothorax by inserting a tube through the chest wall and injecting air into the chest, building up enough pressure to collapse the infected lung and (it was hoped) allow it to heal. Another was to cut the phrenic nerve, which controls the expansion and contraction of the diaphragm, our main muscle of respiration. And lastly, the ribs themselves could be cut apart and removed on the affected side. This particular operation was high-risk, and one which not all patients would survive.

The war against tuberculosis continued to rage inside the walls of the Waverly Hills Sanatorium throughout the late 1920s and all through the 1930s and 1940s, a war which was also being fought throughout many other sanatoriums and healthcare facilities across the United States.

In 1943 there came a breakthrough, with the advent of new antibiotic drugs which could deal with tuberculosis far more effectively than the other treatment methods used up to that point. Streptomycin was now leading the charge against tuberculosis and other infectious diseases, and it began to look as though places such as Waverly Hills had had their day. In the summer of 1961, the facility closed its doors for the final time as a sanatorium. The building was swiftly repurposed as a retirement home for senior citizens, catering to a large percentage of residents who had behavioral illnesses such as Alzheimer's. It served in this capacity for another twenty years; allegations and rumors of patient neglect contributed to it being closed down by the State of Kentucky in 1982.

Passing into the hands of private developers, the Waverly Hills site languished despite a number of proposed new uses. Plans for conversion into a prison were nixed when developers realized that none of the locals wanted one on their doorstep. Another scheme, this time to construct the world's largest statue of Jesus Christ, fell through when the projected multi-million-dollar financing required to fund it failed to reach even five thousand dollars in donations.

The sanatorium and its surrounding buildings all languished, but their salvation would come from a most unlikely source – for nobody had factored the resident ghosts of Waverly Hills into the equation.

Death was a commonplace, everyday part of life at the sanatorium. Tuberculosis is a cruel disease, and can often be fatal, particularly when the proper treatment tools are unavailable. Thousands of people did not leave the sanatorium alive. Much has been made of the high death toll experienced at Waverly Hills. During an interview, one of the owners, Charlie Mattingly, weighed in with his own personal opinion during an interview:

"So, you're talking somewhere around the 18,000 to 20,000 (people) that actually died here and when you think about that much death in one place how could there not be some type of residual spirit of some sort left by somebody, someone who was here before," said Mattingly.

Quite understandably, the doctors and nurses believed that it would be bad for the morale of the surviving patients to see an almost constant parade of dead bodies being wheeled past them on gurneys, on their way out to the undertaker. So, the body chute was devised as a means of bringing some privacy to this macabre but necessary duty — or so it was said.

One of the most terrifying (but equally fascinating) ghosts to inhabit the halls of Waverly Hills Sanatorium is the doppelgänger. In paranormal folklore, the doppelgänger is a term for encountering the apparition of yourself, while you are still alive. Sometimes the doppelgänger is seen by others who mistake it for the actual living person themselves. The few instances of this type of haunting which are recorded in the case files of the paranormal are genuinely eerie, particularly when one considers that the doppelgänger is often regarded as being a harbinger of death.

Paranormal investigator and Waverly tour guide Mike Flickner related his own experience with a doppelgänger to TV host Zak Bagans on the TV show *Ghost Adventures*. While giving a tour of the Sanatorium, Flickner had separated several groups of guests onto different floors of the building, moving between the floors as necessary.

He recalled that the group located down on the third floor seemed to be less than pleased to see him when he arrived at their location after leaving the fifth floor:

"They said, 'You came down here just five minutes ago. You took two steps towards us, then you turned away from us, walked down two doors, then went out onto the Solarium and was hiding from us.' I told them, 'I swear to you, that was *NOT* me.'"

More frightening than the doppelgänger is the apparition known to staff and visitors alike simply as "the Creeper." This is a shadowy figure which lurks on the upper floors of the building, particularly the fourth floor. The Creeper has been seen numerous times by multiple independent witnesses, ducking in and out of the derelict patient rooms, but the most sinister aspect of the Creeper is his (or should we say its) ability to crawl along the walls and ceilings of the old, abandoned corridors.

Many tour guides and visitors at Waverly have experienced a diverse range of physical phenomena. This ranges from the relatively benign (the sensation of an unseen somebody holding their hand when walking through the rooms and corridors) to the downright nasty, such as the case of the guide who was physically thrust out of his chair by a powerful, invisible force.

Headaches are commonplace within the building, sometimes accompanied by aches and pains throughout the body – the chest and areas around the lungs seem to be a particular "favorite" region in which to hurt.

Unfortunately, many of the stories about Waverly Hills that are circulating around the paranormal community have little or no basis in fact. I doubt that these were attempts to actively deceive. Some are simply tales that grew in the telling, half-truths and urban legends that have managed to take on a life of their own.

A good case in point is the purported death toll. As mentioned previously, Charlie Mattingly cited a figure of 18,000 to 20,000. Entering this question into a search engine yields wildly differing results.

One 2017 article bears the headline, "The haunted hospital where 63,000 people died." A 2021 article states, "It's believed that nearly 50,000 people died here." Neither piece of writing, of course, contains any data to support this contention.

Fortunately, two of my good friends, authors Shannon Byers and Troy Taylor have actually done their homework. Both are credible researchers who have worked to actively dispel some of the myths surrounding the world's most famous haunted sanatorium. Taylor quotes former Waverly Hills assistant medical director Dr. Frank Stewart's statement that the maximum number of deaths to occur in one single year was 152. For most years, the number was significantly lower, sometimes dropping down to less than fifty. Taylor concludes that no more than 6,000 people are likely to have died there during its operational lifetime.

In conjunction with a fellow researcher named Pam, Shannon Byers set out to track down the death certificates of every patient that ever died within the walls of Waverly Hills. (You can read about this, and much more, in Shannon's excellent book, *Paranormal Fakelore, Nevermore*). Their project was still a work in progress at the time of publication, but her predicted number agrees with Troy Taylor's: somewhere around 6,000. This means that, when it comes to certain media portrayals, the number of deaths at Waverly Hills has been inflated by a factor of ten — an entire order of magnitude. Byers lists the highest number of fatalities to happen in any given year to be tied between 1945 and 1946, both of which saw 162 patient deaths at the sanatorium.

The evidence shows that, for most of the years that Waverly Hills was actively treating tuberculosis patients, an average of two patients died each week — sometimes three. This means that, despite the gross exaggerations which still persist in some quarters, several thousand people drew their last breath inside this magnificent old building. Small wonder, then, that some of them may still remain after all these years.

Other frequently told stories about the sanatorium focus upon the fifth floor, one of the more active areas. One tale relates the death of a nurse, believed by some to have committed suicide in Room 502, sometime between the 1920s and the 1940s. Her lifeless body was supposedly found hanging from a pipe by the maintenance man when he emerged from the elevator, presumably getting the shock of his life. The story goes that this particular nurse was pregnant, in an era when there was a great deal of stigma to bearing a child out of wedlock.

A variation on this tale holds that the nurse had been diagnosed with tuberculosis herself, and was haunted by the possibility of passing it on to her unborn child. Attending to so many patients on a daily basis who were afflicted by the disease and seeing at firsthand what a painful death could follow, must have preyed on the poor woman's mind. But the story takes an even more lurid and distasteful turn when one factors in the rumor that the father of the unborn child was said to be one of the higher-ups at Waverly Hills, who attempted to perform an abortion on site and ended up accidentally killing the mother along with the baby. According to the guides who went on record with *Ghost Adventures,* the aborted fetus was found in the water system on the fifth floor.

Room 502 is also claimed to be the scene of another fatal tragedy relating to the sanatorium staff: a nurse allegedly leaped to her death some five floors below — although some versions of the story suggest that she may have been pushed.

I asked another friend about the stories. She has given tours at Waverly Hills and knows the building and its history well. Her comments were interesting, and reflect conversations with former employees of the sanatorium.

"One nurse jumped or was pushed from a window on the fifth floor," she told me. "As for the other nurse (this has been pieced together from EVPs from different teams) her name is Sarah, and she was raped by an orderly. The situation was staged to make it look like she hung herself, then a story was fabricated about her being pregnant and having committed suicide. Sarah was found outside Room 502. The rope was hung from an old pipe that is no longer there, due to renovations in later years. She was never hanged *in* Room 502."

I still have a hard time getting past the idea that a nurse taking her own life at Waverly Hills would not have made it into the newspaper, whether suicide or not. Regarding the supposedly true story being told by EVPs, I have never heard any of them personally, and the reader is invited to make up their own mind as to the reliability of this method of gleaning information. As with so many aspects of the paranormal, one's individual mileage will vary.

Shannon Byers also challenges the veracity of the hanging story. She has trawled through year upon year, decade upon decade's worth of local newspapers, and has found not a shred of evidence to support the contention of a nurse hanging herself on the fifth floor. She rightly points out the variability and vagueness of the dates provided (1920s through 1940s) and notes that this is the sort of story that would have almost certainly garnered some column inches in the paper... but it never has.

The same is true of the stories regarding the nurse supposedly falling to her death. Again, I am unaware of even a trace of objective evidence on which to base this story, either in the newspaper archives or the Waverly Hills death certificates. Shannon is a thorough and meticulous researcher. She has done an excellent job in cutting through the layers of folklore (or, as she terms it, fakelore) surrounding a number of the country's most iconic haunted locations. As she likes to tell people, telling the truth about the people who lived and sometimes died in a place is the best way to honor their memory. The reverse is also true. If a story has no provable truth to it, it can become both disrespectful and damaging.

If the reader can point to any concrete evidence which supports these accounts, I will be only too happy to revise my opinion, and also to share the information publicly.

It *is* true, however, that there were a number of violent deaths at the sanatorium. In 1954, a fight broke out between three of the employees, which ended when one of them stamped on the head and chest of his prostrate colleague. The wounded man subsequently died of an intracranial bleed. This *did* make the newspapers. There was also an accidental electrocution, which proved fatal.

Of course, the magic question remains: is Waverly Hills really haunted? Author Troy Taylor certainly needs no convincing. He visited the sanatorium on a dark and stormy (yes, really!) night in 2002. He heard the sounds of doors slamming, seemingly of their own accord — Troy insists that there was no way the wind could have been responsible, as this took place deep within the bowels of the building.

So far, so intriguing, but what really blew Troy's mind was his sighting of a figure in what appeared to be a white doctor's coat, walking directly across his field of vision. This took place on the fourth floor, and the mysterious figure was going into a room to which there was only one entrance and exit. When he looked, the room was, of course, empty. Nevertheless, Taylor and his friend searched the entire floor, to rule out the possibility of a human intruder.

They were all alone.

What he experienced on the fourth floor of the sanatorium was the paranormal investigator's holy grail: unless it was an extremely vivid hallucination, then Troy caught sight of nothing less than a full-fledged apparition. I know people who have spent an entire career in the field without being treated to something like that.

I could only hope to experience something as mind-blowing when I was given access to Waverly Hills myself.

Until the arrival of the TV ghost hunters, Waverly Hills was a relatively well-kept open secret in the paranormal field. Once it began to appear on TV shows, however, interest in Waverly Hills as a haunted hotspot simply exploded.

During their twenty-four-hour lockdown in the sprawling sanatorium, Zak Bagans and his *Ghost Adventures* crew claimed to have experienced quite a bit of unusual activity. Although some of their EVPs were of questionable quality, the disembodied moans and sighs which they recorded during the early hours of the morning are rather interesting.

Perhaps their most intriguing piece of evidence came from the third floor, where a locked-off full-spectrum video camera recorded the stunning sight of a black figure emerging from one room, advancing down the hallway, before disappearing into a different room. Analysis of the footage showed what appeared to be a distinct head with long hair, and upon closer inspection, a second figure crossing the hallway behind the first. Could this be the mysterious Creeper, caught on film for the first time?

Zak Bagans and his team are far from the only media investigators to spend a night at Waverly Hills and roll their cameras on an overnight investigation. The Atlantic Paranormal Society (TAPS) actually beat them to the punch, filming episode fourteen of their second season at the sanatorium in March of 2006, returning with a much longer live ghost hunt for their 2007 Halloween special, before returning in 2011.

Not to be outdone, Yvette Fielding and her team from the British ghost hunting show *Most Haunted* also spent the night at Waverly Hills during the American run of their series. Resident parapsychologist Professor Ciaran O'Keeffe did manage to successfully debunk the movement of a ball in between patient rooms, figuring out that a subtle dip in the floor was the most likely culprit. But he was unable to offer a convincing non-paranormal explanation for the remainder of the ghostly activity that is said to take place at this monolithic, run-down old sanatorium.

It is not my intent to weigh the pros and cons of shows such as *Ghost Adventures, Most Haunted,* et al, right here. Suffice it to say that both shows have their fans, and both have their detractors. It certainly cannot be denied that paranormal "reality" television has served to raise the profile of historic locations like Waverly Hills. Without the publicity — some would say notoriety — that has arisen as a result, and the consequent flood of paying visitors, it would be difficult, if not impossible, for the owners and custodians to keep the lights on. Paranormal tourism is a double-edged sword, to be sure, but without it, a lengthy list of places would have long since fallen into disrepair and ruin.

To be clear, I have no issue with locations charging rental fees so that visitors can investigate. It's a concrete way to help support them and preserve the properties for future generations. Banding together with some fellow Coloradoan investigators, we came up with the $1,000 fee to hire Waverly Hills for one night. That might seem like a lot of cash (and it is) but you get a whole lot of square footage for your money, and it's well worth it to get the full run of the place.

Our small team flew out from Denver early on a summer's morning, before picking up a pair of hire cars and checking into a motel in Louisville. After grabbing some much-needed sleep, we made the drive to what had become a bucket list location for everybody.

The drive was a pleasant one, passing through small towns and miles of rural countryside. They do love their churches in Kentucky; we seemed to pass one every few miles. Finally, we arrived at our destination,turning off the road onto a long and winding paved road named Paralee Lane, which was enclosed with trees on either side. The sun was still fairly high in the sky as late afternoon gave way to early evening, and the air was hot and humid.

We rolled to a stop a few feet away from a metal barrier which blocked the road. On it were painted the words 24 HOUR VIDEO SURVEILLANCE, ON SITE SECURITY, and NO PARKING. I checked my watch. We were a few minutes early. The sense of anticipation inside our car was palpable. I could only imagine it was exactly the same in the other vehicle that made up our small convoy.

Our small group passed the time in idle chit chat. Finally, after what seemed like a lifetime but was in actuality just a few minutes, our guide arrived, right on time. She unlocked the barrier and raised it, then secured it behind us. After a short drive, we emerged from the shadow of the trees into golden sunlight again, and there she was, the grand old lady herself — Waverly Hills Sanatorium.

The building was every bit as awe-inspiring in real life as I had hoped it would be. A little run-down and dilapidated it may have been, but there was a certain indefinable dignity and gravitas to the monolithic structure that truly has to be experienced to be believed. Parking our cars, we got out and walked toward the sanatorium, nothing less than awestruck. I could hardly believe I was actually *here* after all these years. This truly was a dream come true, and I was tempted to pinch myself to prove it was real.

I stood there for a moment, just taking it all in. Many of the windows had been busted out, or were boarded up with plywood. I made a slow circuit, trying not to miss a single detail. A rusty fire escape was attached to the end of one wing, though the lowest flight of steps had been removed — no doubt as a means of keeping trespassers out.

Craning my neck to look up, I could see a line of four gargoyles perched on top of four separate pillars, looking down on the building and its grounds below.

We congregated at the entrance and our guide kindly took a group picture for us. Then we sign waivers, basically agreeing that we will comport ourselves with some degree of decorum, and not hold the owners liable if something goes wrong. That all seems fair enough. Everybody signs with a flourish, eager to get acquainted with the sanatorium.

Over the space of the following hour or so, we were given a guided tour of the building. To be honest, it turned out to be something of a double-edged sword. On the one hand, our guide really knew her stuff, and obviously had a lot of passion for Waverly Hills. The orientation was also good for team safety, always a good thing when you're creeping around an unfamiliar building in the dark. On the other hand, we only had access to the building for eight hours, and the walk through ate into our valuable investigation time.

By the time the tour was over, the shadows of the trees were growing long on the grass outside. Waverly Hills is enclosed by trees, which leads to a sense of genuine isolation. However, even though we were in the twilight hour, it wasn't a particularly eerie feeling.

The walk through had given us all a new appreciation for just how big this place was. Although the sanatorium was designed and constructed in a methodical and commonsense way, it's still something of a maze in there, and I quickly learned that one of the best ways to navigate inside the building was to use the exterior windows and balconies as reference points.

With the majority of her task now done, our guide waved us goodbye and left us to it. We wouldn't see her again for several more hours. The last of the day was fading outside, orange fingers of sunlight spearing through the leaves and branches as the sun began to set...and then, just like that, we were all alone inside one of the world's most haunted places.

"Alright." My colleague, Jason, clapped his hands together and rubbed them eagerly. "Let's get set up." He and his wife, Linda, had brought an arsenal of equipment along with them that wouldn't look out of place in Q's lab in a James Bond movie. They were both very tech-driven, which was no bad thing. We didn't have a sensitive or medium along on this particular trip, so most of our focus would be on recording, measuring, and experiencing whatever we could personally.

The team dispersed in order to run cables, set up cameras and recorders. Waverly Hills is so big, there's no way we could possibly have covered even half the square footage. The place could easily have accommodated a team of fifty, without any of them stepping on each other's toes. There were just nine of us. The flip side of this relatively small team size was the fact that we would find it much easier to reduce noise contamination. Splitting into two or three small groups, we could head to different floors and the opposite ends of the building, secure in the knowledge that the others wouldn't hear a thing.

We got the cameras and mics up and running just in time for nightfall. Although things started to cool off a little when the sun went down, it was still hot and humid. There was obviously no air conditioning, and very little in the way of a breeze stirred the leaves. This was one of those nights when an icy draft of wind or a cold spot would be welcome in more ways than one! Already, our clothes were beginning to stick to our bodies as sweat began to dry. I ran a hand through my hair, which was so slick, I might have just gotten out of the shower.

I walked out onto the second-floor balcony, leaning against one of the vertical supports. The first evening stars were already out, and I took a moment to just experience the place for the first time. Closing my eyes, I cleared my mind and tried to simply *be*. to exist in the moment. The night is still and quiet, save for the sound of crickets and cicadas in the grass below.

After the steady diet of TV shows and stories from fellow paranormal investigators who had been to Waverly Hills before me, I was ready for the place to have been a hotbed of haunting activity. If that was indeed the case, it hadn't started yet. Everything felt still and peaceful. If it wasn't for the heat and humidity, I could quite easily have curled up in a folding chair and drifted off to sleep.

Going from floor to floor, I wandered from patient room to patient room. I felt a sense of kinship with the dedicated medicos who had staffed this place, tending to the sick and the dying while at the same time being afraid of contracting tuberculosis themselves. The sanatorium didn't feel like a place of nightmare and horror to me — in fact, quite the opposite. In a weird way, I almost felt as if I belonged there, on some level. A completely subjective feeling, I know, but it grew stronger as the evening wore on.

I lingered for a while in a room which had once belonged to a patient named Lois Higgs. Using a flashlight, I carefully examined a monochrome photograph of Lois that was taken during her time at the sanatorium. Dark haired and beautiful, she was seen to be sitting on the brick balcony outside the room. Behind her, I could see the opposite wing of the sanatorium as it arched away into the distance. Lois wore a shirt and blouse of the 1950s style, and bore an anxious expression which really tugged at my heartstrings. There was such a sadness on her face, it brought a tear to my eye. What must it have felt like, I wondered, to live here in the full knowledge that many of the residents did not survive the disease which was attacking their lungs? Doubtless she would have seen both friends and strangers die, and had gone to sleep at night hearing the sounds of hacking coughs echoing along the hallway.

Another picture showed Lois standing on the same balcony alongside another woman, who was presumably a friend, and a third captured her resting in bed. In none of the three photographs was she smiling.

Lois's story is particularly tragic. She was married with children, and by all accounts led a happy family life...until she contracted tuberculosis. The 27-year-old was admitted to Waverly Hills in 1955, in an attempt to cure the disease. Despite the best efforts of the doctors and nursing staff, TB killed her. She died on August 18, 1956, aged just 28.

It has become something of a tradition for visitors to the sanatorium to leave flowers in Lois's room as a mark of respect. I wished that I had known that before I arrived, because I had no tokens of remembrance to leave for her. Instead, I just sat in the darkness of her room and spoke softly, offering messages of support and condolence. My voice recorder was running at my side. When I played back the audio file later, no voices other than my own had been picked up. A number of people have gotten EVPs in Lois's room, but I was not privileged to be one of them.

Unbeknownst to me, while I was sitting quietly, my wife Laura was having her own strange experience. She had been exploring one of the lower floors, and then began working her way up. As she climbed the inner staircase, she clearly heard the sound of footsteps coming from behind her. She stopped. After three or four seconds, so did the footsteps. She shone her flashlight down toward the source of the noise. There was nobody there. Puzzled, she resumed climbing again. The footsteps followed suit. She stopped, and once again, so did they.

When she told me about this odd occurrence, I was tempted to simply write it off as an odd acoustic anomaly. Large old buildings such as Waverly Hills can do very strange things to sound, things that are not remotely paranormal. In an attempt to debunk it, I accompanied her back to the staircase and had her descend, then repeat her climb. This time, there was only a single set of footsteps — hers.

"Looks like somebody was taking an interest in you," I tell her, earning myself a single raised eyebrow in return.

We file this one under "unexplained, and intriguing," and move on.

Laura has been a lifelong fan of vintage era music. Her iTunes library was crammed full of songs from the 1920s through the 1950s. She decided to put it to good use by playing a few tunes which would have been in vogue during the sanatorium's heyday. Setting her phone down in one of the doorways, she soon had the strains of Cole Porter and Al Jolson echoing through the long-abandoned hallways and rooms of Waverly Hills. It really did seem fitting, and before long, she was waltzing through the darkness, dancing with an imaginary partner and humming along with the music. I suspected that gramophone players might have been popular back in the day, a way of taking the patients' minds off their woes with a little soothing music.

After ten minutes, silence returned to the sanatorium. "I hope you enjoyed the music," Laura told whoever might have been listening. I couldn't speak for the spirits of Waverly Hills, but I most certainly had.

We took a short break, then set out to explore a different part of the building. So much has been said and written about the infamous tunnel, more popularly known by its ominous nicknames of "the death tunnel" or "the body chute," that it has garnered a lot of attention
over the years.

The team was eager to experience it for ourselves, so four of us headed over there while the others went to explore the upper floors. It's fair to say that, if there was one part of Waverly Hills that felt somewhat unnerving, this was it. Stepping past the heavy door and standing at the top of the shaft, which sloped downward at a surprisingly steep angle, felt very much like we were walking into the opening reel of a horror movie.

It didn't help that we couldn't see the bottom of the chute, which was shrouded in darkness. The team began the long trek downward, treading carefully in order to keep our footing. We were surrounded by concrete and cement, our voices echoing off into the distance each time somebody spoke.

I ran a hand along the side wall as we descended. My fingertips came away damp. The air inside the tunnel was even more oppressive and humid than it was upstairs. Unfortunately, trespassers had defaced the walls with graffiti, showing a massive amount of disrespect to the facility and its history. It was such a shame to see.

Suddenly, there came a *fltfltfltfltflt* sound, followed by a blood-curdling shriek. I felt something disturb the air just inches from my left ear. Laura let out a string of profanities that put us all instantly on edge.

"What is it?" I wanted to know.

"Bat," said my colleague, Seth. A flying rodent had zipped up from somewhere beneath us in the tunnel, almost smacking Laura in the face as it whooshed past her head. I didn't blame her in the slightest for being startled. It's not every day that you end up in such close quarters with a bat, though it is an occupational hazard when you spend nights in as many old and abandoned buildings as we do.

Laura took a moment to slow her pounding heart, then we resumed our descent. The tunnel seemed to go on for miles, though in reality it was somewhere between four hundred and five hundred feet long.

We finally reached the bottom. Sitting down on the relatively cool concrete floor, we set about running an EVP session, clustering around a digital voice recorder. Kira, Seth, Laura, and I all took turns calling out and asking questions, attempting to connect with somebody...with anybody. After running several different bursts and playing them back, however, we were disappointed to find that nobody seemed to want to talk to us.

After half an hour passed, we climbed back to the top of the chute. Other than the somewhat claustrophobic feeling that being enclosed had engendered, it hadn't felt particularly unusual in there. Knowing that the tunnel had sometimes been used to convey dead bodies might creep some people out, but it was important to remember that many rooms in the sanatorium had seen their fair share of death. What made the tunnel so special?

After reaching them on a walkie-talkie, we reconnected with our fellow investigators again and all met up with one another. They hadn't gotten much in the way of results on the upper floors. We traded, with them heading down to the tunnel while we headed up toward the roof.

Most of the rooms had been stripped bare over the years, lacking everything from plaster on the walls to panes in the window frames. The paint was chipped and flecks of it lay on the floor wherever we walked, testament to the fact that most of this building had been open to the elements for many years.

One room contained a child's blue ball, which we found sitting in the far corner. I wondered if it had been used to test the camber of the floor, or had simply been left as a plaything for any child spirits that might have been around.

We explored the third and fourth floors next. All was still and dark. Of the Creeper, one of Waverly Hills' most infamous reported spirits, there was absolutely no sign.

Up in Room 502, I was disappointed to find more graffiti, including an inverted pentagram that was doubtless sprayed on the wall by some wannabe occultist who broke into the place illegally. I had sympathy for the owners. Securing this place had to be an absolute nightmare, considering how big and isolated it was. The sanatorium's worldwide renown meant that there was never a shortage of those who were willing to chance their luck at getting arrested in exchange for the bragging rights of having trespassed there. Some of the vandals even left their names scrawled on doors — Bobby, Jeremy, Nikki...whoever you are, in the unlikely event that you're reading this, I'd like to let you know that you're all complete dicks.

EVP experiments on the upper floor, even the notorious 502, yielded nothing. We were all having a great time, simply *being* in that magnificent place, but it was shaping up to be one of the quieter nights of my paranormal career.

One room which captured everybody's imagination was, we were told by our guide, the former operating theater. A huge, green-stained metal lamp mounted on an armature dominated the room, accompanied by coiled strands of exposed wiring. Vines stretched in through some of the windows, Mother Nature exerting her influence over what was once the most modern tuberculosis treatment center in the United States. The present owners of Waverly Hills poured as much money as they could into restoring and preserving the place, but it was a truly Herculean task — and one that would take tens of millions of dollars to complete. I had sympathy for the sheer amount of work they had taken on, apparently undaunted by its vast scope. It is a battle that may never be won, though I truly hope that is not the case.

After snacks and some caffeinated beverages, we broke up into two different groups and dispersed ourselves throughout the building. The other group opted to spend time in the tunnel. It made sense for us to go to the fifth floor, to ensure that there would be no audio contamination between our two groups.

In the early hours of the morning, we climbed to the top of the building and did a few burst EVP sessions up there, paying particular attention to Room 502 — sadly to no effect. Then we made our way out onto the roof. It was a beautiful night, slightly cooler and with a sky full of brilliant, twinkling stars. The heat was beginning to dial down a little bit. It was sobering to thing that children had once run and played up here, five stories above the ground. The Waverly Hills staff had also taken their work breaks on the roof, enjoying the view and a bit of fresh air — which was once mistakenly regarded as a cure for tuberculosis.

Finally, a light breeze rustled through the trees. It felt blissful to stand there, letting it cool me off. I looked out over the treetops at the lights of civilization, and listened to the sound of insects surrounding us. My fellow investigators scattered to different parts of the fifth floor, each running an EVP session of their own. For my part, I just wanted to soak up the atmosphere and appreciate this place for what it was — a place of healing that, despite its fearsome reputation, deserved its place in American history for almost all of the right reasons.

After about an hour had passed, we went to rejoin the other group. Nothing discernible had happened in paranormal terms, but I felt incredibly grateful to be there, and was overwhelmed by a sense of peace and wellbeing that is hard to describe. I was more content and fulfilled than I could remember feeling in a long time. There was something about the atmosphere of Waverly Hills, something (dare I say it) almost magical.

As things turned out, our colleagues had experienced something rather puzzling. They had been making their way toward the tunnel, following the corridor which leads directly to it, when suddenly they had heard a voice coming from somewhere up ahead.

The voice was faint, but grew steadily louder as they approached the tunnel entrance. My team-mates couldn't make out what was being said, but they had no difficulty in recognizing the voice: it was mine. Not only did it have my accent, they said, but my tone, inflection, and cadence were all spot on.

"It sounded as if you were addressing a group of people," one of them told me. "It was coming from the far end of the tunnel, right down at the very bottom."

As soon as the team reached the entrance to the body chute and shone their flashlights down into the darkness, the voice immediately stopped speaking. It happened so fast, it was almost like a switch had been thrown. My friends went down into the tunnel, searching it to make absolutely sure nobody was there. It was completely empty.

"Where were you at the time?" they wanted to know.

"Up on the roof," I told them, "at the opposite end of the building." I didn't need to add that I had been in plain sight of several eyewitness throughout. None of them thought I was somehow able to fake the phenomenon — after all, how could I? Short of planting some kind of hidden speaker and broadcasting to it, I couldn't see how that would even have been possible.

Huddled together in a group, we tried to come up with a rational explanation...and failed. While it is true that sound carries further at night, it was simply incomprehensible to think that my voice could have carried from five stories up down to the bowels of Waverly Hills Sanatorium, let alone that it would have been loud enough for everyone to hear. I hadn't been speaking particularly loudly on the roof. Waverly Hills has an almost cathedral-like atmosphere, the sort of place which inclines one to a hushed whisper, as a mark of respect. Nobody had raised their voice all night. It just wouldn't have felt right.

Then there was the matter of my voice — if, indeed, it truly was my voice — shutting up the instant my colleagues came within sight. This sounded like a remarkably convenient piece of timing to me.

All of which begged the question: whose voice had my friends heard? As mentioned previously, the sanatorium is renowned for its doppelgängers and imitators. Could something down in that tunnel have decided to mimic me, or was something equally strange behind it all? Another theory floated was that of a time slip, a paranormal event in which the words of either past or future me were somehow sent either backwards or forwards in type. An outlandish hypothesis, you might think, and I wouldn't necessarily disagree...but is it really any stranger than the concept of some invisible entity playing games with its voice?

I didn't think so. The truth was, none of us had any idea what was behind the mysterious voice. Try as we might to debunk it, we were never able to satisfactorily explain this strange occurrence away. When our guide came to collect us a little while before sunrise, I let her know what had happened. She was completely unsurprised, and said that it would be added to the long list of inexplicable things which grew every week there at Waverly Hills.

● ● ● ● ● ● ● ● ● ●

It was a tired but happy group of paranormal investigators that finally piled into our hire cars. The sky was just beginning to lighten on the eastern horizon as we drove slowly down the long, tree-lined lane toward the main road. I couldn't help but turn around one last time and watch the mighty old building recede into the darkness behind us. So many lives had been lived, lost, but sometimes saved behind those imposing walls. I had expected the place to be intimidating, but instead, it had felt very much the opposite...warm and friendly, even welcoming.

We all agreed that it had been a wonderful investigation, and none of us would hesitate to go back if we were offered the chance.

There is a somewhat maudlin postscript to my Waverly Hills Sanatorium experience, one that I cannot help but share here.

It just so happened that, during a routine physical screening, my new employer ran a number of blood tests on me, as health care agencies are wont to do. One of the diagnostics is known as a quantiferon gold test. After being run twice, it came back positive both times. This particular test is the gold standard (if you will pardon the pun) for diagnosing the presence of... tuberculosis.

Sitting in my primary care provider's office, I experienced one of those surreal moments which we all get from time to time. The sense that our world has just changed in some significant way

I have been infected with tuberculosis.

The disease is latent, not active, I hasten to add. My chest X-rays are clear. I am not coughing up blood, waking up in the middle of the night drenched in sweat, and despite my best efforts, weight loss still eludes me. But the little bastard is undeniably there, lurking in my lungs.

Dormant.

Waiting.

It may stay that way for ever, sleeping its way through my life, until I finally die of something else, something completely unrelated. On the other hand, it may wake up some day. Hey, presto, you have pulmonary tuberculosis. If that day should ever come, I will be genuinely worried.

There are prophylactic medications to treat the condition, something which the doctors and nurses of Waverly Hills did not have in their own pharmacological arsenal. They were virtually powerless to help once the disease was entrenched in the lungs of their patients. Early twenty-first century medicine has treatment options that weren't around when Waverly Hills opened, in the age when tuberculosis ran rampant across the land. In every way measurable, I am better off, and have significantly better chances of not dying from TB than even the healthiest person back in the 1920s.

Still, it is a sobering thought. This thing, this invader, is slumbering within my body. Looking back, I almost certainly contracted it while delivering patient care as a paramedic. I have never exhibited any of the symptoms of active infection and, fingers and toes crossed, hopefully never shall. Nevertheless, in my capacity as a paranormal investigator, much like my role as a paramedic, there is a tendency to separate oneself from those whose stories I encounter.

In the world of medicine, students are cautioned to retain their sense of compassion and empathy, despite dealing with a multitude of different medical complaints each shift. The man in bed seven is not a "chest painer," and we should not refer to him as such; he is a father, brother, son, uncle, a human being, with hopes, dreams, aspirations, and fears, who just *happens* to be experiencing chest pain.

The lesson is timeless: never let the complaint overshadow the human that is afflicted with it. I now have an entirely new level of empathy for those who walked through the doorway of Waverly Hills Sanatorium, either in the hopes of being cared for, or those who used everything at their disposal in the one-sided battle against that insidious disease.

Bless each and every one of them.

CHAPTER SEVENTEEN
A QUIET NIGHT IN HELL

Arguably one of the most notorious and sought-after haunted locations in the United States, if not the world, has to be Bobby Mackey's Music World. Located in the sleepy town of Wilder, Kentucky and owned by a Country and Western singer, this roadhouse runs alongside the railroad tracks and abuts the nearby Licking River.

Bobby Mackey's owes much of its prominence as a haunted property to TV shows such as *Ghost Adventures*, which featured the place in their very first season. I'm therefore going to spend a little time discussing the episode, because I think it's fair to say that without the spotlight put on the case by host Zak Bagans and his colleagues, Bobby Mackey's Music World would not have the notoriety among paranormal enthusiasts that it does today.

In an interview with Bobby Mackey himself (who says he has a hard time believing many of the ghost stories that are told about his place) the singer claims that his wife distinctly heard a voice inside the building telling her to "get out!" She now refuses to step foot inside the nightclub.

One of the saddest stories connected with the nightclub is that of Carl Lawson, a friend of Bobby's and a former caretaker. Carl lived in a room upstairs for quite some time, and claimed to have experienced a constant parade of paranormal activity. He said that much of it was dark and malevolent in nature, such as the time an entity tried to drown him in his own bathtub. In order to cope, Carl would lock himself inside each night before going to sleep, and kept a loaded shotgun next to his bed; something that would not work particularly well against a ghost.

When asked by host Zak Bagans whether there was a demonic spirit at Bobby Mackey's Music World, Carl replied that there was more than one – there are many. He claimed to be awoken at six o'clock each morning by a stampede of phantom activity coming from downstairs in the main part of the nightclub.

It is said that Carl's behavior changed, in subtle ways at first, but finally reaching a point where he believed that he was possessed by a dark spirit. This resulted in a six hour-long exorcism being performed on him by a priest – a section of this ritual has been posted on YouTube, and the story has been written about by author Douglas Hensley. According to Hensley, in the aftermath of Carl's exorcism, one entire wall of the kitchen spontaneously burst into flames, requiring the fire department to respond and put it out.

The apparition of a male entity with a handlebar mustache has been reported in the men's restroom, of all places (he likes to throw the metal trashcan around) and bizarre electrical mishaps abound – such as the jukebox playing even when it isn't plugged in.

I have to confess that I'm not a particularly big fan of Country and Western music, but the song *Johanna* sits on my iPod and gets some regular playtime. It is Bobby Mackey's tribute to Johanna, a 1930s-era dancing girl whose lover – a man named Robert Randall – was supposedly murdered by her father when she became pregnant with his child out of wedlock. It's a catchy song, and even today evokes memories of my investigation at Bobby Mackey's Music World whenever I hear it. Some, including Carl Lawson, says that they have seen Johanna's apparition inside the building, and smelled rose perfume which they attribute to her.

In what has to be quite the coincidence, Bobby Mackey's mother named him "Robert Randall Mackey" when he was just one day old...a strange precursor to his connection with the nightclub in Wilder, Kentucky, that lay in Bobby's future.

The remnants of a well downstairs in the basement has been claimed by some to be a literal "gateway to hell," due to its association with a murder and decapitation which supposedly culminated in the victim's head being tossed down there. This claim does not bear up under scrutiny, as we shall soon see.

As Bagans and his colleagues are exploring the basement, they catch sight of what appears to them to be a shadow figure; this is a common report from that particular area of the building, and they were neither the first nor the last to report seeing it. It isn't long before the team claim to be hearing a female voice, upstairs on the dance floor, and posit that this may be the voice of Johanna. They record the sound of what Bagans believes to be a woman crying, followed by that of a man humming or singing (again, this is Bagans' interpretation, not mine).

The *Ghost Adventures* crew begin to taunt whatever entities might be present ("if this is the portal to hell, why don't you come up out of the ground and get us!?") and it isn't long before there are reports of nausea, dizziness, and Bagans stating that his lower back is burning – a flashlight reveals three long vertical scratches running down the length of his spine.

In a consultation with Bishop James Long of the Old Catholic Church, Bagans is told that the number of scratches is significant – three, said to be a number chosen by demonic entities in order to mock the Holy Trinity.

Although Bobby Mackey's Music World has appeared on several other TV shows both before (such as *A Haunting*) and since, I think it is fair to say that the wider paranormal community first became aware of the case thanks to the efforts of Messrs. Bagans, Goodwin, and Groff. The location has remained on the bucket list of many investigatos and enthusiasts ever since.

It has to be said that some of the folklore surrounding Bobby Mackey's Music World is incorrect, either totally or partially, and some of it was given credence and publicized by the *Ghost Adventures* episode. Shannon Byers has carried out her own research into the historical events that took place at this location. She uncovered an article published in the Kentucky Post on November 2, 1915, titled *The Merciless Ax of Time*, which reveals that the stretch of land on which Bobby Mackey's Music World was the scene of so many hangings back in the mid-1800s that it was given the moniker "Gallows Gap" – and that superstitious locals would avoid the place out of fear of the ghosts that haunted it.

Not only did more than twenty people meet their death at the end of a rope in that area, but a little further along the river, forty more were killed (many of them drowned, others suffering brutally traumatic injuries) in an 1892 bridge collapse.

The building that once stood where Bobby Mackey's now stands was never actually a slaughterhouse, however; it *was* a distillery, and far from being used to flush the blood and guts of the abattoir into the river, the well in the basement and its associated tunnel is one of three that was hollowed out in 1876 and used as a part of the liquor-distillation process.

Nor do the stories of devil worship and human-sacrificing cults using the site to carry out occult rituals, bear up under close scrutiny. I have been unable to find any evidence to support that anything of the sort ever took place at what would one day become Bobby Mackey's Music World, or even in the vicinity. The stories may originate from the so-called "Satanic Panic" of the late 1980s, or could simply be tall tales that have sprung up around the location ever since it became famous for its ghosts. One eyewitness account says that a visitor to the basement cut himself and allowed his blood to drip all over a Ouija Board, presumably in some misguided attempt to practice dark magic.

What is demonstrably true, however, is that a murder referred to in the TV episode – the beheading of one Pearl Bryan, did actually take place, in 1896. Pearl's drink was laced with cocaine by her boyfriend, one Scott Jackson, who with the help of an accomplice named Alonzo Walling (his roommate) decapitated her...while she was still alive. Yet despite the gruesome nature of this crime, which took place several miles away from what was at the time the distillery and is today Bobby Mackey's Music World, there is no evidence at all to suggest that Pearl's head was taken anywhere near the distillery, let alone actually thrown down into the well, as modern-day folklore likes to suggest.

All of which goes on to suggest that Pearl Bryan probably isn't one of the ghosts that haunts Bobby Mackey's Music World. However, there are plenty of accounts regarding others that supposedly do.

One of the weirder stories involves a fatality car crash which occurred on Licking Pike Road, almost directly outside the bar. The first police officer on the scene found a single vehicle smashed into a telephone pole. Both the driver and passenger were dead. The doors to the bar opened, and a woman crossed the street. The cop noted that she was wearing a formal evening dress. She handed him two white tablecloths, which he could use to cover up the bodies and afford them a little dignity.

Several days later, the story goes, the officer returned to Bobby Mackey's with the intention of thanking the woman for her kind and compassionate behavior. He was surprised to be told that nobody had heard of the woman, and did not recognize her description. Besides, he was told, the bar hadn't even been open that day. *Nobody* should have been inside.

It's one of those ghost stories which sounds almost too good to be true, something akin to that of Chicago's Resurrection Mary, but considering the source — a law enforcement officer — it has to be taken seriously.

• • • ● ● • ● ● ● • •

After our night at Waverly Hills, the team had gone back to our hotel, and everybody was hitting the hay just as the sun came up. After a solid eight hours' sleep, we found a local restaurant and ate a hearty lunch/dinner combo before setting out for Wilder.

Despite not being the most active place we'd ever investigated, the sanatorium had still made a positive impression. If there was any lingering disappointment, it was just because our expectations had been set so high. It's rare to find a supposedly haunted location that really *does* live up to its reputation. Tales so often grow in the telling, particularly when somebody stands to benefit.

Based on interviews that I'd seen with him, I liked Bobby Mackey's approach to his place being haunted: he didn't seem to really believe it personally, but if it brought customers through the door in order to experience it for themselves, then that was all well and good. He didn't tell people what to believe, and for a few hundred books, you could experience the mysterious goings-on at his place for yourself...

...or not.

Full disclosure: we had paid to rent Waverly Hills, and we were paying to rent out Bobby Mackey's Music World. Neither place was cheap, but the owners of each location were completely honest about what we were getting. Ghosts were not guaranteed by any means, but we had full access to the property, very few restrictions, a knowledgeable guide to chaperone us, and hours to investigate. You can't really ask for more than that.

Still, I always advise people to be skeptical in the paranormal field whenever money is changing hands. You should be skeptical of what you see on TV, where ratings are king; be skeptical of haunted locations who have a vested interest in selling you tickets for a tour or a rental; you should even be skeptical of writers like me, who you're paying good money to in order to read a book like this. Keeping an open mind is essential in all walks of life, and the paranormal is no exception.

The subject of discussion as the miles passed was one of the other things I'm somewhat skeptical about: demons. I may draw some fire for saying this, but I truly do believe that the term is massively overused, particularly on this side of the Atlantic.

When I began my paranormal journey, some twenty years ago (and about 65,000 words back) in the United Kingdom, I had barely heard of so-called "demonic" cases. Great Britain did have a few documented cases which were decidedly sinister in nature, such as the Enfield Poltergeist haunting, but demons? Those were, for the most part, the stuff of Hollywood movies.

There were exceptions, of course, such as the case of St. Botolph's church at Skidbrooke, which is detailed at the beginning of this book. Some believed that whatever inhabited the tower there was not human, and I was never able to explain the animalistic screeching sound that took us all by surprise in the middle of the night. Given the history of occult ritual magic associated with the church, that certainly made sense...but these types of hauntings were few and far between.

Then came paranormal reality television. It wasn't long before the hosts of such shows began finding demons on a regular basis. Dark and negative hauntings were good for ratings, it turned out, and once this became apparent, more and more supposedly demonic hauntings were uncovered.

To clarify, I don't doubt that there is such a thing as a negative haunting. I've worked on a number of them over the years. I am certainly open to the possibility that non-human entities do exist. The question, however, is just how are we to tell whether a violent and angry entity is simply a pissed-off human spirit, or something that was never human at all?

I do realize that I'm on somewhat delicate ground here. I have friends in the paranormal community who hold the title of demonologist. Many of my friends and colleagues — many of them here in the United States — quote scripture and warn of the perils of dealing with demons...

...and you know, maybe they're right. Maybe there truly *are* demonic entities prowling some of this country's most haunted locations. It's not for me to impose my belief system on them, nor they on me. I don't subscribe to their view of the world, and that's okay. As long as we respect one another's viewpoints, we can investigate cases in our own respective ways, and respectfully agree to disagree.

One of the most troubling aspects of the demonic issue is the elephant in the room that nobody seems to want to address: just why is it that the explosion of supposedly demonic American hauntings tracks so closely with the popularity of the TV shows which claimed to encounter them with increasing frequency, beginning in the mid-2000s and continuing throughout the 2010s to the present day? Is this mere coincidence, or is there causation between the two? Having given the matter much thought, I've arrived at my own conclusion. I completely respect your right to form your own opinion.

Do I believe in demons? I'm open to the possibility that they might exist. Whether that is in the literal, biblical fire-and-brimstone sense, I'm not so sure. The D-word, as I like to call it, brings with it a set of religious associations that come with their own preconceived notions. I'm much more comfortable with the term "non-human entity." I will, however, say this: if there truly are such entities, then I am firmly convinced that they are much rarer than some interested parties would have us believe.

Playing devil's advocate, my friend, Hawaiian shirt-wearing, tiki-drinking paranormal pop culturist Aaron Sagers, advanced a fascinating hypothesis. What if, he posited, the increased coverage of demonic cases in the media — on TV, big budget Hollywood movies such as the Conjuring franchise, and in print — has actually caused a genuine increase in demonic activity? Has a sort of "demonic feedback loop" been formed, one in which the massive increase in public awareness of demons has led to the genuine article itself becoming stronger and more prevalent? It's an intriguing notion, and makes a solid counterpoint to my own position.

The key thing is that we do not necessarily have to respect one another's beliefs when it comes to the demonic, or any other subject; we simply have to respect one another's *right* to believe in whatever we wish. There should be room for many differing viewpoints in the paranormal realm, and at the end of the day, there are no true experts. Each and every one of us sets our own bar for what constitutes evidence, and a multitude of different factors play into that... including our upbringing, cultural background, our faith, and countless biases of which we are blissfully unaware.

The bottom line: for me, the jury is still out when it comes to demons. If they are something you, the reader, strongly believe in, I respect your right to do so.

All of which brings us back to Bobby Mackey's Music World. I won't deny feeling a little bit nervous, having read so many accounts of people being shoved, scratched, and otherwise physically attacked at that location. It's one thing to consider yourself a rationalist while sitting around a steakhouse table at three o'clock in the afternoon; it's something else entirely when you're going to be spending the night at what some people claim is the literal gateway to Hell.

On the drive to Wilder, we talked about the location's terrifying reputation. I was trying to adjust my expectations downward, in order to stave off disappointment if the place didn't perform. Pulling into the parking lot, I stared up at the huge red-on-white sign emblazoned on the side of the ramshackle building: BOBBY MACKEY'S, it proudly declared, WILDER, KY.

I'd love to tell you that the place looked ominous and brooding, as Waverly Hills had from the outside, but it really didn't. That might have had something to do with the fact that it was still broad daylight. Ours were the only two cars in the lot. The bar itself was closed that day, and there was no way for us to get inside until our guide arrived, so it was exploration time.

The railroad tracks ran alongside the rear of the building, just a few feet away. Looking both ways for safety, we crossed the tracks and walked into the tree line beyond. The ground suddenly fell away, sloping down toward an embankment. Below that ran the Licking River.

As I mentioned earlier, in 1892, not too far along that same river, a catastrophic bridge collapse took the lives of more than forty men and severely injured many others. Some have posited the idea that paranormal activity at Bobby Mackey's may be connected with this tragic event and the major loss of life. As theories go, it might have some merit, but we must ask why those same spirits wouldn't haunt some of the other properties that are closer to the collapse site. Why would they choose to haunt the honky tonk bar, rather than any other building along the same stretch of river?

We picked our way carefully down the slope, coming to a circular opening about four feet in diameter — the water pipe which led directly beneath Bobby Mackey's Music World.

It was too small for an adult to walk into, but I was able to make my way inside on my hands and knees. The pipe was pitch black. I used a flashlight to see a few feet ahead.

"Be careful," one of my companions called, their voice echoing from the concrete walls. "Watch out for critters."

They had a point. These cramped environs weren't the kind of place you wanted to encounter an angry raccoon — or a skunk. One scenario could result in me getting bitten, and the other would leave me stinking so badly, I'd have to spend the night outside.

The pipe was too narrow for me to turn around, so I shuffled back the way I had come, scraping my knees in the process. Needless to say, there had been no sign of Pearl Bryan's missing head.

By the time I emerged and everybody who wanted to, had gotten the chance to check out the pipe, our guide was pulling into the parking lot. A friendly lady named Angela, she had spent many nights at Bobby Mackey's, acting as a guide or investigating the place with her own team. We warmed to her immediately. She treated us with courtesy and respect, and also had a great sense of humor.

Angela unlocked the front doors and led us inside. The first thing we noticed was the infamous sign.

Warning to our patrons, read a sign inside the building, *this establishment is purported to be haunted. Management is not responsible and cannot be held liable for any actions of any ghosts/spirits on this [sic] premises.*

It would be easy to dismiss this warning as a cynical method of promoting the haunting, something worthy of P.T. Barnum or the movie-maker William Castle. (Castle, who was a master of exploitation movies, once claimed that one of his flicks was so scary, he offered a free $1,000 life insurance policy to anybody who died during a screening. Needless to say, audiences flocked to see it in theaters, and nobody's next of kin ever claimed the cash). Yet Bobby Mackey actually had a perfectly valid reason to post the disclaimer.

In 1993, a patron named J.T. Costigan claimed to have been assaulted in the men's restroom at Bobby Mackey's Music World...by a ghost. On September 29 of that year, Costigan — who didn't find the experience remotely funny, unlike almost everybody else — filed a lawsuit against the country singer, seeking $1,000 in damages.

The way Costigan told the story, he went into the restroom in order to answer the call of nature. This may not have been a wise move on his part, because earlier that night, he had laughed and poked fun at the idea of the bar being haunted. It's unclear how much, if any, alcohol had contributed to his ebullient mood, but if his story is to be believed, J.T. Costigan soon had cause to regret his behavior.

As he was taking care of business, a man with dark hair appeared in the restroom behind Costigan, and suddenly laid into him with his fists and feet. Costigan described his phantom assailant as having a rope — possibly a noose — tied around his neck, consistent with having been hanged. Once the assault was over, leaving the astonished Costigan battered and bleeding, the ghost supposedly vanished into thin air right before his eyes.

It's a fantastic story, and one that has absolutely no evidence to support it, other than the word of one bar patron who tried to make money off it. Did it really happen? We'll never know, but it cannot be denied that the story stretches the bounds of credulity just a little.

In addition to demanding cash, the lawsuit stipulated that the bar post a warning regarding the risks of being attacked by a ghost on the property. Bobby had no qualms about putting the sign up, which can be found there to this day. The lawsuit was dismissed without the $1,000 being awarded.

It's worth mentioning that the following year, 1994, a TV show titled *Encounters* filmed at Bobby Mackey's for several days, focusing mostly on the ghost story. According to a representative of the production company, "the equipment acted funny for four days" while they were there.

The central hub of Bobby Mackey's Music World is the stage, bar, and dance floor. Walking out into the middle of it all, it brought a smile to my face to think of the thousands of people who had danced the night away right there, ever since Bobby first bought the place in 1978. Up there on the stage was where Bobby

Mackey himself had belted out hit after hit, many of which were mounted proudly above the bar, a long row of L.P. records that made my friend, Jason, an avowed lover of all things vinyl, nod approvingly.

We walked around, soaking it all in. In a round leather pit sat El Turbo the Bull. For just six bucks, patrons could ride the bucking mechanical beast and test their skill at clinging on. I walked up to the stage, soaking up the happy vibes.

The building had one heck of a history. It had been a distillery, an inn, a bowling alley, casino, and later a club named *the Primrose*. That, in turn, became *the Latin Quarter* under new ownership, and was well known for its connections with organized crime. Good food, fine wine, and gambling were the order of business back then. Things were more formal back then than they would become under the aegis of Bobby Mackey.

Heading downstairs, Angela showed us the so-called portal to Hell, which was exactly what it looked like — a hole in the ground. Nothing more, nothing less.

The basement had allegedly seen a few executions, courtesy of the building's Mob connection. It was impossible to miss the cluster of bullet holes which perforated one of the wooden doors, at head and chest height. One of the smallest rooms was supposedly used by mobsters for interrogating and torturing people — and sometimes, it has been claimed, execution. Another rumor said that if you were caught cheating at the gaming tables, you would wind up tied to a chair, and got the crap beaten out of you.

A staircase which leads to nowhere, dead-ending at the ceiling, was once used to help hide illegal gambling equipment when the police turned up to raid the place.

I had brought a very specific piece of equipment with me for this part of the building, but I had left it in the car. I went back upstairs and out to the parking lot, returning with a heavy bag. Just as I was securing the front doors, what I can only presume was a local fellow walked past in the street outside. He leered at me, showing a mouthful of jagged teeth, and drew a finger across his throat in one swift motion. Momentarily taken aback, I recovered just in time to flip him my middle finger. Not the smartest thing to do, I admit, and certainly not the most professional, but the show of casual disrespect irritated me.

With hindsight, I regret having done it. I should have been more professional than that, and I only relate the event here to show what not to do. We were lucky not to come back out and find our tires slashed... or worse. Certainly not my finest hour.

Back down in the basement, I unzipped the bag and brought out "Freddy" — a life-size trauma mannequin that I had borrowed from my place of employment (with their permission). Freddy had the head and torso of an adult male, but no arms, and absolutely nothing below the waist. He looked bruised and battered, and several tubes extended from various parts, which medical trainers could use to pump blood through.

I can only imagine what the Transportation Security Administration agents made of him when they X-rayed my checked baggage at Denver International Airport.

I used Freddy to teach my fellow paramedics and EMTs clinical skills, such as managing a difficult airway by inserting a breathing tube, or performing CPR. Knowing the shady history of this location's criminal past, however, I had another use for him.

We set sat him on a chair at the back of the very cramped room and all took turns to "interrogate him." I put the word "interrogate" in quotation marks because this sorry excuse for an interrogation was far from our finest hour.

"Come on, buddy, talk if you know what's good for you."

Slap.

"Give it up, wiseass, or things are going to get bad."

Smack.

"Okay, douchebag, you're really asking for it now!"

Wallop.

I should point out — full disclosure — that these, and so many more tired and painful cliches were all trotted out by the male members of the team. Our female colleagues refused to lower themselves to this kind of melodrama, choosing instead to stand back and try not to let their derision show. In this, they were unsuccessful.

To be fair, after the initial painfully weak swats, we started to give Freddy a few good jabs. We got less hesitant, until we were finally punching him hard enough to rock his head back each time. But it is *also* fair to say that we made for the least intimidating bunch of wannabe mobsters you could possibly imagine. I left a digital voice recorder running to record any EVPs, but nothing showed up on the audio file — not even snorts of derisory ghostly laughter, which would have been totally warranted.

Twenty minutes later, Freddy went back into his bag. We broke into smaller groups and went off to run EVP sessions in different areas of the building. I wanted to follow in the footsteps of what is arguably the best known spirit said to haunt Bobby Mackey's Music World: Johanna.

As a reminder, Johanna was said to have been a showgirl who danced at *the Latin Quarter*. In the time-honored fashion of so many tragic stories, Joanna became pregnant, and when her father found out, he became enraged and had her lover killed. Overcome by grief at the loss of her beau, Johanna fatally poisoned herself.

Stories of Johanna haunting the honky tonk bar abound, so much so that Bobby Mackey himself wrote a song based around Johanna's tale. Several variations of the legend exist, but there is little evidence to support them. Former live-in caretaker Carl Lawson said that he found a journal hidden in the basement, which bore Johanna's name on it, and was an account of her love affair and subsequent suicide. Mr. Lawson also claimed to have encountered Johanna's apparition inside the building.

What happened to this journal? I'm unaware of anybody ever actually setting eyes on it, save for Carl Lawson, who was willing to talk about its contents, but did not seem to want to physically produce it. If the journal ever truly existed, and I cannot say for sure whether it did or did not, then careful analysis might help clear up some of the contradictory information which surrounds Johanna's story.

Be that as it may, we had just one night to investigate Bobby Mackey's Music World, and I was going to proceed on the working premise that whether Johanna was real or not, it was worth making an attempt to communicate with her. To that end, I decided to spend some time in what our guide told us was believed to have been Johanna's dressing room... and, some say, the scene of her demise.

The room was sparse, but there were a couple of chairs. I settled into the least uncomfortable one and sat there, in the dark, with a voice recorder running.

"Johanna, are you here?"

There was nothing but the sound of my own breathing, which was almost deafening in the thick darkness.

"If you, or anybody else would like to communicate, please speak into the red light here at my side." That was the LED indicating that the recorder was operational.

Rather than use multiple burst sessions, I let it run for the next half hour, and tried to engage in a one-sided conversation. I asked about the salient points of Johanna's life — her hopes, dreams, and aspirations — before edging into the murkier waters of her final days.

Wiser individuals than I have pointed out that spirits must get royally sick of being asked the same questions during EVP sessions.

What is your name?
Did you die here?
Were you murdered?

This is, in my view, a very good point. Like a movie star doing the umpteenth round of publicity, fielding the same trite, canned queries from reporters over and over again, why would they even bother to respond? It may also be that asking a spirit questions about their own death could be traumatizing. I therefore restricted these to just a couple, at the end of the session, and tried to keep my tone light, friendly, and above all else, respectful.

Unfortunately, nobody was taking the bait. My own voice was the only one talking when I played the audio back. Nor did I smell Johanna's famous rose perfume, which a number of visitors say they have smelt, a phenomenon that was also immortalized in Bobby's song.

I was a little disappointed when I emerged from the dressing room, but cheered myself with the thought that there was a whole lot of building left to explore. My thoughts turned to Carl Lawson. In many ways, if the alleged haunting of Bobby Mackey's Music World had a star witness, it was Carl — and, seeking to understand him better, it might help me to walk in his footsteps.

Climbing the staircase up from the ground floor, we reached the door to what had once been Carl Lawson's room. Sadly, Carl had passed away in 2012. A Stars and Stripes decal was pasted on the door. Underneath it, the words GO AWAY! had been spelled out in stickers, with two large black arrows added for emphasis. Clearly, Carl had not liked to entertain guests...possibly because of the uninvited and unwelcome paranormal visitors?

Opening the door, we walked inside. To say that the room was a mess would be a huge understatement. It stank of stale cigarettes. Dust and cobwebs coated every surface. A layer of greenish scum marred the white porcelain bathtub and washbasin. I really hoped that Carl hadn't lived in such squalor during his time at Bobby Mackey's, though based on some of the old items that were laying around, it looked as if it was being used as temporary storage.

Several of the ghost stories associated with Bobby Mackey's can be traced back to Carl Lawson. Some of those stories sound as if they were ripped from the pages of a horror novel. Now, I have no idea how valid any of them may or may not be. I never met Mr. Lawson myself, nor did I ever have the opportunity to speak with him. As to whether he was truly tormented by dark forces, or possessed by some kind of entity, your guess is as good as mine. We do know that an exorcism was performed on him by a priest, in an attempt to rid him of what some felt was a malign presence — a demon.

Carl's room was not a pleasant environment in which to spend much time. Nevertheless, we gave it the old college try and ran several burst EVP sessions in there. End result: Zilch. Zip. Nada.

I actually found that rather comforting. More than one visitor claims to have caught Carl's voice on an EVP at Bobby Mackey's. Assuming that those EVPs really are Carl, and not something else imitating him, then I would be concerned to think that he was still in residence. Considering the reports of him being tormented by evil spirits there, it probably wouldn't be considered his happy place...although I could be wrong about that, who knows?

It is my sincere hope that Carl rests in peace.

Our final activity of the evening involved splitting up and running separate sessions throughout the building. I spent some time in the bar and gift shop area, running EVP sessions — all of which yielded nothing. Downstairs in the basement, Linda and Laura both heard what sounded like shuffling coming from somewhere near the staircase. It could possibly have been a raccoon or some other nocturnal critter, but when they went to investigate, they could find no explanation.

We left Bobby Mackey's before the sun came up. It's fair to say that the team felt a little disappointed with our night there, though once again, it was our own fault for having unrealistic expectations. We had been exposed to so many accounts of visitors being scratched, shoved, and otherwise physically affected, that it had colored our attitude before we even set foot inside.

Is Bobby Mackey's Music World truly haunted? I, for one, cannot say. My team and I had no personal experiences there, picked up no EVPs, and gathered nothing in the way of evidence.

Perhaps the conditions were not right. Perhaps we had the wrong mix of people; came on the wrong night; weren't paying sufficiently close attention; or perhaps the place isn't haunted at all.

If there really are ghosts to be found at the friendly country and western bar situated just above the Licking River, they did not interact with me during my investigation — but that doesn't mean they haven't, and won't, continue to interact with others. There is a wealth of eyewitness testimony and a number of intriguing EVPs which suggest there could be more going on at Bobby Mackey's Music World than meets the eye.

Should you, dear reader, ever find yourself in the area, I heartily recommend that you drop in and find out for yourself...and if something inexplicable were to happen to you, don't say you weren't warned. The warning sign is clearly posted for all to see.

ACKNOWLEDGMENTS

I would like to extend my heartfelt thanks to those dedicated paranormal researchers who have mentored me, accompanied me, and hopefully sometimes have learned a little from me, over the past two decades.

Andrew J. Wright and the team from SPECTA
Tracey Robson and the MPI investigators
The men and women of the Boulder Country Paranormal Research Society, past, present, and future:
Anna Choate, Laura Estep, Linda and Jason Fellon, Lucilla Giron, Catlyn Keenan, Miranda and Jeff Metzger, Kathleen
Paulsen, Sean Rice, Jenna Robbert, Joey Stanford, Charlie Stiffler, Kira and Seth Woodmansee.
The Other Side Investigations: Brad Carstens, Robbin Daidone and Randy Schneider
Stephen Weidner and the staff of the American Association of Paranormal Investigators
Chris Balassone of Tri-City Paranormal
Bryan, Carol, and Ginger from Rocky Mountain Paranormal

My heartfelt thanks go out to:
Laura T, for her support, tolerance, and valiant efforts to stay awake

Amy Glaser, for her patience, support, and believing in the project

Doreen Shakesby, matriarch extraordinaire

Aunt Janet, Jean and Roger Newby, Jo, Paulette, and Tracey – for nursing mum in her final months, I can never thank you enough.

Gwynneth Tiberio, for the best snowball fight ever

Vicki Kennedy, who stood by me when it counted.

My brother and sister firefighters in service at Boulder Rural Fire Rescue (Bruce Mygatt, Chief); fellow EMS providers, dispatchers, and support staff at Pridemark Paramedics (Jen Roderick, Clinical Manager – greatest boss EVER); and the disaster response pros serving with me on the awesome Colorado DMAT 3.

My fellow instructors at the Front Range Community College, Health One EMS, and the St Anthony Paramedic Academy.

Mark Pickerel and Gary Micheli, keepers of the historic flame at the Pueblo Fire Department

Carol Byers and the good folks at the MillSite Inn

Mr. Crud, without whom this book would probably not have been written

Rhonda and her colleagues at the City of Longmont

Nick Forte, impresario of the Dragon Con paranormal track

The team at Haunted Happenings, for a great night in London

Annie Lindup, B Jones, and my SFBall family – for your tireless support of the Teenage Cancer Trust, and putting on the world's greatest convention, you guys are the greatest

Lastly, but by no means least, everybody who allowed us into their home in order to investigate. And let's not forget the ghosts themselves...

Richard Estep
Longmont, Colorado
August 2014

Printed in Great Britain
by Amazon

39563869R00149